# FICTION AS WINDOW

## CRITIQUING THE INDIAN LITERARY CULTURAL ETHOS

SINCE THE 1980S

V PADMA

Orient BlackSwan

ORIENT BLACKSWAN PRIVATE LIMITED

*Registered Office*
3-6-752 Himayatnagar, Hyderabad 500 029 (A.P.), India
Email: centraloffice@orientblackswan.com

*Other Offices*
Bangalore, Bhopal, Bhubaneshwar, Chennai
Ernakulam, Guwahati, Hyderabad, Jaipur, Kolkata
Lucknow, Mumbai, New Delhi, Patna


First Published 2009



ISBN 978 81 250 3657 9

*Typeset in* Aldine 401 BT 10.5/12.5 *by*
MacroTeX Solutions
Chennai

*Printed in India at*
Graphica Printers
Hyderabad 500 013

*Published by*
Orient Blackswan Private Limited
3-6-752 Himaythnagar
Hyderabad 500 029

*To my teacher Dr C. T. Indra*

*for teaching me*

*the sanctity of scholarship and research*

# Contents

# List of Abbreviations and Short Titles

| | |
|---|---|
| *Howdah:* | *The Moth-eaten Howdah of the Tusker* |
| *Masterpieces:* | *Masterpieces of Indian Literature* |
| *SS:* | *Saraswati Samman Archives, K. K. Birla Foundation, New Delhi* |
| *Memory:* | *The Memory of Elephants* |
| *GG:* | *Gopalla Gramam* |
| *Red Earth:* | *Red Earth and Pouring Rain* |
| *Themes:* | *Themes in Politics Series* |
| *Untouchables:* | *The Untouchables: Subordination, Poverty and the State in Modern India* |
| *Women and Family Law Reform:* | *Women and Family Law Reform in India* |

# Acknowledgements

I wish to thank the following:
The University of Madras where I worked on my PhD dissertation that was the basis of this book;
The University Grants Commission for their Junior Research Fellowship;
Everybody at SCILET (Study Centre for Indian Literature in English and Translation) at American College, Madurai for providing me with a bulk of the material I have used and for replying so promptly to requests over ordinary mail that I wondered at the need for e-mail;
Madras Institute of Development Studies for allowing me to use their very well-stocked library;
The Bharatiya Jnanpith Foundation for giving me access to much of their material;
The Former Director of Bharatiya Jnanpith, Mr Dinesh Mishra for sparing time to talk to me about literary–cultural ethos in India and about the Jnanpith Foundation;
The K. K. Birla Foundation for allowing me to use a lot of their material including *bhasha samiti* reports and minutes of various meetings that they had used in their selection process of the Saraswati Samman award, and for their permission to cite these sources;
The Director of Saraswati Samman Shri Bishen Tandon for talking to me and making it possible for me to have unconditional entrée into the material;
Mr M. H. Venkateswaran, Officer on Special Duty at Sahitya Akademi, New Delhi for telling me about many things regarding the Akademi and its functioning;
Ms Chandra Chari, Editor of *The Book Review* for her useful insights into the world of review criticism;
Dr C. T. Indra, my PhD supervisor, for always being there, for giving me courage and strength, for teaching me the importance of human values, for letting me be myself and for all the wonderful food;

Dr Indra's mother for simply everything;
My father, for putting up with my moods, madness and questions, for forcing me to ask questions and teaching me to follow my conscience;
My mother, for teaching me self-reliance and multi-tasking;
My sister-in-law Charmaine for the sympathetic ear she always lent me;
My nephews Sean and Shane for the lighter moments of life;
My mother-in-law for constantly telling me to 'take off' from housework;
My uncles and aunts for listening to all my ramblings about my work;
My brothers-in-law Anthony and Dominic for all the bonhomie;
The PhD Club at the English Department, Madras University, for being my second family;
Geetha and Sumathy for believing in me and for critiquing the right things at the right time;
Yasmin, Pavithra and Naga Radhika for being great friends,
Abhirami for all her help when I went to Delhi and her husband Biju for giving me his copies of the papers presented at the Sahitya Akademi Seminar on Criticism;
Dr Bharati, Dr Meenakshi Hariharan and Dr Nirmala for making me realize many things about India and Indian culture;
Dr Prasad for being a great source of encouragement and for the wonderful gender workshop he conducted which gave me interesting insights into the last chapter;
John Ilavarasu for all the material on Parsi literature;
Vikram whose untimely death bereft me of a great friend and Anirudhhan for persuading me to discuss my work;
Dr Azhagarasan, lecturer at the English Department, Madras University, for teaching me that nothing is beyond interrogation;
Dr Rajani, our Theatre professor, for all his coffees, teas and lunches while discussing my work;
Dr Venkataramanan, Dr Armstrong and Vinayaga Selvi, lecturers at our Department for all their support and encouragement;
Thiru Sir, Section Officer, for helping me with all the official work—especially the reports—that I always hated, Kothandam Uncle, since retired, for doing a lot of running around to help me with the administrative part of research and Late Prema Akka for unflinchingly climbing down four floors to get me tea, coffee and milk;

Tintin, Asterix, Archie and P. G. Wodehouse for cheering me up;
Madhavi Menon of Orient BlackSwan for her assiduous editing;
And not least

Neil, my son, for showing me the joys of seeing everything with a child's eye

and

Alistair, my husband, for his encouragement and criticisms, for doubling as my driver all round Chennai, for foregoing home food for days together to enable me to work, for sharing my aspirations and agonies, for teaching me how to keep an open mind and for being the Rock of Gibraltar I could always fall back upon.

# PART ONE

## Mapping Modern India: Literary Cultural Ethos

# INTRODUCTION

The introduction to *India's Literary History: Essays on the Nineteenth Century* (2004) edited by Stuart Blackburn and Vasudha Dalmia begins with what can be read as an admirable summing up of the basic conditions of the literary scene in India since the 1980s:

> Ever since Clifford Geertz transformed the drama of Balinese cock-fighting into a text, and new historicism made the complementary gesture of returning culture to the center of literary studies, students of literature, history and culture have shared a common vocabulary, key concepts and points of reference. This convergence has led to a reorientation in the study of literary history. The periodisation, assessment and attribution that characterized earlier literary historiography have been replaced by an effort to understand the place of literature in history, largely through an analysis of textual production of cultural meaning and the socio-political conditions of creating texts. (1)

The field of literary studies in India since the 1980s has seen a decisive shift towards greater interdisciplinarity. Neither is literature any longer merely a connoisseur's delight nor is literary criticism any more barely an exercise in aesthetic interpretation. Subversive conceptual changes occurring in various spheres of Indian society and culture—economics, politics, the publishing industry etc.—have made it impossible for literature to remain an isolated creative activity. Literary criticism has perforce to encompass these changes and study their relation to the prevailing forms, themes and techniques in literature today using an integrated methodology. Even as creative literature is fast becoming a discursive space where pressing issues and concerns can be debated and discussed, literary criticism is compelled to turn ideological and is showing an increasing awareness, in a self-reflexive manner, of the paradigms and assumptions that inform its own activity.

This study aims at examining the literary cultural ethos in India during this stimulating and perhaps even turbulent period. It attempts to (a) identify recurrent leitmotifs and issues in the literary culture of the period, (b) analyse the implications of these leitmotifs for criticism and (c) examine the ways in which certain works of fiction (across languages) produced in this period engage with the issues identified.

## 1

The period from the 1980s witnessed far-reaching changes in all fields. Politics, for instance, saw a major upheaval after the close shave that India had with totalitarianism during the period of the Emergency in 1975; 1980 marked the year when Indira Gandhi returned to power after having been defeated in the General Elections in 1977 when the Emergency was lifted. After around nine years of political 'stability' that followed 1980, the role played by regional parties in national politics was becoming increasingly potent, throwing into relief regional claims against a national screen as well as making it impossible for any thinking person in contemporary India to ignore regional differences and concerns while dealing with 'national' problems. Defining the nation has become a much more onerous task than ever before and literary historiography has had to contend with the changing perceptions of the nation in the writing of a 'national literary history.' With the multilingual nature of Indian society and the multi-pronged nature of Indian culture with a variety of streams and traditions, pressing more and more not only for recognition but also empowerment at various levels, literary history and literary criticism too have found it necessary to identify varying literary traditions and voices in the amorphous mass of 'Indian literature'.

These changes in the political arena went hand in hand with various economic and social changes that sought seemingly opposite ends. In the 1990s, while opening up India to foreign investors and disinvesting various public sector undertakings seemed to create conditions for faster economic growth to place India in a contending position in world affairs, the legal and legislative advantages given to suppressed and oppressed sections of society not only gave greater scope for 'new' voices to speak but also allowed them to become proactive so as to destabilise majoritarian discourses, and call into question many of the hitherto-taken-for-granted aspects of Indian society. With time, the ideological assumptions of these very reform and development programmes have come to be questioned, especially from gender and caste perspectives. The rise of a wide range of trends—especially those of Dalit literature and women's writing—within the literary traditions of any one language and the acceptance of a variety of literary traditions within the framework of 'national literature' cannot be missed. The consequent problematisation of the very notion of a 'national literature' is perhaps not surprising in an age when the notion of 'India' itself has come under tremendous pressure.

The redefinition of 'India', made necessary by the rupturing of the idea of a 'unified', 'integral' nation, has been further problematised by the emigration of Indians to other countries, which have become spaces from which to use literature as a means of creative criticism of the motherland. The large corpus of literature by Indians from such non-Indian spaces has necessitated not only a reappraisal of the existing native literary tradition, but also the construction of a new set of critical and aesthetic tools with which to read such literatures. As a consequence, the categories in which texts are placed seem to need revisioning, making the creation of new categories almost inevitable.

The period from the 1980s has opened out a plethora of positions from which to see and critique the nation. In the place of the Grand Narratives of nationalism and national development, we have a host of marginalised positions such as gender, caste and sexuality which effectively dispute the claim of a 'monological' 'unified' India. A whole host of media have become the means through which these new and different voices and opinions emanate. And literary studies—with all its allied dimensions such as creative literature, literary criticism, literary history and translation—is one of them.

Using the genre of fiction as a window through which to examine this ethos may seem almost a natural choice for a number of reasons, one of them being the enormous boom that publication, translation and criticism of fiction has seen in the period from the 1980s onwards. Although short fiction, drama and poetry too have received ample critical attention and have witnessed considerable changes, it is the novel that remains the most read, translated and published genre. Also, by virtue of its very form, the novel allows extended discussions on various issues besides providing space for a number of voices to speak within a single text. It becomes, therefore, the ideal form to use when analysing a chequered political and cultural ethos. At the same time, criticism on the novel form has registered colossal changes in the last twenty years. Moving beyond its earlier concerns such as historicising the form, defining it and tracing its pedigree, novel criticism appears to be subject to relentless ideological conditioning and has evidently become as important a space for debates and discussions as the novels themselves. It is however tacitly understood that a study of other genres is necessary and may throw up even conflicting ideas.

The selection of creative and critical texts has also been restricted, as is inevitable in any study, by my own linguistic competence and hence, texts written originally in English, Hindi or Tamil and / or translated into any of these languages have been chosen for study.

The motifs that we can identify in the literary culture of the period are embedded in criticism, literary history as well as in the texts themselves. Many of these leitmotifs are also implicit in the parameters of many institutions which offer patronage to literature. Most importantly perhaps, they can be discerned across languages – in Indian Writing in English as well as in Indian Writing in the *bhashas.*[1] We would therefore, do well to consciously avoid the binary often implied in current literary studies in India between these two linguistic categories. Indian writing in English and literature in the *bhashas* need to be read together and placed on a common platform in order to form an integral understanding of the ethos of fiction.

## 2

The 'literary culture' of any period is an amalgam of a number of diverse aspects. If fiction creatively reflects or critiques social, economic, cultural and political conditions of a time, criticism provides basic tools for reading these texts. At the same time, criticism itself is a discursive space and a product of the same conditions that give rise to particular forms and themes in fiction. It is not merely a 'reading' of a text or an 'interpretation' of it; it is not even 'many' interpretations of a text. Criticism includes seeing the text qua text and simultaneously reading it in the light of non-literary areas and disciplines such as legal debates or development studies. We need to look not only at texts, but also at the impact that these texts had on the extratextual space and examine the cultural, social and political conditions that made such an impact possible. Such a reading need not, as some might fear, take away its 'literariness'; rather, it shows how conditions not entirely 'literary' often affect literary forms and themes. Literature becomes, in this case, a cultural site which actively engages with the world 'outside' the text. The writer, critic, literary historian, translator, publisher—all become part of a larger cultural dialectics where issues jostle each other; and literature—creative literature and criticism—itself becomes a site where the dialectics of these are acted out.

The two parts into which this book has been divided operate as complementary studies to understanding the literary culture of the 1980s and need therefore to be read together. Discursive / non-creative dimensions of literary studies such as criticism, literary history, translation studies and patronage are one part of the fiction-culture that throw light on some central issues cutting across critical traditions; they bring to light the multifarious connections that literature has with the culture and society that produces and consumes it. Novels reveal how fiction has thematically as well in its form, narrative etc. discursively engaged with these issues. Such a division into two parts, however, is not meant to bifurcate the study of the literary–cultural ethos; the first part is not a 'background' against which to study works of fiction. The division has been made more to foreground various aspects of criticism such as sites of production of critical readings, patronage etc. too as a location of literary culture.

Creative and discursive dimensions of literature often have a cyclical relationship. While it is often thought that criticism only follows creative literature, we are living in an era when literary criticism is engaging freely from various other disciplines and is therefore able to create a theoretical framework that creative works can themselves draw upon or question. This is one reason why non-creative aspects of literary culture form the first part of the study. It is only when such similarities and differences are foregrounded that a composite picture of contemporary Indian literature and literary culture can emerge.

## 3

We are time and again reminded that we are living in a post-modern world where notions like 'truth,' 'reality' and the 'nation' have lost their absoluteness. We speak today of these terms in their grammatical plurals, thereby acknowledging that social, cultural and ideological conditioning or affiliations will impinge upon our understanding of these ideas. Our critique of a literary–cultural ethos will necessarily throw up many of these plurals and in doing so, will place us too within a postmodern Indian culture. This is a postmodernism that not only uses a number of perspectives to read individual texts, but also sees literature as a site where a number of positions are articulated.

By blurring the disciplinary boundaries between literature and other discourses and even by seeing creative and critical literature as parts of the same cultural ethos, we are consciously placing ourselves within this postmodern Indian culture. It is a culture in which disciplines do not exist in watertight compartments, but flow into each other; a culture where interfaces between languages and literary traditions keep throwing up new spaces of literary production and consumption, and is therefore a space where new voices and viewpoints can be accommodated.

This is not a denial of any ethical responsibility on our parts; we do not unconditionally say that 'anything goes'. For we are asserting the need for human dignity, even demanding it, within the literary ethos. When asking that legal reforms be made in favour of women and while reading literary texts with this in mind, or when insisting on a space for the articulation of dalit voices within literature, aesthetics and culture or when asking for a critical strategy which would use and forge new methods based on what we need and what we have, we are effectively demanding a space for as many voices as possible so that no single voice subsumes others, so that a clamour is heard. We do not hear *a* reality amidst all this clamour; rather, the clamours together form reality.

It is by so keeping our feet in many places that we can critique a literary cultural ethos. It is a method offered by the very culture we live in for Indian culture has indeed witnessed what we may call, drawing on V. S. Naipaul's text, 'a million mutinies' in every field especially since the 1980s; and literature and literary criticism are no exceptions. As we go on, we will discuss a few of these millions and a few of these mutinies from the vantage point of fiction in its various dimensions.

## Notes

1. '*Bhashas*' is a term used here to refer to Indian languages. This term, used extensively by G. N. Devy in his path-breaking and Sahitya-Akademi-winning critical work *After Amnesia: Tradition and Change in Indian Literary Criticism*, has become part of the critical vocabulary of Indian literary studies today.

## References

Blackburn, Stuart and Vasudha Dalmia. Introduction. *India's Literary History: Essays on the Nineteenth Century*. Eds. Stuart Blackburn and Vasudha Dalmia ( New Delhi: Permanent Black, 2004). Hereafter cited in text as Blackburn and Dalmia, *India's Literary History*.

# 1

# SHIFTING PARADIGMS

The period since the 1980s has been viewed by almost all critical works in nearly all fields, dissenting and assenting, as the most exciting and turbulent one in recent Indian history. Be it politics, international relations, economics, organised protest against various forms of discrimination or literary studies, the period has witnessed perhaps the greatest challenge to foundational thinking on culture. From a subversive moral and philosophical standpoint, we may see this phenomenon as a glorious acceptance of the relativity of Truth and the assertion of the existence of a number of Realities. When dealing with the idea of nation, national identity or a national literature, however, such a multiplicity of positions forces us to reconsider hitherto-taken-for-granted definitions of what constitutes India; now, this assertion of multiplicity calls for a recognition of the plurisignification of Indian life and culture. The traditional view that Indian civilisation has the ability to take in as many cultures as possible may seem a naïve liberal humanist standpoint, but it nevertheless stresses the ability of an average Indian to exist simultaneously on multiple planes. Today, we are experiencing the full social, political, cultural and literary implications of the worn-out phrase 'unity in diversity'. In terms of language, religion, ethnicity, ideology and subject positions, many a discourse since the 1980s projects India as anything but a monological entity.

Consequently, the impossibility of defining the nation in terms of any one cultural group, ethnic identity, religion or language has led to a plethora of critical positions from which to view any issue. For instance, recent debates on what constitutes 'development' and 'progress' have shown a sharp departure from the Nehruvian ideal that saw national development in terms of industrial growth within a socialist economic framework. Recent challenges to this model have come from ecofeminist critics such as Vandana Shiva[1] who point to the male and Western assumptions of maximum (rather than optimal) use of natural resources in such agendas. Shiva's position itself, however, becomes a springboard for caste-based critiques of development by activists like Gabrielle Dietrich[2] who see her arguments as potentially hegemonic. All these voices seek to use the discursive space and resources available to provide the best for the greatest possible sections of society.

At the turn of the last century India had been an uneasy spectator to intense turbulence, the onset of which can be traced to the two decades that preceded it. With political uncertainties prevailing since in the late 1980s and with increasing importance given to regional parties in the central cabinet since the mid-1990s, the opinions and positions of smaller groups have become an important force to reckon with while taking major national decisions. In fact, the very idea of a single-party government at the centre now appears to be a thing of the past. Simultaneously, it has become much more difficult to talk of an 'unproblematic' nation and any major decision-making process needs to consider the opinions and points of view of many communities and groups; especially those who will be directly affected by the major policies of the government.

Literary studies during this period has witnessed a vast increase in the number of subject positions from which authors and texts speak. Traditionally suppressed groups such as Dalits and women are increasingly finding their voices, both in fictional as well as discursive writing. These twin groups also account for two of the most talked-about literary trends in recent times in all languages in India. Just as these subject positions cast doubt on many of the cultural, social and ideological assumptions hitherto taken for granted, they also consciously offer a challenge to what has been seen as 'mainstream literature'. Criticism on these positions therefore too has been compelled to engage seriously with important cultural, social and ideological issues.

There is another kind of 'marginal' position which poses a challenge to many official discourses of development. Here we hear the voices of the people adversely affected by development programmes and reform schemes. The positions of such people and groups have become more prominent after the rightful attention which the Narmada Bachao Andolan[3] has received from the media. Earlier too, the furore over the Silent Valley project[4] in Kerala had become an important political issue in the late seventies and early eighties. Contrary to earlier beliefs that it was inevitable that some communities be made the scapegoats in the path of the nation's march towards development (the strategy of maximum good for maximum number can be seen to be operative here), the tendency today is not only to tell the stories of such people, but also to use these as vantage points from which to critique many of the assumptions of governmental development programmes. Although creative literature has often spoken about and dramatised the plights of such people, criticism on such texts has usually taken the form of the binary between tradition and modernity as the basic critical framework in reading them. Novels now dealing with this issue offer a challenge not so much to the idea of a 'national literature' or 'national aesthetics' but to the government itself. However, with an ever-increasing corpus of texts dealing with such issues, it has become necessary for criticism too to draw from social science discourses while shaping its analytical tools.

New positions, however, need not always be those of victims. The growing body of texts written by Indians residing outside India has made it necessary to create a specific category of expatriate and diasporic literature and to set out the aesthetics of such a position. Although much criticism has dealt with such texts written in English, there is a growing body of similar writing in many *bhashas* as well: Mauritian writing in Hindi, Sri Lankan writing in Tamil are just two such examples. Reading these texts has necessitated a foray into issues such as the economic and cultural implications of migration etc. Even traditional concepts such as 'home' and 'homeland' have taken on newer, more expansive meanings.

V. S. Naipaul's book *India: a Million Mutinies Today*, might be a useful reference point from which to approach these multiple positions in the Indian literary–cultural ethos. Naipaul's text evokes the picture of a nation where a number of voices are emerging, each challenging the other. What Naipaul has spoken of as a cultural, political, social phenomenon also has a literary *avatar*. The multiple subject positions from which literature is now being produced, consumed and critiqued can be seen as 'mutinous' in so far as they refute and openly challenge the way in which the nation and its inhabitants have been represented in earlier literature. The sheer number of these positions makes the task of redefining either the Indian nation or the 'national culture' a daunting one. The growing interdependence between literature and various non-literary aspects of culture is what marks the literary ethos in India from the 1980s. This period, its turbulence, the literature it has produced and the parameters used for critiquing that literature are what we will be looking at.

## THE POSTCOLONIAL DISPUTE

A striking feature of the late twentieth century has been the felt need to redefine certain aspects of society and culture that had for long been taken for granted. In fact, the need to problematise and redefine the concept of the 'nation' evident in various fields such as literature, culture and politics points to a recurring motif in many of the other connected aspects of the age – that of defamiliarisation and reconstruction. Notions and ideas that had for long been held sacrosanct and had been un-problematically idealised, suddenly became topics of intense debate. The 'nation' was perhaps the first to face this embarrassing arraignment – the overarching question of 'what is a nation?' is the motif behind many of the literary and critical endeavours of the period. The question seems to have drawn sustenance from many political, social and cultural movements, some of which, perhaps unwittingly, sought to redefine this area so far considered unproblematic. Added to this are the troublesome questions: how do we define India? what coordinates are we to choose? who is a 'true Indian?' and by extension, 'what is a real "Indian" text?' While the discourse of nationalism and patriotism before and after Independence set the 'nation' above the values of region, gender, caste or language as a matrix of identity, the period from the 1980s saw a massive reversal in perspectives. It was now the smaller matrix which gained visibility, thereby leading to a veritable fission in the concept of the nation and to a corresponding understanding that region and nation may be totally contradictory ideals. We might remember that the discourse of nationalism too had propagated the mutual exclusivity of these two and in the process, held the nation supreme. The dissenting mood of the late twentieth century reversed the hierarchy; however, it did not really manage to move out of the binary implied in it.

This reversal is the underlying deep structure in the various shapes and forms that postcolonial criticism has taken in the last few years in the field of literary studies. A look at the changing fortunes of this critical method would lead us willy-nilly into various disputable areas which criticism in India—in a variety of languages—has focussed upon.

Largely responsible for taking Indian writing in English to the global arena, postcolonial criticism was initially welcomed heartily (at least in English) into the Indian literary scene. It was primarily and perhaps single-handedly responsible for rupturing the notion of 'English literature' as that produced only in England and marginally in America, and for creating an alternative canon for the discipline. Many motifs current in literary studies such as the value of non-standard language, of history and narrative etc. have in some way stemmed from postcolonial criticism. That a suppressed group can successfully use and simultaneously subvert the language of the oppressor in order to 'write back' to them is an idea that is in vogue even today. The now much-debated issue of cultural consciousness of a text was also a product of this very same school. Postcolonialism made the writing and reading of literature an act of patriotism, as an act that would privilege the culture that generated the text and its reading. For example, readings of canonical texts from postcolonial perspectives also illustrate this position. Recent readings of Shakespeare's plays (for instance, those that see Prospero in *The Tempest* as the coloniser of the island and Caliban as the wronged colonial subject) and especially of early English fiction that was written during the heyday of British imperialism (like interpretations of *Robinson Crusoe* as dramatising the process of colonisation and the increased focus on the Crusoe–Friday relationship as depicting the stereotyped colonial-master–colonised-slave relationship) attempt to centralise the colonial experience of marginal characters in them. Postcolonial criticism also successfully subverted the notion of form and problematised it. Novels written in an apparently fluid manner, with a non-linear temporality, partly in mythic and partly in realist modes, came to be seen less as aberrations and more as assertions of a native world view. Postcolonialism made it possible to look differently at the form of Indian novels in English such as *All About H. Hatterr* (1948) by G. V. Desani or *The Silver Pilgrimage* (1975) by M. Anantanarayanan, which were now seen as deliberately recasting the novel form in modes and shapes familiar to the Indian psyche. It also made possible alternative readings of early *bhasha* texts like the Tamil *Pratapa Mudaliar Charitram* (1870) by Vedanayagam Pillai and Malayalam novels like Chandu Menon's *Indulekha* (1889), allowing for critics like Meenakshi Mukherjee in *Realism and Reality* (1985) to see them as showing deep interconnections between a western realist mode and a pre-colonial oral narrative tradition. A similar change can be seen in criticisms on early twentieth century writers in English too. Initially, literary criticism in the nationalist phase took note, for instance, of Raja Rao's special use of English as a tool to reflect Indian metaphysical sensibility. R. K. Narayan's language was also regarded as typical of the features of South Indian speech. However, after the emergence of postcolonial theory, such writing came to be seen as a deliberate mode of 'writing back to the Empire.' It has today become passé to see Raja Rao's use of native Indian words in *Kanthapura* and his use of the *sthalapurana* when writing modern Indian history as deliberate attempts to 'Indianise' the novel form. The *Routledge Encyclopaedia of Post-colonial Literatures* (1st edition) pays special attention to the form of *The Silver Pilgrimage* focusing on its fusion of recipes, criticism on drama, philosophical discourse and fiction. Such a form is seen as a deliberate attempt to move out of a European, realist model.

Despite these advantages, the postcolonial paradigm in the form in which it was received in India in the 1980s, has today been largely, if not fully, discarded as a valid one for studying Indian texts.

One of the chief objections to the paradigm was that it primarily dealt with literature in English. This monolingual bias of a paradigm that had broken new ground in the Western academia spelt danger to the projection of India through its literature to the West – for it created an impression that literature written in English predominated creative activities in India. This belief became the centre of much controversy after Salman Rushdie's (in)famous statement in his Introduction to the *Vintage Book of Indian Literature* (1997) that

> . . . the prose writing – both fiction and non-fiction – created in this period by Indian writers working in English, is proving to be a stronger and more important body of work than most of what has been produced in the 16 'official languages' of India, the so-called 'vernacular languages', during the same time; and, indeed, this new, and still burgeoning, 'Indo-Anglian' literature represents perhaps the most valuable contribution India has yet made to the world of books. (x)

This statement, offensive to many Indian writers and lovers of literature, denigrating the value of an entire corpus of literature written in the *bhashas*, provoked, naturally enough, substantial opposition. In a bid to answer back to the writer who had ostensibly answered back to the colonial powers, the *bhasha* writers and critics began to question the value of English literature produced in India. Issues such as the foreign origin of English were resurrected and were conflated with ideological issues regarding the class and caste of the writers of English literature, thereby effectively placing Indian writing in English and Indian writing in the *bhashas* in opposite camps. This controversy, a crucial aspect of modern literary studies in India, will be dealt with in detail later.

The centrality of English in postcolonial criticism was further strengthened by the stress it put on non-standard uses of English (what the authors of *The Empire Writes Back* christened as 'english') in particular and not any language in general. The two-way relationship between creative literature and criticism paved the way for a large number of critical studies of these very English texts, further giving the impression that all English texts from India dealt merely and always with the themes of identity (a misplaced belief that Indians are grappling with Indian and western aspects of identity every day of their lives), colonial history etc. Taken together, this was further seen to create the misconception that all literatures from India were 'postcolonial.'

Reactions against such tendencies of postcolonial criticism came quite early. Aijaz Ahmed in 'Jameson's Rhetoric of Otherness and the "National Allegory"' (his famed response to Fredric Jameson's essay 'Third-World Literature in the Era of Multinational Capitalism') was one of the first of them. Apart from the familiar disagreement with Jameson's assertion that all Third-World literature must be read as national allegories, the essay also points out that due to the unavailability of translations, the few accessible English texts from India are seen as 'representative' of the sub-continent. This awareness of the unequal projection of *bhasha* literatures and Indian Writing in English testifies to the 'great divide' between Indian writing in English and Indian writing in the *bhashas* which seems to have become all-consuming in recent times in literary studies in India and can be seen as yet another manifestation of the need to define India in terms of an 'Indian-ness.' The distrust regarding the English language and literature itself has compelled readers to address issues of class and caste rather than merely literary merits and demerits.

Apart from the distrust of the monolingual bias of early postcolonial criticism, there has been much debate on the themes and motifs that it tended to recognise – namely, the insistence on nationalism, freedom, the valorisation of the native, vilification of the coloniser and a one-sided view of colonialism as utterly bad and evil. The critical attention given to these issues created a canon wherein only texts that glorified a pre-colonial, 'pristine,' native way of life were regarded as 'authentic.' Any deviation from this was viewed almost as treason. Although such a practice did 'turn the tables' on the earlier Eurocentric view of literature, literary form and canon, it also disallowed any nuanced understanding of the two-way cultural dialogue that the colonial period would necessarily have engendered.

Despite this, there is, among the critics from the erstwhile colonised world, the fear that the postcolonial paradigm merely recreates the very same hierarchy that it seeks to denounce, leading ultimately to the continued centrality of the colonial period itself. One of the earliest voices in this regard was that of Salman Rushdie. In 'Commonwealth Literature Does Not Exist' in his collection of essays *Imaginary Homelands* (1991), he makes a case against this kind of categorisation. In arguments which are based largely on the thematic isolation implied in the term 'commonwealth', he points out that to expect all literature from the former colonies to deal with the same set of themes i.e. valorisation of nationalism, assertion of national identity and vilification of colonialism, is to place these texts in a further straitjacket. The inability of the model to fully understand other positions that may have an ambiguous attitude towards colonialism is addressed by critics like Arun Prabha Mukherjee: she sees the model as totally incapable of understanding the position of a thinker like B. R. Ambedkar for whom the coloniser would have provided a means of social uplift by secular education that was denied to the Untouchables by traditional society because of their caste (Trivedi and Mukherjee, 'Interrogating Postcolonialism: Some Uneasy Conjectures'). The ways in which colonial hegemony worked with or against various kinds of native hegemonies like gender and caste are, however, yet to be fully analysed. In either case, an unqualified use of the postcolonial model may not prove very useful.

That postcolonialism as a critical model is becoming increasingly suspect is clear from the fact that writers themselves have in recent times objected to the use of the nomenclature 'postcolonial' to define them. One such voice was that of Amitav Ghosh in his letter to the Commonwealth Award Committee (dated 18 March 2001) declining the award for his novel *The Glass Palace* (2000). The letter brings out the inadequacy of the nomenclature of 'postcolonial literature' when dealing with a multilingual and multicultural society like India:

> I have on many occasions publicly stated my objections to the classification of books such as mine under the term 'Commonwealth Literature'. Principal among these is that this phrase anchors an area of contemporary writing not within the realities of the present day, nor within the possibilities of the future, but rather within a disputed aspect of the past. (www.amitavghosh.com, 18 March 2001)

The letter goes on:

> As a grouping of nations collected from the remains of the British Empire, the Commonwealth serves as an umbrella forum in global politics. As a literary or cultural grouping however, it seems to me that 'the Commonwealth' can only be a misnomer so long as it excludes the many languages that sustain the cultural and literary lives of these countries (it is surely inconceivable, for example, that athletes would have to be fluent in English in order to qualify for the Commonwealth Games).(www.amitavghosh.com; 18 March 2001)

That postcolonialism continues to place the colonial experience at the centre is its undoing, argue critics like T. Vijay Kumar who in 'Post-Colonial or postcolonial: Relocating the Hyphen' see the very prefix 'post' in 'postcolonial' as a graphological marker of its ideological bias (Trivedi and Mukherjee). In other words, there is now a clearer understanding that the paradigm tends to validate precisely that which it seeks to negate namely, the centrality of the West over the non-West.

The suspicion regarding the eurocentrism of postcolonialism is somewhat exacerbated by the popularity that the model has received in the Western academia. That the prominent theorists of the model teach in Western academic institutions and publish primarily in Western journals has led many writers and critics to suspect them of playing to the Western academic gallery. The glaring example of such a theorist is Gayatri Chakravarty Spivak. That these theorists are only remotely acquainted with, if not untouched by recent debates on caste and gender within India and therefore are incapable of using them in their discussions, is another accusation against them.

Yet, many critics in India with varied ideological orientations have used several aspects of postcolonial criticism in their own debates. The case of non-standard use of any language has already been mentioned. Even as postcolonial criticism encouraged the use of 'native' versions of 'english' and saw these as a mode of destabilising the colonial power structure, Dalit literature in various Indian languages has questioned notions of standard forms of any language. The celebration in Dalit literature and criticism of the use of dialectal versions and the apotheosis of hitherto denigrated cultural items share much of the spirit of postcolonial theory. Similarly, the conscious assertion of a different perception of the world in feminist critiques of patriarchal cultures and texts, and the attempts to find different forms of resistance to patriarchy too share their methodology with postcolonial criticism. Such attempts point to fruitful adaptations of the approach of postcolonialism to suit different positions and stand in opposition to either outright denials of the value of the paradigm or its uncritical use.

Suspicions of the postcolonial critical framework point to a historical need to redefine the projection of Indian literature and India to the outside world. That literature is one of the sites where the nation can not only be constructed, but also projected in particular ways to the outside world underscores its value. The antagonism against the model is not an issue involving language alone but needs to be seen in the context of the growing suspicion of English itself as a language that can be used for national self-projection.

Texts like Raja Rao's 'Preface' to *Kanthapura* (1936) had stressed the dilemma of an Indian using a non-Indian language – English – to represent an Indian reality. For long, this was the main subject for discussion. These debates were linguistic (concerned with the relationship between language and culture) and literary (how good can such writing be). By the 1990s, however, the shape of this criticism had drastically changed. English was distrusted not so much because it was a foreign language, but because within India, it is the language of an elite and privileged group. The fear that *bhasha* texts suffer from the over-projection of English texts on the literary scene needs to be read as articulating the apprehension that such an over-projection of English novels might misrepresent India as a homogeneous entity to the outside world, leading in turn to a denial of urgent social problems and issues which affect the life of the ordinary Indians as opposed to the elite. This has led, in its turn, to a scrutiny of the caste and class affiliations of earlier writers in a bid by criticism to reiterate that it works as an effective corrective to any projection of India as a homogeneous if not monolithic mass, through English novels. Tabish Khair's analyses of R. K. Narayan, Raja Rao and Mulk Raj Anand as representing an upper-class, upper-caste milieu in *Babu Fictions: Alienation in Contemporary Indian English Novels* (2001); Makarand Paranjape's review of the major writers from the point of view of their caste in *Towards A Poetics of the Indian English Novel* (2000); his study in the same work of the translations of only elite words, phrases and proverbs in Raja Rao's works; the refusal by literary awards institutions such as the K. K. Birla Foundation which has instituted the Saraswati Samman, and the Bharatiya Jnanpith to consider English texts for their awards, are all different manifestations of this suspicion of English, and by extension, of majoritarian discourses.

There is also a perceptible change in the way in which non-Western 'English' is viewed. For long, such uses were seen as positive markers of the 'Indianisation' of English whereas today, critical focus has shifted its perspective. C. N. Ramachandran, for instance, in his essay 'Critical Response to Rushdie' calls attention to the fact that although Rushdie's use of English is seen as being 'born out of a creative consciousness' and a 'subversion of English language,' 'it is actually a mere chutnification and serves only to reinforce the Western idea that Indians use a form of pidgin English or Butler English' (31). Vikram Chandra mentions in an article titled 'The Cult of Authenticity' which appeared in *The Boston Review* (Feb/March Issue 2002), that Meenakshi Mukherjee saw his use of Sanskrit words like *dharma*, *artha*, *kama* etc. as chapter titles in *Love and Longing in Bombay* (1997) as a strategy to entice a Western audience. The implication was that by using these terms from Sanskrit philosophy the novelist was 'giving in' to the Orientalist Western notion that Sanskrit – a classical 'elite' language associated with a particular and hegemonic class, caste and gender – is the representative language of India. As a writer, however, Vikram Chandra foregrounds the philosophical and popular meanings that these words still carry in the minds of the common public. He goes on to list a number of Hindi films carrying the word 'dhrama' in it, testifying to the real, lived meaning the word has in India today. Amit Choudhury says in his introduction to the *Picador Book of Modern Indian Literature* (2001) that postcolonial hybrid language need not be confined to exotic words alone nor need it 'be worn like a national costume' (xxvi). He wishes to stress the point that often, such a use of language is natural for many, thereby subtly questioning the tendency in postcolonialism to pick out any instance of linguistic aberration as a conscious attempt to recast language. We can see here already a shift in critical perspective – away from the purely literary and aesthetic to a greater interaction and dialogue with the issues and concerns current in society, mostly those related to equity, self-esteem and privileging.

Suspicions concerning the postcolonial model bring us to an important motif in criticism in recent times in India – the divide between the insider and outsider positions – leading to an almost irresolvable question of the authenticity of the speaking voice. This trend has to be seen in the context of the general suspicion of any idea or concept that comes from a privileged position. A reappraisal of tradition and culture has called for affirmative actions that try to correct the social inequities of the past. Highly commendable though this trend is in politics and public spheres, it also needs to beware of merely reversing hierarchies, and in the process getting more deeply entrenched in the oppressive social structure. The tendency to doubt any critical stand stemming from a privileged position – be it caste, class, gender or culture – has led to the articulation of a number of problems with the postcolonial model. The feeling that a privileged position is incapable of fully understanding the difficulties faced by people *living* in marginal / suppressed communities is very strong. This naturally brings up the question of the authenticity of the speaking voice. Who can speak for a culture, especially for a culture that has long been suppressed? Not surprisingly, an outsider's voice is regarded with immense scepticism. There is the belief that the outsider's position 'naturally' makes her / him a victim of the ideological biases of her / his community. Hence, novels about India written by Indians living outside the country are received with a degree of reservation, for, living with the privileges that the West allows, it is assumed that they are highly likely to be unaware of urgent problems related to caste, gender and environment, confronted by the Indian masses. Needless to say, novels set in and dealing with India but written by non-Indians are scarcely given any serious critical attention. Barring older writers like Paul Scott, Rudyard Kipling, E. M. Forster and John Masters, there are few critical appraisals of novels written by say, Martin Kämpchen or David Iglehart (both European writers whom Ashokamitran identifies in his article in the Tamil magazine *Kumudam* as writing from an admirable 'insider' position) or for that matter, the most recent novel of the Australian woman writer Inez Baraney, *Neem Dreams* (2003), which captures the tumult surrounding the question of Intellectual Property Rights in India. Even the recent attention given to novels like *Jahanara* (1989) by Lyanne Guillane and *White Mughals* by William Dalrymple has been restricted to slender reviews, and that too is partly because these novels deal with a particular phase of the past in Indian history. Novels dealing with present-day India and written by non-Indians are assumed to naturally harbour an Orientalist attitude. The critical centrality of the victim–insider position can be seen to emerge all the more strongly in Dalit writing, where any text on Dalit issues written by a non-Dalit is immediately not only suspect, but also actively discarded. In the case of women's literature, the issue of whether men can be 'feminists' and understand a woman's position has become so polemical that 'men in feminism' has itself become an entry in anthologies of critical viewpoints. However, in the Indian academic scene, the question of the ability of men to address women's problems does not seem to appear with much persistence.

In other words, the tendency in criticism is more towards the privileging of a position where the insider and the marginal coincide. Necessary though this literary affirmative action is, it should not blind us to the fact that we need to critique a text and an idea for itself as much as we need to critique it for the position from which it comes. The use to which Dalit criticism has put the methodology of postcolonial criticism is a case of using a suspect tool in the best interests of the critic employing it. Similarly, English literature is out of favour in some quarters precisely because it uses a language that is not 'Indian' in origin but was a colonial imposition and, secondly and more importantly, because even within India, it represents the lifestyle and attitudes of the elite and privileged classes and castes. The issue needs to be looked at more openly and critically.

This suspicion of English literature produced from India has given a more or less self-defensive tone to much criticism that supports or even merely analyses English texts. Almost as though to counter the accusation that this literature is a foreign bird in Indian feathers, most analyses of English novels devote much space to highlighting their Indian-ness. Again, the reciprocal relationship between creative and critical literature has tended to make novels themselves foreground their 'Indian identity'. One important area of literary studies in this context has been that of narrative and narratology. Although the study of narratology has, for long, been a critical favourite, the purely structuralist mode has today given way to a cultural critique firmly rooted in a historical context.

That there is a narrative tradition peculiar to the non-West in general and to India in particular is today a critical cliché. Many novels written in English have been following a narrative model that is a far cry from the linear, single-'story-ed' narrative of the Victorian novel or even the loosely flowing stream-of-consciousness narrative of the modernist novel. The apparently formless form of the novels written from the 1980s onwards is generally seen as owing this structure to the self-conscious narration employed by Rushdie in *Midnight's Children* (1981). Although the form itself was in use in earlier novels such as Raja Rao's *Kanthapura*, M. Anantanarayanan's *The Silver Pilgrimage* etc., *Midnight's Children* brought to it a self-consciousness that made it impossible for critics to ignore the implications of such a use. This form – marked by stories-within-stories, a denial of the linearity of time, the use of a narrator rather than a writer thereby stressing orality, the use of storytelling to narrate history and the self – has become so common that it has been critically acclaimed as one of the features of the 'New Indian Novel in English' as the novels published after 1980 are christened. Rushdie himself helped bolster this connection in various interviews and articles by citing oral narrative traditions as having influenced him much more than Latin American and Western magic-realist writers like Gabriel Garcia Marquez and Günter Grass. Witness for example, this remark:

> The other thing about form is that it has to do with the structure of the oral narrative. For a long time, I have been interested in that. If you listen to anybody – your grandmother or a public storyteller telling stories, it is also never beginning–middle–end. . . . It seems random, but let us assume that the same is a deliberate one and not accidental because the shape has settled . . . that form is part of the enjoyment of the story. (Interview with Shanta Gokhale)

In yet another interview, he commented on the form of the oral narration itself:

> The oral narrative does not go from the beginning to the middle to the end of the story. It goes in great swoops . . . spirals or in loops, it every so often reiterates something that happened earlier to remind you and then takes off again . . . . Sometimes there are Chinese Boxes where there is a story inside a story inside a story inside a story . . . it

> has the appearance of being random and chaotic because this shape conformed very exactly to the shape in which people liked to listen. (qtd. in Malak, 114)

The focus on oral narration and its contours and trajectories has gained greater critical currency as many of the features of such narration are seen to be similar to those of post-modern narratives. Viney Kirpal in her introduction to *The New Indian Novel in English: A Study of the 1980s* (1990) studies the tendency on the part of critics to equate the technique of loose structure with the deliberate discontinuity in postmodern narratives. In her opinion, 'Quite often, the complexity latent in oral narrative structures (which are metaphoric in nature) get mistaken for the consciously created technical complexity of modern / post-modern works' (xvi).

The focus on narrative – and by extension form – is not without its political implications. The disjointed narrative structure of the novels has forced a critical reconsideration of the novel form itself and this reconsideration has also been linked to the construction of national form. In his introduction to *Indian Fiction of the Nineties* (1997), R. S. Pathak indicates that many novelists are aware that the 'issues pertaining to the Indian subcontinent cannot be easily and simplistically rendered' and that therefore, 'all of them have made use of a complex narrative technique' (x) which results in a break from the old fictional form. In an exclusive interview with Jonathan Noakes, Rushdie echoes the same opinion when he says: 'India is not neat and restrained and highly selected and so on. India is crowded and excessive and vulgar and overblown and far too much for anyone to take in at any given time. So you have to have a literature of that kind of excess, of too muchness' (Reynolds and Noakes, 12). However, in his introduction to *The Picador Book of Modern Indian Literature*, Amit Choudhury sees this tendency to view the novelistic form as synonymous with the shape of the nation, and what is more, justify it by an appeal to magic-realism, as a critical anomaly. It amounts, he feels, to a paradox that despite the avowals of anti-realism, such an analogical thinking follows a mimesis of form, where the bulk of the book is directly related to the bulk of India.

Such a critical connection made between national form and novelistic form has led to a veritable redefinition of the nation itself as plural and multiple with a variety of voices, many contradictory, but each with a validity and ground of its own. This is quite different from the earlier notion of India as an idealistic homogeneous nation where differences of race, caste, gender and language were seen as antitheses to the idea of unity and were effectively subsumed or reduced in potency.

However, it is doubtful if such a connection between the two 'forms' is an aspect of literary studies of *bhasha* texts, for it appears in English studies to be an instance of criticism trying to prove its 'Indian-ness' in the face of a hostile denigration. The focus on disjointed, structureless narrative is a critical coordinate in the analyses of many *bhasha* texts too as the readings of novels such as Vishwas Patil's Marathi novel *Jhadajhadati*, the Gopallapuram chronicles (*Gopalla Gramam* (The Gopallam Village) [1976] and *Gopallapurathu Makkal* (The People of Gopallapuram) [1990]) in Tamil by Ki. Rajanarayanan and Thakazhi Sivasankara Pillai's Malayalam novel *Kayar* (Coir) (trans. 1997) show. Indeed, given the structure of the narrative in them it would be impossible for criticism to ignore it. However, there is no pressure to connect such a narrative to national form or to see it as a definite marker of an 'Indian-ness.' The discussions, by Nuhman and Ashokamitran regarding the Gopallapuram chronicles for example, focus on how these texts virtually redefine the concept of the novel because of the absence of a linear structure and of a single protagonist. The various reviews of *Jhadajhadati* merely mention its disjointed narrative without interpreting it in terms of the structure of the nation. *Kayar* however, is an exception, for criticism on the novel *has* tended to relate its narrative to that of the Mahabharata and the Ramayana and even to identify coordinates of the *pauranic*[5] structures in it, thereby definitely relating it to an 'Indian' context. Ayyappa Panikker's analysis is one such:

> With appropriate change, several of these features may be found built into the structure of *Kayar*. It is a long narrative in prose dealing with what has been handed down from the past through various oral traditions. Sarga and Pratisarga here will have to be interpreted differently as indicating the process of land reclamation, revenue settlement, land survey [etc.] . . . The synchronic narration of the histories of several families of Brahmins, Nairs, Christians, Muslims, Ezhavas and Pulayas is reminiscent of the Vamsavali found in Sanskrit puranas. The desertion of land ... corresponds to the dissolution of the world in some of the puranas. One need not, however, overstress the point, differences are natural and to be expected. ('The Narratology of *Kayar*' 103)

The author of the novel, Thakazhi Sivasankara Pillai, had himself made the connection in his Jnanpith Award acceptance speech:

> The modern novel and short story have their roots in the West. There, they are deeply connected to life as is lived in the West. We have had our own different kinds of narrative traditions and techniques which were partly in poetry. Ramayana and Mahabharata are examples. Why do we not try to evolve a form of our own? This is what I have tried to do in a humble way in *Kayar*. This novel has in it the life and social conditions of Kerala in the last 250 years. This could not have fitted into any Western mould. (*Jnanpith Puraskar: 1965–1990*; translation mine)

Many reviews of the novel too have argued along similar lines. Vanajam Ravindran points out that the technique of the novel is directly drawn from the Mahabharata in that it weaves various stories and themes without allowing them to be 'subsumed by an overarching central theme' ('This Mortal Coil'). Along a very similar vein, R. A. Asher points out that despite the influence of many Western thinkers, Thakazhi's greatest influence was the Indian style of storytelling ('Kerala's Greatest Modern Writers'). Talking of *Kayar,* Ayyappa Panikker mentions the compulsive historian Achoma Kurup 'who cannot take rest unless he passes on the tradition of story-telling, along with the inherited and accumulated stories of the community to the new generation, both the tale and its telling, both the history and its historiography. Thakazhi has gone on record that he learned this dual art from Vyasa, the author of *Mahabharata*' ('The End of Historiography?' 1).

It is this binary between Indian narrative/ historiography and a Western one which is exploited by various kinds of criticisms of English novels in order to stress their 'Indian-ness'. Blurbs of novels often pick up the narrative and its Indian-ness. Publications of *Red Earth and Pouring Rain* [1995] have blurbs that constantly refer to its Arabian Nights structure and Scheherzade; those of *Love and Longing in Bombay* to the insistent appearance of the 'controlling narrator' motif while blurbs of *A River Sutra* (1993) remind us of the disjointed narrative structure. Reviews frequently take note of the connections between such a structure and the reinterpretation of history (again as in the case of *Red Earth and Pouring Rain* and Amitav Ghosh's *In an Antique Land* (1992). A reinterpretation of Indian history, especially colonial history, from an Indian perspective is thus a staple point of 'Indian-ness' in novels.

Needless to say, such a critical model assumes a binary opposition between the coloniser and the colonised and is definitely an exercise in postcolonial criticism. The underlying belief here is that Indian history has been mutilated and prejudicially interpreted by British historians, both in form and content. Much critical space, theoretical as well as textual, has been taken up in expounding this claim. Such critical endeavours are very much concerned with the low esteem in which Indian modes of historiography have been held and consequently attempt to regain a sense of pride in native historiographic traditions. Essays like those written by G. N. Devy in *Of Many Heroes* (1998) and the collection *Narrative: A Seminar* (1994), which is an outcome of a seminar conducted by the Sahitya Akademi and Ayyappa Paniker's *Indian Narratology* all contain ample analyses of the 'different' modes of narrative employed by Indians in writing history and in valorising these over the Enlightenment model followed by the British. The same preoccupation with a differential historiography can also be seen in many of the essays that make up the various volumes of *Subaltern Studies*. Textual analyses of novels cast in the native modes of historiography tend again to relate their cyclical structures, formlessness etc. to a historiographic method that is peculiarly Indian. This too appears to be a case peculiar to English criticism from India as, except for the above-quoted instances from Thakazhi, few *bhasha* texts have felt it necessary to reinterpret historiography itself.

However, we also need to pause to see what is being projected as this 'Indian' alternative for a colonial model. In most of the cases cited above, we find the insistence on a *pauranic* mode and a recurrent return to the Mahabharata, the Indian epics and oral narrative traditions as the alternative. However, a dogmatic promotion of only the loose epic model tends to blind such critics and readers to other non-European modes of writing history that have been used in *bhasha* texts. A signal instance is that of the Persian *dastaan* mode used specifically in Qurratulain Hyder's Urdu novel *Aag ka Dariya* (1959) (*River of Fire*; trans. 1998). Given the history of the Urdu language, it would seem almost the natural narrative choice especially since the novel itself deals with almost thousand years of Indian history and stresses on the multi-ethnic, mixed nature of Indian culture. Mohammad Umar Memon describes the features of the *dastaan* when it was collected and written down: 'It referred all causality to supernatural rather than to human or natural agencies. It offered a different notion of time and its characters were unavoidably two-dimensional. Stripped of individuality, they were commissioned to personify abstract ideas' ('Modern Urdu Literature: An Introduction' 1). He says that 'until it was finally written down and printed in the nineteenth century, [it] was an oral and anonymous composition, narrated by professional story-tellers for the entertainment of a feudal or metropolitan aristocracy, though often also for the amusement of the masses' ('Modern Urdu Literature: An Introduction' 1). The importance of the *dastaan* mode in reading *Aag ka Dariya* would be heightened if one were to place this novel in the context of the history of the mode. J. B. Paksoy analyses the *dastaan* mode as it was practised in parts of Central Asia:

> Dastans commemorate the deeds of fearless and capable men and women. They rise from among the people when critically important tasks need to be performed. Often this task is to fight for the independence of a polity, or group of polities which we now refer to as confederation. (Paksoy, 'The Dastan genre in Central Asia', 1)

He goes on to analyse the political and social uses to which it was put:

> Various propagandists have sought to utilize the dastans as platforms to carry new messages. Various Islamic propagators attempted to inject their religious philosophy into a number of dastans in the hope of making the newcomer religion to Central Asia more palatable. (5)

He adds that, 'After the Russian invasion and occupation of Central Asia, the local populace vehemently opposed the new alien invader and began collecting and publishing the *dastaans*' (5); he adds that 'dastans were used in their customary way against Russian power during the 1916–1930 Turkistan Liberation Movement, called by the Russians the Basmachi Movement' (5). He goes on to tell us that from 1925 onwards:

> . . . dastans were collected by the authorities in order to be hidden away; reciters were killed. At the same time, Central Asian intellectuals began cleansing added elements and publishing the dastans in forms as close as possible to their originals. Many paid with their lives. The message of that era was, once again, freedom. (6)

Hyder's novel, written in Urdu a few years after independence and stressing the cosmopolitanism of Indian culture, can be legitimately read as consciously using the *dastaan* mode to posit a view of Indian culture that questioned definitions of India invoked by a nascent nation. Yet, much available criticism on the translated version of the novel continues to read it in the light of the structure of the Mahabharata (like reviews by Shohini Ghosh and Aamer Hussein). Such criticism also relates the schemes of different temporality used in the novel as a conscious means employed to stress its Indianness. Few, if any, even mention the *dastaan* mode and this can, in fact, be a fruitful area for further research.

The other alternative mode of writing history that criticism has not taken into account is of the kind we find in texts like Ki. Rajanarayanan's Gopallapuram chronicles. In this Tamil work, history is written in the form of everyday, ordinary stories of people belonging to a community. Such a writing fills the aporia in official versions of history, by documenting the lives of ordinary people in a way as cannot be seen in academic historiographies. Postcolonial criticism in India, however, has often been blinded by its zeal to foreground the *pauranic* mode of historiography as the only alternative to its Western counterpart and methods / modes such as the *dastaan* and everyday historiographies have remained relatively unexplored.

The nationalist zeal which has caused much literary criticism in the country to question the validity of English writing from India, alleging that it is 'false' because of its foreign origin and latterly its Western orientation, is itself postcolonial in nature. For, it tends to fall back upon the staples of postcolonial criticism, namely, the insider–outsider divide and the valorisation of the insider–native position. It is surprising that critics who deride the postcolonial model, also exploit its implications in positioning themselves. For instance, the critical school christened as 'nativism' seeks to oust English writing from India altogether. Its main proponent Bhalchandra Nemade quite vociferously questions the value of English in India based not on its current social and cultural use, but rather on its past. He sees English literature from India as an aberration in the Indian literary scene because it is not 'rooted' in India; and as 'an abnormal case of a historical development' (qtd. in Mehrotra, *An Illustrated History*, 17) because the 'mode of operation of English ... has been cultural–written–formal rather than social–oral–conversational' (qtd. in Mehrotra, 18). He goes on to assert that 'It is time we realised the fact that beyond our own "language group" all that we do smacks of mediocrity' (qtd. in Mehrotra, 19). The underlying criterion here is again that of 'authenticity' and insidedness. Such critical positions view

English and all of english literature from India with contempt, and can be said to be the cause of much of the self-defensive tone of criticism in English. Hence the anxiety to identify the markers of Indian-ness.

Such an antipathy has also impelled the *desi* / nationalist spokesperson to place Indian writing in English and writing in the *bhashas* in two opposite categories. In an article significantly titled 'Midnight's Orphans' in the magazine *Outlook* (25 Feb. 2002), this debate was acted out by drawing upon a series of interviews with *bhasha* writers. U.R. Anantamurthy, the noted Kannada writer and academic, was sore that 'There are any number of top-quality regional writers who don't get international recognition only because their language is not the global language of America' (Reddy, 54). Similarly, the Hindi novelist Nirmal Varma felt that 'Indian writers in English find themselves in a strange place; the emotional content is missing, as is the real core of the Indian experience' (Reddy, 62). The Tamil writer Ashokamitran likewise thought that

> Being rooted eludes writers like Naipaul and Rushdie. Rushdie is extremely clever and he does try to be Indian, but not successfully . . . This distance from the community the IWE[6] have, their sense of not belonging anywhere, their lack of emotive content, makes them prime candidates for a spiritual life, not writers. (57)

Such a distrust of Indian writing in English is only reinforced by the belief that its authors are quite imitative of the kinds of narrative and themes currently accorded critical attention in the Western academia. On the other hand, the regional writers claim that they learn more from writers from say, Latin America directly, and that in this respect, Indian writing in English certainly lags behind. Jayamohan, a Tamil writer, believed that: 'the experiments happening in Tamil and Malayalam fiction are far bolder than anything happening in Indian English' and that 'The IWE are writing a standardised form of fiction. They read like assembled works put together by some clever editor. The core of a literary piece nowadays is the style and mode of expression. In regional languages, there is vast scope for experiments in expression, but I don't find this happening in IWE' (62). Nirmal Varma was convinced that: 'The best writers in regional languages are coming from a different class than IWE – the middle class and the lower middle class. Their writing portrays contemporary India, its folklore, encompasses the entire epic flow of their life' (62).

A closer look at the arguments so far listed will bear out that the basis for denying value to Indian writing in English lies largely in identifying the alleged lack of a sense of 'belonging' or rootedness and in the fact that only a particular class of people is represented in such writing. However, we need to look at the arguments in a far more pragmatic manner. A sizeable number of Indians writing in English (by no means all of them) write from outside India and their very 'derootedness' which is decried in the above interviews becomes, in fact, the theme of their novels. Chitra Bannerjee Divakaruni's *The Mistress of Spices* (1997) depicts the racial problems faced by Indians in America; Sunetra Gupta's novels dramatise the fate of a generation that is constantly on the move and is consequently homeless; Abhay's story in *Red Earth and Pouring Rain* (1995) tells us about the inability of an Indian of his generation to feel at home in India or America; while Rohinton Mistry's novels keep returning to India as a place from where to draw sustenance when he himself was settled in Canada. This is an experience of a particular class of Indians and its literary articulation cannot be dismissed on account of its expatriateness.

Secondly, Indian writers in English are fast moving out of the earlier tendency to write only novels that depict the colonial period or ones that only contain particular imitative kinds of experimentation. A novel like Kaveri Nambisan's *The Scent of Pepper* (1996) captures the changes taking place in a small village in the Coorg region of Karnataka and is quite as region-specific as are the Gopallapuram chronicles and *Kayar*; Kiran Nagarkar's *Cuckold* (1997) and *Ravan and Eddie* (1995) are remarkable for drawing thematically upon Indian sources – the former from Indian history and the latter contemporary Mumbai *chawl* (set of houses in a lower / upper-middle class area) and for also beautifully exploiting the element of humour; Boman Desai's *The Memory of Elephants* (1980), analysed in detail here in Chapter 4, chronicles the history of the Parsi ethnic community in India and draws quite successfully from Gujarati linguistic registers in English; Amitav Ghosh's *In an Antique Land* (1992) does critique colonialism, but is quite devoid of the attempt to reverse the power relationship implicit in that historical process; Githa Hariharan's *When Dreams Travel* (1999) depicts the problems of women in a mythic and fabulous form while her *In Times of Siege* (2003) censures the contemporary rise of Hindutva as a political and cultural ideology – and the list is potentially endless.

We might then say that Indian writing in English is moving out of the thematic and narrative constraints of the postcolonial model and looking for and at contemporary concerns – a fact that criticism, caught in the binary between Indian and non-Indian, authentic and inauthentic, inside and outside, appears not to have taken serious note of.

## Critical Categories

The very act of placing texts in categories – at the time of production or consumption and the parameters used for this reflect many of the cultural and political debates of the day. A discussion on this would also bring out how the concepts of literary identities and national identities are linked together.

Traditionally there have been three major parameters for the categorisation of literary texts: a. genre, b. period and c. language. Of the three, no one can really be said to be more important than the other. In the following discussion, the parameter of genre will be eschewed as we are studying only the novel.

Language has for long acted as an important identity matrix of a text. Its inevitable use as a paradigm of classification and the debates over it discussed above underscore many features of current critical thinking in India. So overpowering has been the role of language that for long, discussions were confined to texts from a single language alone, thereby disallowing a cross-cultural or even a multi-cultural understanding of 'Indian' literature. It is only in recent times that language has not been so restrictive a category and criticism has opened itself out to reading texts from different languages together. In other words, criticism has begun to implicitly regard texts as simultaneously belonging to more than one critical category.

The division of literature according to particular periods is part of the practice of literary historiography that attempts to place texts in the political and cultural contexts of their production. A more or less common format can be traced across the literary histories of all Indian languages wherein literature is divided into the following periods: a. classical (referring to literature written either in Sanskrit or under the heavy influence of Sanskrit / Persian literary traditions), b. Renaissance (referring to the literatures produced during the period referred to as the Indian renaissance, i.e. in the last half of the nineteenth century), c. nationalist period / Gandhian period (referring to the literatures written during / under the influence of the freedom struggle), d. modernist (the literatures written during the 1960s and 1970s showing definite influences of the European modernist movement and the existentialist philosophy) and e. post-modernist (literature written during the 1980s, 1990s and since). These or very similar divisions can be found in almost all languages, including English writing where the first category alone is not relevant for obvious historical reasons. These divisions, often the primary principle of grouping texts along with language, recur in a number of essays, articles and multi-volume books. The four-volume work titled *Encyclopaedia of Indian Literature* (1987) published by the Sahitya Akademi carries entries arranged simultaneously along all the aforementioned categories: witness entries such as 'Novel: Tamil' or 'Modernism: Kannada' etc., thereby fusing language and period as bases for categorisation. A very similar trend can be seen in Meenakshi Mukherjee's very influential book *Realism and Reality* (1985) which analyses novels written in various languages during the same period, namely, that of Indian renaissance, and uses the same parameters – the interactions between the print media, social reform movements and the novels of the period. Interestingly, it takes up also *Rajmohan's Wife* (1864) by Bankimchandra Chatterjee, the first English novel to be published in India and analyses it along the same lines. By so placing different literary traditions together, the book effectively displaces language as the final, definitive and restrictive principle of identifying a literary tradition. The same inference can be made when we look at anthologies of essays dealing with particular themes or periods. For instance, an anthology like T. W. Clarke's *The Novel in India* (1970) recounts the story of the rise of the novel form in various Indian languages, thereby providing a multilingual picture of the genre in the country. Other such books include collections of essays like Indra Nath Choudhary's *The Genesis of Imagination: Selected Essays on Literature* (2001), *Theory, Religion and Culture, Regionality and Comparative Literature: Papers in Comparative Literature: Seminars and Workshops 1993–1998* (1998) edited by Sudha Chakraborty Dasgupta, *Narrative: A Seminar* (1998) edited by Amiya Dev (a collection of papers presented at a Sahitya Akademi seminar), *The Growth of the Novel in India* (1989) by P. K. Rajan, Prabhakar Machwe's *Four Decades of Indian Literature: A Critical Evaluation* (1976); *Literary Criticism in India* (1976) edited by Nagendra that deals with the history of criticism in various languages. Significantly, there is also the trend of dividing the languages according to their region: *Routes* (2000), for example, anthologises, as its subtitle reveals, short stories from the South Indian languages alone that represent the 'West' in different ways; Sivasankari's four-volume collection titled *Knit India through Literature* (1998 onwards) is also divided along zonal lines, with each volume covering the languages of one zone. The last method can be seen in the *Kshetra Samiti* i.e. the zonal level of selection of the Saraswati Samman Award which will be discussed in detail in Chapter 3.

All these collections and anthologies, by dealing with a single theme across a variety of languages, create a space wherein commonalities can be identified. This in effect manages to create possibilities for fruitful dialogue between different languages from different regions. Criticism is a sphere where such a dialogue can occur. The importance of such an exercise becomes clearer when we look at marginalised and protest literatures such as Dalit writing and women's literature. These are areas where literature has been used as a forum for carrying on the social and cultural war for securing dignity and equal rights. In such a situation, it is important that commonalities be identified and nurtured across languages so that a common map can be created and modes of resistance be charted out. It becomes an act of political survival that texts by women and/or Dalits across various languages be read together and hence, it is today becoming possible to place along the same plane writers as diverse as Indira Goswami (who writes in Assamese about the problems of women), Bama (who writes in Tamil about Dalits and women), Ambai (who writes in Tamil mostly about upper caste women) and Mahasweta Devi (who writes in Bengali about women, tribals and other marginalised groups) and also place these women alongside other male writers like Sharankumar Limbale and Lakshman Mane who address the issue of caste.

Such an endeavour to overcome the finality of language as a divisive paradigm has been complemented by the publication of anthologies of creative as well as discursive writing that carry translations of texts from various languages into English. This marks an important move towards a shifting self-perception and self-projection of India through literature as most of these anthologies are brought out by publishing houses which are the Indian sections of well-known international publishing houses like Penguin (India) or Orient Longman and therefore have a worldwide market. They are also being increasingly used as textbooks in colleges and universities in

India and outside. Some examples are *The Picador Book of Modern Indian Literature* edited by Amit Choudhury, Sivasankari's four-volume *Knit India Through Literature*, Lalitha and Susie Tharu's two-volume *Women Writing in India* (1991) etc. These anthologies also come with informative and critical introductions which make it possible for the reader to understand the context of the publication of their entries from across various languages.

The form of anthology calls for a different kind of reading practice where individual pieces need to be seen in the context of the overarching theme of the anthology and need also to be placed against each other. An anthology by its very nature has a single thematic framework/ motif/ controlling metaphor running through it. Entries are selected based on this common thread. However, by selecting entries bearing in mind the linguistic plurality of the country, anthologies of criticism and creative literatures published recently in India force us to read the extracts / entries alongside each other and trace similarities and differences among them. For instance, Lalitha and Susie Tharu's *Women Writing in India* puts writings by saints and religious women in the tradition of women's writing. Although the feminist slant in the songs of female saints like Meera has already been noted by many modern critics, this anthology places them along with similar saints from various religions (for example, interestingly, Jain and Buddhist nuns) and forces us to consider cultural and linguistic similarities and differences in the ways in which all of them handled the gender issue. Other anthologies like T. W. Clarke's *The Novel in India* (1970) and P. K. Rajan's *Growth of the Novel in India* (1989) place the history of the novel of various languages in the same space and thereby facilitate a sharper comparative understanding of the cultural and literary processes which assisted the growth of the form in different languages. The critical introductions to the anthologies as well as the individual introductions to sections in the anthologies can offer very useful clues regarding the avowed aim of the compilation or regarding the thread that is to be traced across and along the various entries. Along with the entries themselves, these introductions can be read as a different kind of criticism – one that traces underlying themes / motifs / patterns implicit in other creative or critical works. As we have already noted, the critical introduction to *The Picador Book of Modern Indian Literature* by Amit Choudhury is a case in point. Many of the assertions made there regarding the importance given to the novel form by postcolonial criticism and concerning 'postcolonial' hybrid language are amply borne out by the selections themselves which include children's fiction, excerpts from autobiographies, letters etc. Although this anthology has been rightly and widely criticised for putting together all South Indian languages homogeneously and for excluding Marathi and Gujarati altogether, it does offer a view of Indian literature as comprising a number of literary as well as linguistic traditions. Further, by including Indian writing in English in this anthology, it silently questions current critical attempts to slot Indian writing in English and Indian writing in the *bhashas* in adversarial categories. A similar case can be made for Lalitha and Susie Tharu's *Women Writing in India* where women's writings from across linguistic traditions (including English) are placed together, thereby allowing for a trans-cultural understanding of women's creative expressions and as the critical introduction to the anthology tells us, their modes of resistance. Divided as it is into historical periods, it also allows us to have a simultaneously synchronic and diachronic view of women's writing. That women have been using writing as a mode of resistance in a given language right from the initial stages of that language, including English, is made clear by such a reading and is reiterated by the introduction. This also sensitises us to the political and social uses to which English was put and thereby subtly interrogates the binary of Indian writing in English and Indian writing in the *bhashas*.

A difference needs to be made here between two kinds of anthologies. *The Picador Book of Modern Indian Literature*, *Growth of the Novel in India*, *Women Writing in India* etc. are anthologies where there is a multiplicity of languages or themes. Therefore they can be used to offer a challenge to official / monologic definitions of Indian literature. On the other hand, a number of anthologies which are being published today attempt to compile critical viewpoints on a particular author. These anthologies do not overtly offer any alternative view of Indian literature, but they do point to a tendency to bring existing criticism on the author within a single space and thereby allow the reader to trace different contours of a critical tradition. Compilations of criticism on writers like R. K. Narayan and Raja Rao etc. or entire series of anthologies like B. R. Publications' *Writers of the Indian Diaspora* are of this kind. The last includes writers like Rushdie and Vikram Seth and these anthologies reflect the current importance given to expatriatism and diaspora as critical categories.

The categories of expatriatism and diaspora have become a critical commonplace in literary studies. With a growing number of Indians migrating to the West and using their position from there to produce creative literature, criticism has been forced to categorise their texts and experiences differently. Writers living outside India are labelled 'diasporic' writers and their texts are seen as reflecting the experiences of such a subject position. A distinction can be made here between the expatriate and the diaspora. The former suggests alienation from the mother culture, whereas the latter connotes negotiation and a feeling of being at home in both cultures.

A large number of critical works have emerged that deal with the basic features and characters of such a subject position. Viney Kirpal in her critical work entitled *The Third World Novel of Expatriation: A Study of Émigré Fiction by Indian, West African and Caribbean Writers* (1989) identifies the markers of expatriate writing – a sense of nostalgia, a tendency to homogenise the differences prevailing in the mother country and a corresponding refusal to return there. The identification of such themes has also led to a reappraisal of earlier writers, notable among them being Raja Rao. Rao, who was for long seen as the quintessential Indian writer in English and his reworkings with the language were also noted with great favour by critics. With the growing importance now given to the marginal and 'inside' positions however, Rao had come under a very different kind of criticism. His non-translation of lower-caste and class words has already been noted. This tendency, as well as his projection of India as a metaphysical entity and almost a Hindu nation, especially in *The Serpent and the Rope* (1960), are today seen as marking him out as an expatriate writer. We may recall that for long, his domicile in America and France were treated as inconsequential biographical details.

Caste and gender have today become important subversive literary and critical leitmotifs in nearly all Indian languages. Histories of literatures of the contemporary period like those provided by the *bhasha samities* of the Saraswati Samman Award include Dalit and women's writings as distinct streams. Both within separate literary traditions, as well as when taken nationally, the rise and growth of Dalit and women's literature occupies a special position. This by itself has generated many a heated debate. Many women writers feel uncomfortable being described and discussed as an exclusive group and assert that by assigning 'women's writing' under a separate category, the marginal position of women is only reinforced. Dalit literature on the other hand, is quite vociferous regarding its separate identity from mainstream writing. In both cases, issues pertaining to the parameters of categorisation come into play. Is a text to be categorised based on the position of the author or on its thematic content? With special reference to Dalit literature, this question will be addressed in detail in Chapter 5. The discomfort of women writers to be so called and classified also brings into question the subversive character of their writing. The novelist Shashi Deshpande mentioned in a seminar (Stella Maris College, Chennai on 18 September 2002) that she found the separate categorisation humiliating; Ambai holds the same view in her critique of Tamil literary ethos in *The Face Behind the Mask* (1984). Nonetheless, it was a feminist critic like Susie Tharu who was instrumental in bringing to light many long-forgotten texts written by women and exposing the ideological machinations that had caused these texts to hibernate for so long. Ambai herself makes incisive critiques of the construction of the Tamil feminine subjectivity through literature and points to the conformist attitude even in reformist / revolutionary writers such as the nationalist poet Subrahmanya Bharati (*The Face Behind the Mask,* 50) and the 'radical' writer Jayakantan (*The Face Behind the Mask,* 170). We find therefore, that despite avowals to the contrary, there is a definite need to understand the ways in which a women's literary tradition has emerged and has nurtured subversive techniques and themes. To this effect, we might see the necessity to juxtapose this tradition against the mainstream without necessarily considering the 'mainstream' as superior. This also throws into relief the power of narrative and the idea that to tell one's own story is to have power to articulate and determine the terms of discourse – an idea which has found much favour today and which can be seen as the source of much of the insider–outsider debate.

The critical centrality of the position of the writer is not a new idea in criticism. Yet, the kind of return dealt with above seeks to put the political and cultural coordinates of the texts completely in alliance with the domicile or residence of the writer. For instance, Ashokamitran has commented with some surprise in *Kumudam* that Rohinton Mistry, living in Canada, should show such a deep understanding of the Indian Parsi way of life as most diasporic writers, he feels, are 'unrooted'. Similarly, critical attention to Attia Hossain, on her single novel *Sunlight on a Broken Column* (1979) has placed her in the tradition of Indian writers in English, Indian women writers in English, diasporic Indian women writers in

English etc. Few readings try to trace her tradition along Muslim women writers in India of which there is a strong line. The critical tendency to see Boman Desai's Parsi novel *The Memory of Elephants* as expressing the sentiments of a diasporic community could also be largely due to the author's domicile in America while the text itself seems to show little inclination to so seeing the Parsi community. It is on the basis of similar ideas that Ambai in *The Face Behind the Mask* asks why a woman writing about women's experiences and issues is immediately seen as a 'woman writer' while the same does not hold true for a man (61).

We also, however, need to realise that such an act of categorisation is not the sole prerogative of criticism. Publishing houses themselves evolve many such categories. Novels like *Karukku* (literally meaning 'Palmyra Leaf'; 1992, trans. 2000) were published by Macmillan India under two heads: 'The Macmillan Modern Novels in Translation Series' and 'Dalit Writing in Translation' thereby already evolving two critical categories – Dalit writing and translation. These bring out the shift in parameters for categorisation from merely invoking genre, period and language to more ideological issues, creating more or less a multiple set of positions for a text. In such a scene, language is but one of the many parameters. Hence, among the texts studied in Chapters 4 and 5 here, *The Memory of Elephants* belongs to the traditions of the post-1980s Indian novel in English, Parsi writing in English, Parsi writing from India and diasporic literature, while *Red Earth and Pouring Rain* belongs to The New Indian Novel in English tradition, the postcolonial Indian novel in English and possibly the postmodern Indian novel in English. Among the novels studied from other languages, the Gopallapuram chronicles form part of Tamil literature from India, 'regional novel' or 'country writing' and ethnographic novel, while *Karukku* belongs to the traditions of the Tamil novel, Tamil Dalit novel, Tamil Dalit women's novel and, as we are using the translation, Tamil Dalit literature in translation.

## Changing Literary Histories

The recognition of such multiple affiliations of any text also makes a simplistic rendering of the literary history of any language untenable. In many ways, literary history itself has had to undergo a variety of changes in the last twenty years or so, making space for the inclusion of a number of traditions within any language and for many languages within the nation.

The discourses of literary historiography and national history are intricately connected to each other, the former being one of the ways in which the nation itself is conceptualised and constructed. While in most monolingual nations—one should wonder whether there is any monolingual or monocultural nation left at all in the world now—the two discourses almost have a one-to-one relationship to each other, in a multilingual nation like India the writing of literary history is all the more complicated. To depict the literary tradition of any one language as representing the literature of the nation is to run the risk of silencing and marginalising various other languages and the various literary traditions in those languages. As in the case of thematic and formal studies, the literary history of India is today represented largely in collections of essays and anthologies where there is ample space for the analysis of the traditions of a number of languages. The brief analysis of the category of the anthology attempted earlier in this chapter made clear that the very use of such a form requires this change. A single essay does not provide the necessary scope for the analysis of even a few languages even if a single theme is considered. The choice of the form of the anthology therefore becomes an important one. Histories of the growth and development of a single genre need to be seen in the context of a number of languages and each essay in the anthology, therefore, needs to be read as forming a part of the whole. This is true especially of works like T. W. Clarke's *Growth of the Novel in India*. It is only when all the essays in the collection are read simultaneously synchronically and diachronically that one can reach a better understanding of the literary history of one genre or period, as argued earlier.

At the same time, the need created to recognise not merely linguistic plurality, but also the simultaneous existence of a number of traditions even within a single language—traditions that can have common features across languages too—has made it impossible for literary history to ignore political or cultural history. This is not to say that such a dimension was not at all considered in the literary histories written earlier, but to point out that in many of the literary histories written before the 1980s, history was seen more or less as a background providing the basic themes and motifs for literature. The histories of literatures of various languages published by the Sahitya Akademi are one instance. Take the other example of M. K. Naik's periodisation of English writing from India. He divides them primarily on the basis of the political climate that was reflected in the themes of the novels. Quite ornamentally, he calls them 'The Pagoda Tree (Beginnings to 1857),' 'The Winds of Change (1857–1920),' 'The Gandhian Whirlwind (1920–1947)' and 'The Asoka Pillar (Independence and After)' (*A History of Indian English Literature*). It may be remembered that K. R. Srinivasa Iyengar too tended to see history as a setting for Indian writing in English. The division of the literatures of various languages into periods such as 'Renaissance Phase', 'Nationalist Phase', 'Post-independence Phase' etc. implies an awareness of the political and historical basis of literary trends. That awareness, however, does not impinge on the critical analysis. If a critique were to be written today, it will definitely take a different tone.

A decisive shift can therefore be seen in the literary histories written after the 1980s. History is no longer merely a background; it interfaces with literary forms and modes and helps in the creation of consumer conditions that facilitate the growth of new themes and forms. A variety of book-length studies and essays can be cited to show this new trend. Meenakshi Mukherjee's *Realism and Reality* sees how the introduction of the print media and western education helped in the creation of a new literary form, namely, the novel, which nevertheless continued to owe allegiance to older native oral narrative modes:

> In almost every major novel of the nineteenth century, behind the obvious European influences can be found the bedrock of a different narrative structure and value systems. Chandu Menon, who proclaimed in his introduction to *Indulekha* his desire to write in Malayalam a realistic novel 'in the English style', forgot the intention by the time he finished the story. The concluding lines echo the sentiments with which the oral recital of a Purana traditionally ends: 'All the characters mentioned ... have reached the summit of human happiness, and now may God bless us and all who read this tale.' The last line of this passage reveals the persistence of pre-novel conventions of narrative in spite of the author's conscious adoption of the European mode and his deliberate debunking of the mythic imagination. (15)

This perception reflects yet another aspect in current literary historiography in India that relocates the novel form itself. Earlier literary historians like Srinivasa Iyengar in 1962 saw it merely as a Western import:

> The 'novel' as a literary phenomenon is new to India. Epics, lyrics, dramas, short stories and fables have their respectable ancestries going back by several centuries, but it is only during a period of a little more than a century that the novel – the long sustained piece of prose fiction – has taken root in India. One might, of course, protest and say that Sanskrit works like Bana's *Kadambari* and Subandhu's *Vasavadatta* are also novels, but the description would not really fit; and besides, these were isolated marvels. *(Indian Writing in English, 314)*

The more recent trend is to see the form as having arisen out of a deep cultural interaction between existing oral narrative forms and the imposed British form. Meenakshi Mukherjee herself takes this stance in her entry on the Indian novel in English in Sahitya Akademi's *Indian Literature.* The same trend can be noticed also in the Tamil critic Tamizhnadan who, while accepting that the novel form was 'imposed' upon the Indian literary scene, nevertheless points to the processes that made such an imposition inevitable: the banning by the British of publication of Indian texts like the Mahabharata and the Ramayana and the consequent creation of a reading public that was in a way forced to depend upon British novels, are some of the reasons he cites ('Mudal Indiya Navalgal', 3). This rethinking of the history of the novel form can also be seen in Makarand Paranjape's *Towards A Poetics of the Indian English Novel* where he seeks to find a master narrative for the Indian novel in the oral religious discourses like the *harikathas*.

It is not, however, merely the history of the novel form that has been cast differently; themes and motifs in fiction too are perceived as inextricably embedded in cultural and political matrices. Bina Srivastava, in *Hindi Upanyas ka Vikas aur Madhyavargeeya Chetana* (Bourgeois Mentality and the Growth of the Hindi Novel, 1981) makes a study of how the rise of the Hindi novel was intimately related to the growth and expansion of the newly created bourgeois class. Madiyazhagan in *Naveena Ilakkiya Sindanaigal* (Thoughts on Modern Literature, 1995) too makes a somewhat similar critique of the earliest three novels in Tamil—*Pratapa Mudaliar Charitram*, *Kamalambal Charitram* and *Padmavathy Charitram*—by studying them against three parameters: as products of their political, socio-literary–cultural ethos and as part of the literary output of the author. He also points out that the authors of these works (Vedanayagam Pillai, Rajam Iyer, and A. Madhavaiah respectively) were all in the employ of the British government, and therefore, belonged to an educated class that had access to British literary forms. In a very similar vein, V. C. Harris in his introduction to the English translation of Sethu's *Pandavapuram* (1995) places the novel within the history of the Malayalam novel tradition and sees the history of the form in Malayalam itself as intricately connected to the social history of the communities involved:

> From *Indulekha* to *Pandavapuram* thus, the Malayalam novel traverses a 90-year history that stands witness to a continual process of redefinition and rearticulation of various projects, strategies, concepts and contracts which Kerala society has sought to engage with, and negotiate, the grand narrative of colonial and / or cultural (in other words, post-colonial) modernity. (ix)

This shift in perspective in literary historiography is part of the trend that increasingly views literature as being in close contact with other aspects of culture. Most of the motifs mentioned in this chapter—the privileging of the insider and marginalised position, the inclusive view of literature, the shifting perspectives in literary history and the changes that the very form of critical writing has undergone—all point to a definite reorientation in the idea of the 'nation' and nationhood. In the privilege it provides to the marginal and insider position, criticism is becoming increasingly suspicious of majoritarian discourses and aesthetics. In other words, literary criticism, like literature itself, has become the locus where the ideas of nation, national culture and identity can be discussed and debated.

The recognition and identification of multiple streams/ kinds of literature even within a single language points to yet another rupture in the nature of literary historiography. Not only is it difficult to write the history of national literature in a simplistic, uni-directional way, it is equally difficult to do so within a single language/ literary tradition. Many of the books and essays mentioned above identify a number of streams within literary traditions – Dalit writing, Marxist writing, women's writing etc. The various write-ups delineating the history of a given literary tradition under consideration provided by the Saraswati Samman committees (which will be discussed in detail in Chapter 3) are another example where the writing of literary history displays a move away from a simple, linear, singular model. An important book in this regard is *The Illustrated History of Indian Writing in English* (2003) edited by A. K. Mehrotra. This deals with a number of literary forms and modes and simultaneously historicises them.

For almost the first time, it includes an essay on nature writing in India in English, thereby virtually recasting the literary history of English in India and bringing in writers like Salim Ali into it. The anthology itself forces us to reconsider the idea of the literature of any one language as following a straightforward path to development of new forms and speaking subjects. Rather, the stress is on the simultaneous existence of a number of streams and voices, thereby almost detonating the very idea of Indian literature and dispersing a number of voices. It is the necessity to follow precisely such a model that G. N. Devy calls for in *Of Many Heroes* where the title itself points to the necessity of pluralism, drawn as it is from the two models of history proposed by Rajashekhara in *Kavyamimamsa* and in referring to a history that has multiple centres.[7]

Plurality and multiplicity then appear to have become important motifs in criticism in India in recent times. These are aspects that are constantly being projected as being inherently non-Western and peculiarly Indian, be it in the realm of narrative, historiography or literary history. In many ways, there is a tendency to stress the 'difference' between Indian and non-Indian literary motifs and aspects, both within texts and without. This trend also points to an anxiety to precisely define Indian literature in terms drawn fully from India and even within this, to privilege a marginal and silenced position. Arguments against such cultural consciousness came as early as 1977 from critics: Raji Narasimhan who said in *Sensibility Under Stress* that 'were it not for the presence of totally valid literary grounds [Indian writers in English reflecting] Indian-ness would be overdone nationalism' (4). K. S. Ramamurthy in *Rise of the Indian Novel in English* (1987) similarly, warned against 'Indian-ness' becoming an obsession with the writer:

> A novel written by an Indian will certainly be Indian without any conscious effort on the part of the writer to the extent that it depicts Indian life and culture, reflects faithfully the life and spirit of the Indian ethos and grapples with the problems and tensions generated by the rather peculiar way in which an individual's life and character are determined by home, family and society . . . . But any deliberate attempt made by the writer to make his novel Indian or to design it for a Western audience will make it artificial and unreal. (4–5)

Yet, we may argue that there is an increasing tendency to critique an idea or motif based on the place of its origin rather than by its intrinsic worth. The instances mentioned earlier regarding the suspicion of

Indian writing in English, and even in this field, of diasporic and expatriate writing, all point to a growing anxiety to somehow purge Indian literature of all external influences. Novels themselves may not, however, so much demand such a purging as call for an inclusive world view as the analysis in Chapter 4 hopes to show. These aspects of criticism are the focal points in the next two chapters.

## Notes

1. Vandana Shiva, *Staying Alive: Women, Ecology and Survival in India* (New Delhi: Kali for Women), 1988.
   Vandana Shiva and Maria Mies, *Ecofeminism* (New Delhi: Kali for Women), 1993.

2. Gabrielle Dietrich, 'Women, Ecology and Culture'. *Gender and Politics in India*. Themes in Politics Series, ed. Nivedita Menon (New Delhi: Oxford UP), 1999, 72–95.

3. The Narmada Bachao Andolan, literally meaning *Movement to Save the Narmada*, is a movement asking for proper rehabilitation of over a lakh people who will be evicted for building the Rs 1000-crore multipurpose dams over the Narmada river. The movement is led by activists like Medha Patkar and Baba Amte. The writer Arundhati Roy has also joined the struggle in recent years.

4. The Silent Valley Project proposed by the Kerala State Electricity Board (KSEB), was an attempt to build a dam straddling two hillocks across the Kuntipuzha river in what is called the Silent Valley. This triggered off one of the most controversial environmental concerns in the late 1970s, concerns that flowed into the 1980s. The proposed dam would have irrevocably destroyed what research revealed was the last evergreen rainforest in which flora and fauna had evolved to the fullest possible extent. Moreover, the valley was home to large numbers of medicinal plants and almost extinct species of animals. Academics from the Kerala Shastra Sahitya Parishad (KSSP), also entered the fray, armed with detailed results of research. A fierce controvery raged between the KSEB and the environmentalists, until Prime Minister Indira Gandhi advised the State Government to shelve the project and in 1985 declared the Silent Valley a national park. The early years of the 1980s in Kerala were marked by this controversy and writings about this evergreen forest made up much of the polemical discourse in Malayalam at this time.

5. '*Pauranic*' means drawn from the *puranas* and a '*pauranic* structure' refers to a narratology and mode of writing history drawn from the eighteen Mahapuranas that form an important corpus in the canon of sacred Hindu texts.

6. IWE is the term generally used to refer to, depending upon the context, Indian writing in English or Indian writers in English.

7. In *Kavyamimamsa*, Rajaśekhara identifies two kinds of histories: *parkriya* is a kind of history that has just one protagonist (he gives the example of the *Ramayana*) and *purakalpa* is a history with many heroes (he gives the example of the *Mahabharata*).

## References

Bama. *Karukku*. 1992. Trans. Lakshmi Holmström from Tamil into English (Chennai: Macmillan India Limited, 2000).

Chandra, Vikram. *Red Earth and Pouring Rain* (New Delhi: Penguin, 1995).

———. 'The Cult of Authenticity'. *Boston Review*. Feb–March 2001. 15 June 2001. <http://www.bostonreview.com>

———. *Love and Longing in Bombay* (New Delhi: Penguin, 1997).

Chaudhuri, Amit. Introduction. *The Picador Book of Modern Indian Literature*. Ed. Amit Chaudhuri (London: Picador, 2001).

Choudhuri, Indra Nath. *Genesis of Imagination: Selected Essays on Literature, Theory, Religion and Culture* (New Delhi: Sterling Publishers Pvt. Ltd, 2001).

Clarke, T. W., ed. *The Novel in India* (London: George Allen and Unwin, 1970).

Dasgupta, Sudha Chakraborty ed. *Regionality and Comparative Literature: Papers in Comparative Literature: Seminars and Workshops 1993–1998* (Jadavpur: Jadavpur UP, 1998).

Desai, Boman. *The Memory of Elephants*. 1988 (Kent: Sceptre, 1990).

Dev, Amiya, ed. *Narrative: A Seminar* (New Delhi: Sahitya Akademi, 1994).

Devy, G. N. *Of Many Heroes: An Indian Essay in Literary Historiography* (Mumbai: Orient Longman, 1998).

*Encyclopedia of Indian Literature*. 4 vols. (New Delhi: Sahitya Akademi, 1987).

Ghosh, Amitav. 'Ghosh Letter to Administrators of Common wealth Writers Prize' (18 March 2001), 23 Nov. 2001. <http://www.amitavghosh.com>

Ghosh, Amitav. *In an Antique Land* (New Delhi: Ravi Dayal Publishers, 1992).

Ghosh, Shohini. 'A Transcreation'. Rev of *River of Fire* by *Qurratulain Hyder*. *The Book Review* 23, nos. 1 & 2(Jan.–Feb. 1999): 69–70.

Gokhale, Shanta (Interview with Rushdie). 'Writing in the Oral Tradition'. *The Indian Express Magazine*, 4 Mar. 1984, 5.

Hariharan, Githa. *In Times of Siege* (New Delhi: Penguin, 2003).

———. *When Dreams Travel* (London: Picador, 1999).

Harris, V. C. Introduction. *Pandavapuram*. Sethu. Trans. Prema Jayakumar. Macmillan Modern Novels in Translation (Madras: Macmillan, 1995).

Hussain, Attia. *Sunlight on a Broken Column* (New Delhi: Penguin, 1979).

Hussein, Aamer. 'Chaos and Upheaval.' Review of *River of Fire* by Qurratulain Hyder. *Times Literary Supplement,* 6 Nov. 1998: 25.

Hyder, Qurratulain. *River of Fire*. 1959. Trans. Qurratulain Hyder from Urdu into English (New Delhi: Kali for Women,1998).

Iyengar, Srinivasa K. R. *Indian Writing in English*. 1962. (Bangalore: Sterling Publishers Pvt. Ltd, Rev. ed. 1987).

Khair, Tabish. *Babu Fictions: Alienation in Contemporary Indian English Novels* (New Delhi: Oxford UP, 2001).

Kirpal, Viney. *The Third World Novel of Expatriation: A Study of Émigré Fiction by Indian, West African and Caribbean Writers* (New Delhi: Sterling Publishers, 1989).

———. ed. *The New Indian Novel in English: A Study of the 1980s*. (New Delhi: Allied Publishers, 1990).

Lakshmi, C. S. ( Ambai). *The Face Behind the Mask: Women in Tamil Literature*. Women in Society Series (New Delhi: Vikas Publishing House Pvt. Ltd, 1984).

Machwe, Prabhakar. 'The Regional Novel and Neo-Realism.' *Four Decades of Indian Literature: A Critical Evaluation* (New Delhi: Chetana Publications, 1976).

Madiyazhagan, M. *Naveena Ilakkiya Sindanaigal*. Tamil. (Thoughts on Modern Literature) (Pondicherry: Breith Veliyeettagam, 1995).

Malak, Aman. 'The Shahrazadic Tradition: Rohinton Mistry's *Such a Long Journey* and the Art of Story-telling.' *Journal of Commonwealth Literature* 29 (1993): 109–16.

Mehta, Gita. *A River Sutra* (New Delhi: Penguin India, 1993).

Mehrotra. A. K, ed. *An Illustrated History of Indian Literature in English* (London: Hurst and Company, 2003).

Memon, Md. Umar. 'Modern Urdu Literature: An Introduction.' 22 Feb 2002. <http://www.shelterbelt.com>

Mukherjee, Meenakshi. *Realism and Reality: the Novel and Society in India* (New Delhi: Oxford UP, 1985).

Nagarkar, Kiran. *Cuckold* (New Delhi: HarperCollins *Publishers*, 1997).

———. *Ravan and Eddie* (New Delhi: Penguin Books, 1995).

Nagendra, ed. *Literary Criticism in India* (Meerut: Sarita Prakashan, 1976).

Naik, M. K. *A History of Indian English Literature*. 1982 (New Delhi: Sahitya Akademi, 1995).

Nambisan, Kavery. *The Scent of Pepper* (New Delhi: Penguin Books, 1996).

Narasimhan, Raji. *Sensibility Under Stress: Aspects of Indo-English Fiction* (Delhi: Ashajanak Publishers, 1971).

Paksoy, H. B. 'Dastan Genre in Central Asia.' 6 Feb 2002. <http://www.ku.edu.>

Panikker, Ayyappa. 'The Narratology of Thakazhi's *Kayar*'. Anu Chitra Publishers, 101–9.

———. 'The End of Historiography?' *frontlineonthenet*, 16, 9 (24 April–07 May,1999),2/08/2008. <http://www.frontlineonnet.com/fl1609/16091110.htm>

Paranjape, Makarand. *Towards a Poetics of the Indian English Novel* (Shimla: Indian Institute of Advanced Study, 2000).

Pathak, R. S., ed. *Indian Fiction of the Nineties* (New Delhi: Creative Book, 1997).

Patil, Vishwas. *Jhadajhadati*. 1990. Trans. Gajanan Chauhan from Marathi into Hindi (New Delhi: Vani Prakashan, 1995).

Pillai, Thakazhi Sivasankara. 'Excerpts from Acceptance Speech.' *Jnanpith Puraskar: 1965–1990*. (Hindi). Ed. Bishen Tandon (New Delhi: Bharatiya Jnanpith Prakashan, 1991).

———. *Kayar.* (Coir). Trans. N. Sreekantan Nair from Malayalam into English (New Delhi: Sahitya Akademi, 1997).

Rajan, P. K. *Growth of the Novel in India: 1950–1980* (New Delhi: Abhinav Publications, 1989).

Rajanarayanan, Ki. *Gopalla Gramam* (Tamil. Sivagangai: Selma, 1976).

———. *Gopallapurathu Makkal*. 1990. 2nd ed. (Tamil. Sivagangai: Selma, 1993).

Ramachandran, C. N. 'Critical Responses to Rushdie.' *Writers of the Indian Diaspora*. Ed. R. K. Dhawan (New Delhi: Prestige Books, 2001), 27–35.

Ramamurthy, K. S. *Rise of the Indian Novel in English* (Bangalore: Sterling Publishers, 1987).

Ravindran, Vanajam. 'This Mortal Coil'. *Indian Review of Books* 7, 11 (16 Aug.–5 Sep. 1990), 39–44.

Reddy, Sheela. 'Midnight's Orphans', *Outlook,* 25 Feb. 2002: 54–63.

Reynolds, Margaret and Jonatha Noakes eds. *Salman Rushdie: The Essential Guide* (London: Random House Publishers, 2003).

*Routledge Encyclopedia of Post-colonial Literatures*. 2nd edition Eds. Eugene Benson, L. W. Conolly (London Routledge.)

Rushdie, Salman and Elizabeth West, eds. Introduction. *The Vintage Book of Indian Writing: 1947–1999* (Vintage: London, 1997). Hereafter cited in text as *The Vintage Book*.

Shiva, Vandana. *Staying Alive: Women, Ecology and Survival in India* (New Delhi: Kali for Women, 1988).

Sivasankari. *Knit India Through Literature*. 4 vols. (Chennai: East West Books Pvt. Ltd., 1998).

Srivastava, Bina. *Hindi Upanyas ka Vikas aur Madhyavargeeya Chetana*. (Hindi). (Bourgeois Mentality and The Growth of Hindi Literature). (New Delhi: Macmillan India Ltd., 1981).

Tamizhnadan. 'Mudal Indiya Navalgal.' (The First Indian Novels). *Melum*. (November 1990): 1–7.

Tharu, Susie and Lalitha, eds. *Women Writing in India.* 2 vols. (New Delhi: Oxford UP, 1991).

Trivedi, Harish and Meenakshi Mukherjee, eds. Interrogating Post-colonialism: Theory, Text and Context (Shimla: Indian Institute of Advanced Study, 1996).

Varma, Nirmal. 'Nammul Uraiyum Kadal'. (The Raging Sea Within Us). Interview with B. A. Krishnan. *Kalachuvadu* 37(Sept.–Oct. 2001): 32–40.

Vishwanatha, Vanamala et al. *Routes: Representation of the West in Short Fiction from South India* (Chennai: Macmillan India Ltd. and the British Council, 2000)

# 2

# CRITICAL PRACTICE

While criticism in India has been invoking nation, caste, class and language as matrices of identity, there is also the corresponding criticism that there is no 'native' critical tradition to speak of in India which can deal with such emerging concerns.[1] This anxiety about a critical tradition is also an anxiety about empowerment; for, to trace an 'Indian critical tradition' would complement our notion of a national literature. Among the first to voice this concern was G. N. Devy who, in his influential book *After Amnesia: Tradition and Change in Indian Literary Tradition* (1992), regretted the lack of a native critical tradition in the *bhashas*. He bemoans the practice of relying entirely upon Sanskrit theories that are temporally removed from present-day Indian literary ethos or upon Western theories that are spatially removed. Historicising the condition, he detects a cultural amnesia about the medieval period—during the Islamic rule—that does not allow our critical knowledge to access that period. The same anxiety can be traced in many books and articles on criticism itself. In his introduction to *Samakaleen Hindi Alochana* (Modern Hindi Criticism, 1998) Paramanand Srivastava complains that Indian criticism has today become synonymous with Sanskrit criticism. Similarly, Ka. Na. Subramaniam in *Vimarisanak Kalai* (The Art of Criticism, 1984) had regretted that the novel was largely neglected in Tamil criticism and that there was definitely a need to wean criticism away from *Tolkappiam* the ancient classical Tamil text on poetics. This statement implies that the heavy dependence upon classical theories of criticism which were historically unequipped to deal with the novel has led to the critical neglect of the form. Jasbir Jain expresses the same sentiments in the notes to her essay 'Towards the 21st Century: The Writing of the 1990s':

> We sadly lack an effective critical tradition and if some voices are being heard, one needs to know where they are and to whom

> they belong. A lot of criticism is in response to theories/ critiques/ opinions floated abroad. The dialogue is with them: not horizontally with writing / writers in India and in Indian languages . . . it is not even chronologically with our own critical past (though nativist criticism presents one facet of this). (23)

The modern Tamil writer Ashokamitran too, in his article in *Kumudam* already cited, has remarked that there is a dire need for critics who would tell with some degree of certainty what books were and what were not worth reading. He regretted that criticism was fast becoming an elitist activity written by and for academics.

## Is There a Critical Tradition in the Country?

The debate on the very existence of a critical tradition in India had become so much part of the Indian literary scene that the Sahitya Akademi also conducted a seminar on the topic in February 2002. The various papers presented at the seminar echo the sentiments mentioned so far. H. S. Bhatia's survey of Punjabi literary criticism in 'Meta Criticism and the State of Panjabi Literary Criticism' sees the pre-1950s critical scene in Punjabi as 'elementary, emotive, poetic, appreciative, impressionistic and restricted to literary appreciation' (6). His paper goes on to trace the shifts in the thrust of criticism and points out how Marxism, semiotics, formalism etc. (all Western theories), have influenced major critics in their appreciation of texts. In the same seminar, Prafulla Kumar Mohanty is bitter that 'Indian literature is being evaluated by critical canons borrowed from the West' ('Towards a Search for A Pan-Indian Literary Theory' 1). However, he also reminds us that 'each *bhasha* literature has its own canon of criticism smacking of an impressionistic variety' before pointing out that indigenous theories derived from 'the great Indian tradition of critical antiquity, *rasa–dhvani–ouchitya*, remain mostly an academic pastime or patriotic flag' (1). Similarly, Ravindra Tripathi draws attention to the fact that while Hindi critics easily drop names and theorists like those of Foucault and Derrida, they are not equipped enough to deal with the problems thrown up by their theories ('Hindi Mein Alochana: Ek Sandigdh Upasthithi?' 1)

Such criticisms about criticism—shall we say metacriticism—need to be looked at more carefully. The previous chapter dealt in some detail with the changing contours of criticism in India and also referred to the large number of issues that are common to criticisms in different languages. The anxiety about the existence of criticism itself can be seen as part of the anxiety to define India in terms of 'pure' insidedness. This anxiety about the existence of a 'native' critical tradition removed from classical Sanskrit theories in turn reflects the suspicion of majoritarian discourses current in social sciences; for there is an implicit fear that the purely aesthetic discourses of ancient times will tend to subsume the many new and so-far silenced voices which are clamouring to be heard today. This point is made by G. N. Devy in *After Amnesia* where he places recent critics such as Krishna Rayan and Nagendra against Dalit and *grameen* critics (critics of village/country literature). While the former group is keen on 'bringing back' classical Sanskrit criticism in the analysis of modern texts, Devy argues that Dalit and *grameen* literature (rural/village literature) may find them especially irrelevant and quite useless in the kind of cultural polemics they are engaged in. When India as a whole is placed against the West, the same fear of majoritarian discourses underlies the desire to oust any theory that has its roots in the Western academia. In fact, it was one of the major arguments against the use of postcolonialism as a critical model. The fact that even Indian academicians who used the model did so in journals and articles published in the West was an argument against the model. The anxiety about the supposed non-existence of a critical tradition is voiced—at least by Devy—with specific reference to the *bhashas*. This again has to be seen in the context of the history of literary criticism in the *bhashas* themselves.

The anthology *Literary Criticism in India* edited by Nagendra (1976) carries a very useful introduction where the major trends in criticism in the *bhashas* are traced. The first one he traces is in the medieval period, which witnessed the translation of works of Sanskrit poetics into the *bhashas*, adaptation of some Sanskrit theories and especially the enunciation of the concept of *rasa*. Nagendra then divides the period of modern criticism into various phases, namely a. the beginnings where criticism existed in the form of notes in journals, reviews etc., and an assessment of classics, of cultural topics and their influence on literature; b. the maturing of academic criticism which also saw a return to Indian standards of analysis, discussion of philosophical issues, of characterisation etc.; c. (what Nagendra terms) 'The Golden Phase' i.e. the period from the fourth and fifth decades of the twentieth century onwards which witnessed a feeling of discontent with classical values, the growth of the Progressive

Writers Movement that was basically Marxist in orientation, the introduction of romantic modes into criticism in the importance given to inspiration and spontaneity, the introduction of Freudian psychoanalysis as a critical tool and the pronounced use of New Critical and Formalist methods of criticism. Nagendra goes on to divide the growth of theoretical criticism too into three phases: a. translation of Sanskrit theoretical works, b. their elucidation in the light of new theories and c. the evolution of a 'new code.' These phases can be traced also in the various essays that discuss the critical scenes in all the languages recognised by Schedule VIII[2] of the Indian Constitution and do give the impression of a sustained effort at creating a critical tradition in the *bhashas*. At least the first of these phases—the medieval phase which saw the translation of Sanskrit theoretical works into modern Indian languages—is reiterated by Devy in *After Amnesia* where he makes a detailed mention of the earliest critics who were instrumental in bringing Sanskrit theories into various *bhashas*.

In the light of this literary chronicle, the lamentation that there is no relevant critical tradition appears to be rather a criticism of the historical antecedents of the parameters that criticism is using in the analysis of texts than the absence of one. The new set of codes that has evolved in the period following the massive changes of the 1980s consists primarily of the introduction of modes of criticism such as postcolonialism, postmodernism, new historicism etc. They are today looked at with suspicion by some because of their Western origin. We might, in fact, add that recent metacriticism has also tended to look askance at older models such as psychoanalysis, high modernism and existentialism, especially the last two, due to their imitative quality. We can discern here a return of the same motif that we had traced earlier – the anxiety of authenticity and the concern about defining India in 'purely' Indian terms. This, in effect, suggests that to 'read' an 'Indian' text 'correctly', one needs an exclusively 'Indian' model. The large number of single quotation marks in the previous sentence is mark enough of the difficulties with which such a task is beset; for it involves the definition of India as a nation, of 'Indian' as a cultural coordinate and of authenticity, in no uncertain terms. P. K. Rajan mentions in his essay titled 'Paradigms in Plurality: Search for a Regenerative Principle in Indian Criticism' that the search for this 'Indian' critical model might also construct an artificial structure of unity that defies the pluralism which we are at so much pains to stress (349). We might add that to see Indian criticism as merely an imitative field of enquiry is to be blind to the number of issues addressed, the various forms in which this is done and the numerous sites whence this criticism is disseminated.

Indeed, the last chapter tried to show the different patterns that were and are emerging in the critical field in India today, the deep structure of many of which can be traced in the above contentions as well. Still, many of the arguments regarding the existence of a critical tradition require to be placed in a historical context.

Criticism, like literature, is an institution. It needs support and canonisation for existence and survival. For literary criticism to become solidified and established in any language, the language itself first has to be institutionalised; it has to be taught and must evolve into a written format. It is only when this occurs can the literature of that language be academically critiqued. Sanskrit and Persian—the two classical languages used in North India—were court languages at different points in Indian history and subsequently developed a strong literary and corresponding critical tradition. The various *bhashas*, however, have had a different kind of history. Having emerged as descendents of these two languages, the first phase of criticism in them naturally showed a deep influence of the aesthetic theories in the parental languages. This was perhaps bolstered by the fact that many of the early literary texts written in the *bhashas* were classical in form, following the tradition set by these reigning languages. The simultaneous existence of the Dravidian languages effectively divided the Indian literary tradition into two large linguistic hemispheres. While Malayalam, Kannada and Telugu all form part of this family of languages of which Tamil is the oldest member, the former three languages showed a definite influence of both the Dravidian and the Sanskrit traditions. Translations from Sanskrit theoretical texts formed an important part of the early phase of theoretical criticism in the modern phase in these languages. Medieval Tamil literature too showed a similar trend. Despite this derivativeness, many critics see these very early works as asserting the individual identity of these *bhashas*. G. N. Devy, for example, deals in some detail with Jnanadeva's exposition of the Bhagavadgita in *Bhāvarthāpīthika* and talks at length about the glorification of Marathi over Sanskrit in it. Hailing the text as one that 'pioneered a new literary aesthetic and founded a new literary language' (*Of Many Heroes,* 46), Devy affirms that Arjuna is presented in it as an advocate of Marathi, constantly asking Lord Krishna to explain things to him in that language. Jnanadeva's text is, however, only one of the many such early Bhakti texts that claimed a greater respect for the *bhashas* and literally created a new literary language. Similar claims have been made for Balarama Das's Oriya Ramayana by K. C. Sahu (*Masterpieces of Indian Literature,* 1039), for the Andhra Mahabharata (by Nannaya, Tikkana and Errana) by N. V. R. Krishamacharya (*Masterpieces*, 1409) and for Madhava Kandli's Assamese Ramayana by Rancharan Thakuria (*Masterpieces*, 65).

While this trend would have been quite congenial to the emergence of a critical tradition in the *bhashas*, such an emergence would have also necessitated the growth of an independent literary tradition (assuming that literary criticism emerges in relation to creative literature). Before that could happen, however, the strong influence of European culture and education opened out the *bhashas* to newer literary forms and modes of perception. Although English education itself did not become compulsory till the middle of the nineteenth century, the encounter with an antithetical culture had an inevitable reactionary effect and a consequent return to classical moral, ethical and literary values can be seen across the entity we today call 'India,' almost rejuvenating Sanskrit literature and literary criticism. The interest in them was further heightened by the importance that the West itself came to give Sanskrit literature. The various translations of Sanskrit texts by Western scholars (like Max Muëller and William Jones) were often projected as being the 'real' Eastern texts and they sparked off a corresponding interest in the Sanskrit tradition among Indians themselves and marked a return to conservative literary values, thereby perhaps stunting the growth of *bhasha* literatures and correspondingly also impeding the development and establishment of a critical tradition in the *bhashas*. With English education being made compulsory and with the growth of nationalistic fervour, the need to define 'India' caused a further return to Sanskrit literature and philosophy as representing the 'true' India. The *bhasha* literatures moved rather directly under the influence of Western thought and literature – witness, among other things, the rapid growth of the novel form in the *bhashas*. The parameters of criticism too underwent corresponding changes in the *bhashas*, with the accent shifting first to social reform and then to nationalism. Many of these ideas showed a direct influence of egalitarian and liberal humanist European thought. The result, of course, was that historically, the *bhashas* showed more influence of Western thought and ideas – an aspect that is today being severely criticised in some conservative literary quarters.

However, we also need to point out that critics in the *bhashas* have not blindly used and espoused Western thought. There have been consistent attempts made—sometimes unconsciously—at modifying and altering their ideas to suit Indian culture. Thus, an early review of the Tamil novel *Pratapa Mudaliar Charitram* praises the author's attempt to transpose a European form into the Indian landscape. The famous Hindi critic Pandit Mahaveer Prasad Dwivedi said in the middle of the nineteenth century that 'anybody who knows about human nature, who can express her / his thoughts in well-wrought phrases, who knows the general direction in which society is heading and also has a knowledge of what will and will not help the society can write good novels without the knowledge of Western theories' (qtd. Naval 53; translation mine). The novel therefore could adapt itself to any new culture rather than remain merely a Western literary form. Similarly, the method of realism that became an important critical tool in the mid-1800s was adapted to form a kind of social realism that would suit the fire of reformist zeal which was raging around the country at that time. It needs to be mentioned that such a method came in more useful at that historical point rather than the traditional discourses—what was collectively called *Dharmasastras*—which laid heavy stress on caste and gender hierarchy, mandating a strict adherence to them, thereby giving very little scope for the kind of resistant reading that the social realist model allowed critics like Pandit Mahaveer Prasad Dwivedi and Acharya Ramchandra Shukla. Premchand, one of the best known Hindi writers, brings to his Marxist views on literature a slant that would make it suitable for depicting the class and gender hierarchy of the kind peculiar to Indian society. In fact, Marxism and psychoanalysis have been two of the important critical models used and adapted by literary critics in India in nearly all languages. Of these Marxism was the more widespread. Foremost among critics who have used the Marxist model in literary analysis include Premchand and Ramvilas Sharma in Hindi, Damodaran and Induchudan in Malayalam, Pendse and Suthankar in Marathi, Attar Singh in Panjabi, Majnūn Gorakhpuri and Ehteshām Hussain in Urdu and Kailasapathy in Tamil.

Apart from these, today we find that a group of feminist and Dalit critics have emerged using the matrices of gender and caste in their readings of literary texts. The rise of these forces of criticism has been complemented/ necessitated by the rise of a significant body of creative literature by and about Dalits and women. Although literature by and about women is in no way a new phenomenon, the manner in which texts address gender issues, and therefore the ways in which such texts are being read or indeed need to be read, are vastly different. One can discern attempts at theorising and the backup of strong theoretical texts drawn from various sources. Poststructuralism has, in fact, proved quite useful in this regard as it allows Dalit intellectuals like Raj Gautaman in Tamil to deconstruct not only ideas and concepts that creative literature is dealing with, but also literary forms (especially the autobiography) and aesthetics at large. The attempt by certain critics to regain pride of place for the classical Sanskrit *rasa* and *dhvani* theories is being strongly contested by Dalit intellectuals who see in these majoritarian discourses an attempt at aestheticisation of the same world view that led to their suppression in the first place.

Feminism, on the other hand, appears more confined to texts rather than emerging as theory or criticism. The criticism on texts dealing with women's issues appears more comfortable without theorisation; indeed, the absence of theory is praised in many reviews of Indira Goswami's *The Moth-eaten Howdah of the Tusker* (1988), an aspect that we will deal with in detail in Chapter 5. However, feminist critiques *have* been made in various other fields—culture studies, legal reforms, development studies, economics etc. That the supposedly egalitarian and progressive institutions such as the law and the legislature have fought shy of addressing the gender issue has been much written about. Vandana Shiva's sharp criticisms of development programmes of the government from ecofeminist perspectives, the criticisms of legal experts such as Zoya Hasan and Archana Parashar or the attempts by people such as Urvashi Butalia and Ritu Menon to record the oral histories of women victims of historical events like the partition of India all form an important part of the growing attempts made by women to claim intellectual equality. Although not literary, many of these essays and readings provide useful models that literary criticism can draw upon. At the same time, there has also been commendable effort made to bring out different kinds of contemporary histories of women by compiling and chronicling the struggles of ordinary women. Important books in this regard are Anees Jung's *Unveiling India: A Woman's Journey* (2000) that tells the struggles of ordinary women who face different kinds of antagonism every day of their lives, C. S. Lakshmi's project for the SPARROW workshop that similarly documents the resistance of the average woman and Namita Gokhale's *Mountain Echoes* (1988) that documents the stories of four women from the Kumaon region of North India describing their points of view of the freedom struggle. The last does not offer any kind of alternate history, but it does point to the importance of using a female voice as the speaking subject while historicising. These sociological efforts are complemented in the literary scene on the one hand by efforts like those of K. Lalitha and Susie Tharu in *Women Writing in India.* They also share the concern of publishing houses such as Stree and Kali for Women. K. Lalitha and Susie Tharu have not only brought women's writing from across India and over centuries together, but they have also resurrected many such texts which were left in cold storage, mostly deliberately. The introduction to the anthology provides ample evidence of the archival and rejuvenation work that went before its publication. Kali and Stree have created a platform where such resurrected and newly constructed material can be given publicity. These are ideologically oriented publishing houses which also sponsor translations into English of works from various Indian *bhashas*.

The criticism regarding the absence of criticism is itself then a reflection of some of the anxieties identified in the previous chapter: they form part of the attempt, as already mentioned, to define an India in purely Indian terms eschewing anything Western and resisting hegemonic influences. It is interesting here to take a look at the values upheld by the Grand Narratives, namely patriotism, stability of social formations, humanism and so on. Although some reviews do give importance to these parameters (witness the critique of Goswami) most critics seem to steer clear of them. There is an increasing awareness that neither can problems be simplistically defined, nor can the answers be so simplistically found. Yet, these very same parameters appear to become important when texts are considered for national literary awards. Although it is only the following chapter that will deal at length with the critical implications of the selection processes of three Indian literary awards (the Bharatiya Jnanpith, the Saraswati Samman awarded by the K. K. Birla Foundation, and the Sahitya Akademi), we need to mention here that both in the souvenirs of these awards as well as the citations given to the winners we can get a clue regarding the critical parameters that the committees of these awards consider important. We find that the very same paradigms of nationalism, humanism etc.—the Grand Narratives that are shelved in academic criticism—become at times the governing parameters for these awards. Masti Venkatesha Iyengar, the Kannada writer, has been commended for presenting the 'human face' of history in his novels and short stories *(Jnanpith Puraskar: 1965–1990).* Similarly, Amrita Pritam, the Punjabi writer has been acclaimed for her complex portrayal of women characters *(Jnanpith Puraskar: 1965–1990).* The Maithili Sahitya Akademi winner for 2001, *Pratijna Pandav* by Babuajee Jha 'Ajnat' is praised for having 'advocated the need for peace, national integrity and morality' (*Sahitya Akademi Souvenir 2001*). Of the winner for Rajasthani in the same year, *Gharano* by Abdul Vaheed 'Kamal,' it is said: 'the compact narration, the effective depiction of the inner conflict of the characters and the *social reformist* content of the novel call for recognition of this work as a major achievement' (*Sahitya Akademi Souvenir 2001*) (italics mine). We may note that the necessity of social reform was certainly acknowledged earlier as well. But it could not be at the expense of the holistic structure of the society and the general set of values upheld as characteristic of Indian culture. Towards the end of the twentieth century, however, social reform can no longer be governed by such ideals as some of the more recent award-winning texts testify. Take, for instance, the following selection from citations and souvenirs: Vijay Tendulkar's *Kanyadaan* (Saraswati Samman, 1993) has been commended for its critique of the Dalit movement and for revealing the 'human conditions' of ideological confrontations. Manubhai Pancholi Darshak's *Kurukshetra* (Saraswati Samman, 1997) is commended for portraying the need for racial unity in India. The same is said for Indira Parthasarathy's Tamil play *Ramanujar* (Saraswati Samman, 1999); its questioning of the caste system and the portrayal of an attempt to create a casteless society have been highly commended.

The reasons as to this divide between the criteria upheld by awards institutions and academic criticism would lead us to some speculation. One possible explanation could be that as public institutions, the awards organisations find it necessary to uphold values that have been valorised for many years. However, this would also imply that academic criticism is becoming increasingly ghettoised, with the ordinary reader being completely left out of the critical process altogether. To this, we need to add two observations. Firstly, values such as humanism, social relevance (and the word is used in all its current ambiguity), nationalism etc. cannot be said to have lost their merit completely. Although the currency given to the advocacy of the relativity of truth and morality may have made us sceptical of them, they do play an important role in our everyday lives and consequently should do so in literature and criticism. What perhaps we need is a balance between liberal humanist values and the assertion of contrary humanist values.

Secondly, the form in which criticism is produced is no longer entirely academic. Book-length studies, essays, articles etc. no doubt, remain an important form of critical writing, but other forms too are emerging that are attempting to blur the boundaries between academic and non-academic writing.

## THE LITTLE MAGAZINE

One of the earliest sites where criticism began in the modern period in India was that of journals and magazines called today the 'little magazine'. The little magazine culture played a crucial role in the dissemination of critical ideas and concepts nearly all over the world. The avant-gardism of little magazines has itself become an institution. They are defined in a variety of ways, all of which emphasise their keen interest in non-mainstream literature. For example, they are defined as magazines that are 'primarily literary, often experimental and typically unfettered. Virtually all have a small circulation, and they are usually published, edited, and financed by one person or a small group of persons . . . without a profit motif' (Pollack qtd. in Sivakumar, 2). They are also defined as magazines that

> '. . . usually [begin] with the object of publishing [a] literary work of some artistic merit which is unacceptable to commercial magazines for any one or all of three reasons – the writer is unknown and therefore not a good risk; the work itself is unconventional or experimental in form; or it violates one of several popular notions of polite moral, social or aesthetic behaviour.' (Hoffman qtd. in Sivakumar, 3)

The little magazine culture in India (as anywhere else) has played an important role in creating a literary ethos. In Tamil for example, the history of little magazines includes contributions made by *Sudesamitran* and *Manikkodi* which were the platform that brought to light architects of the modern short story like 'Pudumaipittan'. The other important name in this context in Tamil is C. S. Chellappa who, it is said, ran his magazine *Ezhutthu* with great financial problems. It was magazines like *Ezhutthu* and later *Kachatathapara* (the name refers to the main consonants of the Tamil alphabet) that introduced many Western modernist literary critics to the Tamil scene by carrying translations of essays of F. R. Leavis, Cleanth Brooks and others during the 1960s and 1970s. *Kachatathapara* was also among the first of little magazines in Tamil to include arts other than merely literature and to carry the translations of lectures and speeches of award winners.[3] *Kaalachuvadu* is performing quite a commendable task today in the little magazine scene in Tamil. We also need to mention that important selections of essays, short stories etc. from most of these little magazines have now been published as compilations. *Kaalachuvadu* also has its publishing firm that routinely publishes both collections of writers who have been introduced by the magazine as well as translations from other languages.

Another point therefore, to note is that these little magazines are quite transcultural in character, carrying translations from various international languages and various arts apart from literature alone. One glaring lacuna is the relatively smaller number of translations from different Indian languages, but that of course, can be attributed to the difficulty of getting good translators. *Kaalachuvadu* however, is increasingly publishing translations of creative pieces from various Indian languages.

Today in English, journals like *Biblio*, *The Book Review* and *The Little Magazine* may be said to have taken over this role; they not only carry reviews of the recent books from all humanities and social science disciplines, but also essays analysing important and current issues. For instance, *Biblio* carried an article in its Nov.–Dec. 2000 issue regarding the Booker Prize (VI, 7 & 8 (Nov.–Dec. 2000)). The scene of great expectation that was then created by the media had evoked a sense of curiosity (and at times indignation) about it. The article analyses the Booker Prize and a few other awards focusing on the role that the Booker (now the Man Booker Prize) plays in the literary world. Another article in Biblio looked at the contemporary little magazine scenario in India (VI, 7 & 8 (Sept.–Oct. 2001)). *The Book Review* periodically carries special issues on various topics like translation or on translations from various languages.

Non-academic magazines also play a not-insignificant-role in creating a critical climate. Although largely political or merely 'popular' in tenor, a number of these magazines carry sections devoted to literature and literary studies where a similar shift in emphasis can be seen. Earlier, *The Illustrated Weekly of India*, which went out of circulation almost twenty years back, carried articles on many issues related to culture and literary studies. A number of essays by Raja Rao were published in this magazine; feminist historians and critics like Radha Kumar too published their work here. One can see here a subtle shift in emphasis to marginal concerns. Today, the Literary Review section in *The Hindu* acts as a forum where recent books are reviewed, issues analysed and classics revisited. Other popular political magazines like *The Week* and *Frontline* too carry articles and essays on the latest literary and critical trends. In recent times in all these spaces, more attention is being paid to translations and non-Anglo-American texts in keeping with the general literary trend spanning almost the entire globe.

We should also acknowledge the contributions of academic journals / periodicals, old and new, such as *The Literary Criterion*, *The Journal of Aesthetics and Ideas*, *Littcrit*, *The Critical Endeavour*, *Points of View*, *Quest*, *Setu* etc. as well as literary and culture studies journals brought out by various universities. Mostly academic in character, these journals accommodate readings on postcolonial literatures, Indian responses to canonical European and American texts and debates on current literary issues and concerns. The Pencraft series of publications deserves special mention for providing yet another forum for issue-based discussion. Increasingly, translations are being included for discussion in many of these journals while the book reviews in them make more recent publications known to the academia. Ideologically oriented journals such as *Dalit Murasu* (Tamil), *The Dalit* (English) and *Manushi* (English) (the first two focus on caste, while *Manushi* focuses on women's issues) not only carry special issues on ideological concerns, but also rehistoricise Dalit and women's movements. *Manushi* is also an extension of a social organisation that is an active political and legal participant in debates concerning women and carries reports of the cases it has fought for women, thereby placing gender-based critiques of legal and development issues together with literary and culture critiques. In fact, some such reports along with a few editorials have been gleaned from back-issues of *Manushi* and published as a book titled *Off the Beaten Track: Rethinking Gender Justice for Women* (New Delhi: Oxford UP, 1999). Since the book carries articles written over a number of years, it also provides a historical overview of the contours of women's resistance in India.

## Blurbs

Many of these reviews and critical points of view are re-used by publishing houses as advertisements. The strategies employed for popularising a book also double as critical endeavours, especially the blurbs. Very often excerpts from the reviews in journals / magazines are printed on the back cover or the front flap as blurb when a book is reissued. Often it is the blurbs that make a prospective reader decide to buy a book from a store or hire it from a lending library. The emphasis given in these blurbs often points to popular expectations from texts; expectations that are frequently conditioned by previous successes or critical enterprises. For instance, after the publication of *Midnight's Children* much publicity was given to narrative style, treatment of history, the fusion of personal and the political and the mingling of magical and fantastic elements with the ordinary.

The blurbs may not openly use the critical terminology, but the focus on important critical issues is nevertheless present in them. The blurb of Amitav Ghosh's *The Shadow Lines* (1988) reads:

> All the while private lives are mirrored by public turmoil – the Blitz in war-time London, civil strife in post-Partition Dhaka, a riot in Calcutta . . . . This novel focuses on the meaning of political freedom in the modern world and the force of nationalism, the Shadow line we draw between people and nations, which is both an absurd illusion and a source of terrifying violence.

This focus on the relationship between personal and national history and the writing of different histories is one of the important aspects touched upon in many blurbs.

The other point of highlight is the use of a non-linear narration. The blurb to Boman Desai's *The Memory of Elephants* (1988) quotes from *The Observer:* 'Homi Seervai, a young Parsi scientist . . . who . . . plunges into the collective unconscious . . . Desai's device is clever; he uses it to advantage, turning Homi into a witness to historical events.' That of Amitav Ghosh's *In An Antique Land* says, '*In an Antique Land* is subversive history in the guise of a traveller's tale' and adds extracts from reviews by A. K. Ramanujan who says: 'Amitav Ghosh's new novel weaves together personal lives and public events' and from Girish Karnad who says: 'Ghosh uses to great effect a matrix of multiple points of view in which memory, mythology and history freely interpenetrate'. The back cover of Vikram Chandra's *Red Earth and Pouring Rain* (1995) carries the following reviews from *The Hindustan Times* and *India Today* respectively:

> One of the most ambitious Indian novels of the nineties . . . if the Booker prize is awarded for innovation in technique and the achievement of a fresh cultural nuance to the form of the novel, then Vikram Chandra surely deserves to be in the running

and

> Hundreds of intriguing stories tied and bound and fused in tight circles that spiral with overlapping strands of violence and passion, nobility and chicanery, knowledge and inevitably, grief. There you have it, all the classic ingredients of good storytelling.

The blurb of his next novel *Love and Longing in Bombay* also carries references to its narrative in phrases such as 'The stories are linked by a single narrator' and 'tightly controlled'. Githa Hariharan's *When Dreams Travel* too is commended for 'its sharp and lively blend of past and present, its skilful reworking of the historical tradition' etc. The blurb of *Gopallapurathu Makkal* (1993) similarly says that the novel, using history as background, deals with the lives of ordinary people, thereby implying a relationship between history and the individual.

The importance given in these blurbs to historiography, storytelling, narrative and a fusion of the personal and the political can be contrasted to the blurbs in publications that came out earlier. The largely synoptic model of these earlier blurbs left little scope and space for critical insights beyond a few commendations regarding language and characterisation. 'Evocative language' and 'brilliant characterisation' (worded differently) appear quite often in them. Although praise by well-known writers was a common inclusion, there is little attempt at drawing upon reviews from newspapers or popular journals. Take for instance, B. K. Karanjia's book *More of an Indian* published by Orient Paperbacks in 1970. The novel describes the romance between a Parsi girl and a Hindu boy and, in the process, allows us a glimpse of the Parsi way of life. It is also set during the period of language riots in North India in the late 1950s, and has quite a bit of the history of the age woven into it. The blurb of the book, which carries a tribute by Khushwant Singh, as well as the one review included in the first page—which cites praise by *The Illustrated Weekly of India*—only faintly mention the centrality of ethnic identity in the text. Other parameters include the author's description of places (Singh praises it saying, 'I have not read Bombay better described') and his characterisation (*The Illustrated Weekly* extols it saying, 'Karanjia is best in descriptions and characteristics [sic]'). As can be seen, this is in direct contrast to the blurb of *The Memory of Elephants* where the focus is definitely on the ethnic identity of the characters and the text.

The shift from synopsis and praise of evocative language and good characterisation to a keener sociocultural consciousness can be perceived when we turn to a more recent novel like Githa Hariharan's *When Dreams Travel* where the blurbs focus upon the reinterpretation of tradition and received culture.

These comments are added as advertisements to sell the book and it is in the nature of advertisements to eulogise what is already held to be important. That is the reason why the blurbs of so many recent novels touch upon the narrative, the use of history and also the fusion of the real and the magical points to what the reader—both academic and non-academic—*expects* of a text. The way non-linear narrative techniques and an interrogation of history have caught the popular imagination and percolated to the Common Reader or intelligentsia is evidenced by the use of these paradigms as advertisements for novels. The discourse of academia is put in circulation through the blurbs which draw from reviews, even if they are from newspapers or magazines. Increasingly, people from the academia also write in such spaces. Hence the circulation of motifs, critical vocabulary and methods of analysis is maintained.

This process in a way ensures a wider reach for critical models and can help in blurring the boundaries between the academic and non-academic reader. By viewing blurbs, critical introductions etc. as spaces where the critical practice is carried on, the impact and reach of these same practices can be widened.

## Critical Introductions and Translations

These comments in the blurbs are often expounded at length by critical introductions to the books themselves. Although such introductions are more common in and perform a greater function in translations, their very existence makes it possible for the Common Reader to have access not merely to the text, but also to the criteria by which to analyse and read the text. For instance, the Oxford edition of Amitav Ghosh's *The Shadow Lines* (1988) has three critical essays by Meenakshi Mukherjee, Suvir Kaul and A. N. Kaul, all of which look at specific aspects of the novel. Meenakshi Mukherjee's essay also places it within a Bengali literary tradition. The Selma edition of *Gopallapurathu Makkal* carries not only a long introduction by Venkat Swaminathan (translated into Tamil from English), but also the text of Ki. Rajanarayanan's Sahitya Akademi Award acceptance speech.

However, it is in the translations of works that such introductions play a bigger role. The sudden boom in translations into English from the *bhashas* since the 1980s has made the Common Reader more aware of the literary traditions in various Indian languages and is making possible a greater dialogue between these traditions. Translation works at once as a critical paradigm, an academic and creative practice, a patronage issue and an ideological subject and is a very important medium in India today. It helps in creating and fostering a much-needed dialogue between the multifarious languages of the nation, a dialogue that the division of states on an ethno-linguistic basis in 1956 had drastically reduced. Prior to Independence, translation acted as a medium for the percolation of nationalist and reformist ideologies. For example, magazines in Tamil like *Kalaimagal* and *Vivekachintamani* carried translations from various other languages, especially Bengali and Marathi. It is said that V. S. Khandekar, the Marathi novelist, was more popular in Tamil Nadu than in Maharashtra, while in Karnataka it was long thought that Bankimchandra and Saratchandra were native speakers of Kannada! This kind of active translation is woefully absent today. The 1956 division has more or less ghettoised each language and literary tradition within itself. The challenge to the unitary or holistic definition of India and Indian literature has created an awareness that there *is* a need for the various linguistic traditions to meet and engage in fruitful dialogue and has today resulted in an increase in translation activity, at least from the *bhashas* into English.

The publication of these translations has somewhat filled the gap that Aijaz Ahmed had spoken of. The critical introductions to many such translations—especially those published by Macmillan, Katha, Oxford University Press etc.—help the reader to get an idea of the literary history of the source language and a glimpse of the major themes as well. In the process one gets initiated not only to that particular text and author but also to contemporary Indian fiction in general. Such introductions form yet another mode of critical writing and open up the possibility of including these texts even in college and university syllabi.

Translation has, of course, emerged as a major literary activity today in India. More and more space is being devoted to translated works in bookstores, libraries, and even in review journals and newspapers. It also plays the important role of bridging the gap between Indian writing in English and Indian writing in the *bhashas*. This is made possible largely by the fact that translated texts can fill many of the lacunae identified in Indian writing in English, namely the absence of Dalit writing, the deficiency of writing from non-bourgeois sections and the relative dearth of a 'native' idiom. Translations into English from the *bhashas* have effectively made use of a different kind of 'english' from those used in Indian writing in English: witness translations such as *Kosla* (originally in Marathi by Bhalchandra Nemdade, translated into English by Sudhakar Marathe, published by Macmillan in 1997), *Akkarmashi* (originally in Marathi by Sharankumar Limbale, translated into English by Santosh Bhoomkar, published by Oxford University Press in 2003), *Karukku* (originally in Tamil by Bama, translated into English by Lakshmi Holmstrom, published by Macmillan India in 2000).

As a critical paradigm, translation is somewhat like the proverbial curate's egg; for it is difficult to assess the route that it is taking. One major debate is the question regarding the placement of a translated text – is it part of the source language tradition or are we to see it as part of the target language? This question has not been directly answered and existing criticism seems to unconsciously read a translation more as part of the tradition of the source language. This is most evident in the critical introductions to the translations. Mostly written by experts in the source language, these introductions, as already mentioned, place a translated text neatly within the literary history of the source language tradition, but rarely deal with its impact on literatures from other languages, or even on the possible impact of the translation on the literary tradition of the target language. For instance, although Sudhakar Marathe's introduction to his translation of *Kosla* locates the text within the context of modern Marathi literature and discusses its position as the pivotal text of modern Marathi fiction, there is no attempt to see this translation as part of the history of Indian writing in English. The same can be said of most other critical introductions as well. While many of them provide an admirable history of the literary tradition of the source language, there is rarely an attempt made to see interconnections between the translation and Indian Writing in English per se. In other words, the critical introductions provided in many translations are admirable in themselves and act as solid background material for an academic reading of the texts. However, they are singularly incapable of reading the translation as occupying a dual position—in the literary history of the source as well as the target language. Perhaps the addition of another critical introduction—this from experts in the target language—might provide a more wholesome picture. Yet another lacuna in the analysis of translated texts is the comparative absence of attempts to trace influences between different languages. For instance, the language used in the translation of Bhalchandra Nemade's *Kosla* is syntactically and semantically a far cry from those used even in the most unorthodox works in any language and does offer a repertoire of styles that other translations as well as English writing from India can draw upon. But there is little or no critical material that can trace such instances or speculate on the reasons for the absence of any such connections. Another example can be given here of caste issues. One of the accusations levelled against Indian writing in English was that it lacked the equipment/ know-how to address the caste issue. This lacuna was mostly linked to the class / caste from which most writers of English fiction came, namely the upper and privileged ones, whose concerns did not include caste in the sense in which it matters to a writer hailing from the under-privileged groups.[4] However, with the increasing number of translations from *bhashas* into English of texts written by Dalits dealing in far more intensive way with dalit issues, there is a growing awareness of the pressing nature of caste issues among writers, critics and readers. In this context, it is interesting that a novel like David Davidar's *The House of Blue Mangoes* (2001) should deal with the caste issue although it is written in English. The ways in which this novel handles the issue and deviates from the treatment in *bhasha* texts can be a fruitful area for research.

Yet another feature of reading translations and critiquing them is the tendency to see them as 'secondary' and to compare them to the 'original'. Although critics like G. N. Devy and Ayyappa Panikker are two of the many critics who are trying to change this attitude and to evolve an alternative paradigm for analysis of translations, it is present in the various reviews that always tend to read a translation against its original. In such assessments, deviations are frowned upon despite constant assertions by critics that ancient and medieval India consistently encouraged deviations in translations. A translated text is worst hit in reviews where the reviewer has read the 'original' text. This is perhaps best seen in the reviews of Qurratulain Hyder's *Aag ka Dariya* which was first published in 1956, but was translated (by the author herself) only in 2000. Shohini Ghosh sees it as a good translation because it does not read like one ('A Transcreation' 69), while Shama Futehally, having read the Urdu novel, tellingly calls her review 'Classic Let-down' viewing the rendition into English as distancing the reader. Moreover, she sees it as employing a language that comes not from 'felt need' but as one that was merely deemed fit for its subject (37). Most other criticisms—in the form of reviews or essays—merely mention that the text is a translation. The focus is largely on how it treats the concept of time and on the notion of Indian culture that emerges.

It is often the case that when we know the 'original' language, we very rarely find any translation good enough; that it misses an 'essence' is a common enough accusation. The reviews of Giriraj Kishore's Hindi novel *Dhai Ghar* (trans. 1996) note that much of the dialectal variations have been lost in the translation and the reviews of the English version of Thakazhi's *Kayar* point to the inability of the translation to capture much of the wry humour of the Malayalam text. Not knowing the 'original' however, we may be handicapped by not being able to compare, but it may also allow us to be more open to the translation itself.

Given the multilingual culture that prevails in India, the translation activity perforce needs a via media – a language that can reach out to a relatively large number of people and this role is fulfilled by English. The much-spoken about 'boom' in translation has created a substantial corpus of texts translated from various regional languages into English. Sujit Mukherjee's complaint in 1981 in *Translation as Discovery* that we do not have any author, barring Tagore, a large body of whose works have been translated into English, can today be successfully countered: a number of novels of M. T. Vasudevan Nair, Thakazhi Sivasankara Pillai, Vaikom Mohammad Basheer and Lalitambika Antarjanam from Malayalam; Ashokamitran, Ambai, Lakshmi Kannan, Jayakanthan, Sundara Ramaswamy and Indira Parthasarathy from Tamil; Sunil Gangopadhyay, Mahasweta Devi from Bengali; Indira Goswami from Assamese; Manoj Das and

Pratibha Ray from Oriya; Qurratulain Hyder, and Ismat Chugtai from Urdu have been successfully rendered into English. In fact, the works of earlier writers like Tagore have been translated more than once, Sujit Mukherjee's own recent rendering of *Gora* being an instance.

There has, however, been a rebellion, and expectedly too, against the use of English as a via media for bridging the gap between languages; an attitude that can be seen as yet another manifestation of the anti-English syndrome. Nirmal Varma, for example, himself a Hindi author and a translator of Czech texts into Hindi, said in an interview that

> we should give up the habit of approaching world literature through the medium of English. We should establish a direct contact with French, Czech, Spanish, German, Swedish traditions. Only then can we come to a sensible conclusion regarding which novelists to translate and who will be acceptable to the Indian . . . Our inferiority complex in the face of English has made us incapable of experiencing the best in world literature. ('Nammul Uraiyum Kadal' 37).

However, such an attitude has resulted in the positive practice of translating texts into regional languages directly from other languages. This mode is the preferred one with publishing houses such as Cre-A in Tamil which shows a great deal of sophistication and critical thinking in its output. However, direct translations either from Indian languages or from other languages are hard to come by due to practical difficulties. There are precious few people in India who are proficient enough to translate texts between two *bhashas*; even if people *know* two *bhashas*, they need not be capable of translating between them. Ms Chandra Chari, editor of *The Book Review* echoed the same sentiments in an interview:[5]

> But intra-lingual translations are still very much at a premium in India. NBT is doing some. Sahitya Akademi is *supposed* to be. . . . If you want to do a translation from Hindi to Malayalam, just imagine how difficult the task is. Hindi is perhaps not a good example. If you wanted a translation from Malayalam to Bengali, now how many people would know Malayalam and Bengali well, the language and the culture well enough to do the translation? Certainly, the knowledge of Bengali will have to be very good and Malayalam will have to be more than a simple working knowledge. You can count people who fulfil all these criteria on your fingers. That's going to be a major hurdle. (15 March 2002)

In the absence of such large-scale translations, the option is perhaps to rely on translations into English. True though it is that statistically, the number of people who know and can read English translations is very small, it is also a fact that among these readers can be found translators who can render these English translations into other *bhashas*. For instance, it may be difficult to translate an Assamese novel directly into Tamil; but it is possible and relatively easy to translate an English translation of the text into Tamil.

This process may, however, meet with stiff opposition because of the antagonism towards the English language that both nativist and regionalist discourses display. However, English does have the ability to reach out to people across languages. It has the added advantage of making a text visible to the world community. Moreover, the point made earlier about 'original' English novels being projected as representative of Indian literature in the absence of translations, can be partially rectified by encouraging translations into English.

It is true that such a practice would keep the translated text at two or three removes from the 'original' ideal text and thereby drastically reduce its value and credibility. But we may say, like the narrator in Rushdie's *Shame* (1983) that 'it is generally believed that something is always lost in translation. I cling to the notion . . . that something can also be gained' (29). This would also mean that translation codes and methods vis-à-vis English need to be standardised to a great extent and spruced up in quality. Translation as a patronage issue (which will be dealt with later) will then indeed be closely related to the actual practice of the activity. Translation practice definitely impinges upon the critical practice and vice versa.

The task of creating a group of people who can carry out efficient translations between Indian languages is an onerous one. We might perhaps rely upon the associations of various states / languages to undertake this. In Chennai, for example, we have the Kerala Association, the Assam Association, the Bihar Association and the Maharashtra Association, to name a few. While embassies and consulates of other countries (the Max Mueller Bhavan for German and the Alliance Francais for French) train students in the art of translation, the activities of these associations are often confined to cultural activities. If these associations were to undertake the task of training people to translation between their mother tongue and another *bhasha*, direct translations between *bhashas* may become somewhat easier and more practical.

At the same time, we need to come to an impartial understanding of the nature of English in India and in the world today. The tendency to see English as the tool of the coloniser or his *chelas* even as late as the twenty-first century has been somewhat checked by the increasing uses to which it is put. The postcolonial model greatly helped in understanding the nature of assimilation of a new tongue in a different country by proposing the model of 'englishes' – the nearly complete surgery on Queen's English and the transplant of native organs into it. That the validity of these transplants has been accepted by the world community (and not only by the English-speaking one) is evidenced by the inclusion of a large number of these words, like *Hindutva*, *chai*[6] etc. into the Oxford English dictionary ('All For English'). It may not be long before our computers will not give a red squiggle when we type *janata* or *kolam*. The fact remains that English is fast becoming perhaps the one language that can be understood anywhere in the world. Moreover, it is the language of international commerce. These facts should alert us to the possibility that English can offer us the necessary intermediary space for reaching out to the outside world. At the same time, we need also to remember that translations into English are not made entirely for a Western audience. Many Indians too get to know of *bhasha* texts only through translations into English. Amiya Dev brings out the importance of an intermediary language in his essay 'Conscience, Activism and Jaidev's Location' by saying: 'In fact, as a vehicle of intra-Indian communication English is more and more turning out to be a function, not authority. Its link-language status has by and large been a useful piece of pragmatism' (71).

The issue of intra-lingual translation brings us also to the question of what languages and genres are considered for translation. The case of languages is quite easily answered, for it is only the twenty-two or so languages recognised by Schedule VIII of the Indian Constitution which are—indeed can be—considered as source languages. The importance of state sponsorship and institutional patronage for the very existence of a literary and/or critical tradition—at least in the forms in which we know them—can be gauged from this.

Recognition in Schedule VIII of the Constitution of India means more than a mere entry into official records. It ensures that these languages are taught; schools can use them as mediums of education, college level degrees can be provided in them and their literature can move out of anthropological or ethnographical studies into literary studies. Recognition in Schedule VIII also ensures that texts in the recognised languages get printed and therefore attain greater publicity. Such state support further implies that texts from these languages get into popular circulation, are open to translation into other languages and that consequently, a critical tradition will evolve that would also historicise the literary tradition in these languages. The discussion of the awards institutions in the next chapter will needs return to this issue as languages not accorded state recognition cannot be considered for awards.

The implication here is that in any consideration of 'Indian literature', we face this severe handicap of being unable to deal with it in its entirety, for a group of languages is always left out. Even the most comprehensive study or group of studies on Indian literature cannot include all languages. Since it is well nigh impossible to overcome this handicap, we might do well to work with it and refrain from considering the literary or critical tradition of *any* language as being fully representative of India.

Secondly, although novels, poetry collections and plays are being translated on quite a large scale—with of course, novels taking centre stage—critical works are yet to be rendered from one language into another on a larger scale. The result is that although criticism has today become quite a self-conscious discipline, it is difficult to trace similarities or differences across languages. One is forced to take recourse to stray mentions about critics in various languages. In this area, awards institutions can play an important role as most of them depend upon the critical reception of a given text to decide on an award. This in turn necessitates translations of available critical material in *bhashas* into at least English, if not other Indian languages.

We can see how any study of the literary ethos of the period under consideration has to take into account the existing critical practices, the challenges to orthodoxy in literary appreciation and the emerging forms and practices which are necessitated by the shift in the literary, cultural and critical paradigms. The attempt here has been to throw light on the different facets of the critical practice today which is embedded in the ideological premises of discursive writings and literary output.

## Notes

1. Parts of this chapter have been published in an article entitled 'Is There a Critical Tradition in This Country' in the journal *Littcrit* 32, Nos. 1&2 (2007), pp. 116–24.

2. Schedule VIII of the Indian Constitution contains the list of languages that the Indian Government recognises.

3. Little Magazines have played an important role in most *bhashas* as well. Magazines such as *Orunoday* and *Jonaki* in Assamese, Lankesh's *Lankesh Patrike* in Kannada etc. played a very important role in creating and fostering a literary–cultural ethos in them. However, information on them is rarely translated into other languages and this could be an area for further research.

4. U. R. Anantamurthy's Kannada novel *Samskara* did deal with issues related to caste; its translation into English by A. K. Ramanujam made the text available to a wider readership, both 'lay' and academic. The position of *Samskara* as a 'Dalit' text, though, is highly debatable.

5. These remarks were made at an interview given by Ms Chandra Chari to me on 15 March 2002 at *The Book Review* office at New Delhi.

6. The second edition of the *Oxford English Dictionary* contains *Hindutva* and *chai* while the eleventh edition of the *Oxford Learner's Dictionary* carries the same words.

## References

'All For English'. Editorial. *The Hindu*, 14 Feb. 2003, 10.

Ashokamitran. '*Tharkala Ulaga Ilakkiyathaip Pattri Talavay Sundarathidam Ashokamitran Pesugirar*'. (Tamil). ('Ashokamitran Talks to Talavay Sundaram about the Position of Contemporary World Literature'). *Kumudam International: Deepavali Malar*, 4 Nov. 2002: 280–87.

Bama. *Karukku*. 1992. Trans. Lakshmi Holmström from the Tamil into English (Chennai: Macmillan India Limited, 2000).

Bhatia, H. S. 'Meta Criticism and the State of Panjabi Literary Criticism'. Paper Presented at '*The State of Literary Criticism: Trends, Texts and Issues*' seminar. Sahitya Akademi Auditorium, Rabindra Bhavan, New Delhi, 21–23 Feb. 2002.

Chandra Chari. Editor. *The Book Review*, Personal Interview, 15 Mar. 2002.

Chandra, Vikram. *Red Earth and Pouring Rain* (New Delhi: Penguin), 1995.

Chandra, Vikram. *Love and Longing in Bombay* (New Delhi: Penguin, 1997).

Davidar, David. *The House of Blue Mangoes* (New Delhi: Penguin, 2002).

Desai, Boman. *The Memory of Elephants*. 1988 (Kent: Sceptre, 1990).

Dev, Amiya. 'Conscience, Activism and Intellect: Jaidev's Location'. *The Politics of Literary Theory and Representation*. Ed. Pankaj K. Singh (New Delhi: Manohar, 2003), 67–73.

Devy, G. N. *After Amnesia: Tradition and Change in Indian Literary Criticism* (Bombay: Orient Longman), 1992.

———. *Of Many Heroes: An Indian Essay in Literary Historiography* (Mumbai: Orient Longman, 1998).

Futehally, Shama. 'Classic Let-down'. Review of *River of Fire* by *Qurratulain Hyder*. *Indian Review of Books* 8, 4 nos. (16 Jan.–15 Feb. 1999), 36–37.

Ghosh, Amitav. *In an Antique Land* (New Delhi: Ravi Dayal Publishers, 1992).

———. *The Shadow Lines* (New Delhi: Oxford UP, 1988).

Ghosh, Shohini. 'A Transcreation'. Review of *River of Fire* by *Qurratulain Hyder*. *The Book Review* 23, nos. 1 & 2. (Jan.–Feb. 1999), 69–70.

Gokhale, Namita. *Mountain Echoes: Reminiscences of Kumaoni Women* (New Delhi: Lotus Collection Roli Books, 1998).

Goswami, Indira. *The Moth-eaten Howdah of the Tusker* (1984). Trans. Indira Goswami from Assamese into English. *The Search for the Sea: The Fictional World of Indira Goswami (Mamoni Raisom Goswami)*. Ed. Satarwala Kaikous Burjor (New Delhi: B. R. Publications, 2002), 187–338.

Hariharan, Githa. *When Dreams Travel* (London: Picador, 1999).

Jain, Jasbir. 'Towards the 21st Century: The Writing of the 1990s'. *Indian Writing in English: The Last Decade*. Ed. Rajul Bhargava (Jaipur: Rawat Publications, 2002).

Jung, Anees. *Unveiling India: A Woman's Journey* (New Delhi: Penguin, 2000).

Karanjia, B. K. *More of an Indian* (New Delhi: Orient Paperbacks, 1970).

Kishore, Giriraj. *The Knight's Move*. Trans. Prajapati Sah from Hindi into English (New Delhi, Sahitya Akademi, 1996).

Kishwar, Madhu. *Off the Beaten Track: Rethinking Gender Justice for Women* (New Delhi: Oxford UP, 1999).

Lakshmi, C. S. *Payanappada Padaigal: Katchi Vadiva Varalatrup Payilarangil Penn Kalaignargalin Padivugal*. (Tamil). (*Untrodden Paths: Sound and Picture Archives on Women Artistes*). Compiled by A. Srinivasan and M. Shivasubramanian (Mumbai: SPARROW (Sound and Picture Archives for Research on Women), 2001.

Limbale, Sharankumar. *Akkarmashi: The Outcaste*. Trans. from Marathi by Santosh Bhoomkar (New Delhi: Oxford UP, 2003).

*Masterpieces of Indian Literature*. 3 vols. Ed. K. M. George (New Delhi: National Book Trust, India, 1997).

Mohanty, P. K. 'Towards a Search for a Pan-Indian Literary Theory'. Paper Presented at *The State of Literary Criticism: Trends, Texts and Issues* seminar. Sahitya Akademi Auditorium, Rabindra Bhavan, New Delhi, 21–23 Feb. 2002.

Mukherjee, Sujit. *Translation as Discovery* (Hyderabad: Sangam Books, 1981).

Nagendra, ed. *Literary Criticism in India* (Meerut: Sarita Prakashan, 1976).

Naval, Nandkishore. *Hindi Alochana Ka Itihaas*. (Hindi) (The History of Hindi Criticism), (New Delhi: Rajkamal Prakashan), 1981.

Nemade, Bhalchandra. *Cocoon*. Trans. From Marathi by Sudhakar Marathe (Chennai: Macmillan, 1997).

Pillai, Thakazhi Sivasankara. *Kayar: Coir*. Trans. N. Sreekantan Nair from Malayalam into English (New Delhi: Sahitya Akademi, 1997).

Rajan, P. K. Ed. Paradigms in Plurality'. *Indian Literary Criticism in English:* Critics, Texts, Issues (Jaipur: Rawat Publications, 2004), 339–82.

Roy, Nilanjana S. 'Judgement Day: An Analysis of the Booker Prize and its Literary Cohorts.' *Biblio: A Review of Books*. 6, Nos. 7 & 8 (Nov.–Dec. 2000). 1 page. 26th March 2003. <http://www.biblio-india.com/archives>

Rushdie, Salman. *Midnight's Children*. 1981 (London: Picador, 1982).

———. *Shame* (New Delhi: Rupa and Co., 1983).

*Sahitya Akademi Souvenir, 2001.*

Sivakumar, R. (Unpublished Dissertation). 'Literary Avant-gardism in American Little Magazines with Special Reference to *Poetry* and *The Little Review*'. M. Phil. University of Madras, 1989.

Srivastava, Paramanand. 'The Story of a Dying Order'. Review of *The Knight's Move* by Giriraj Kishore, *Indian Literature* 37, no.1 (Jan.–Feb. 1994): 112–16.

———. Introduction. *Samakaleen Hindi Alochana. (Hindi). (Contemporary Hindi Criticism)* ( New Delhi: Sahitya Akademi, 1998).

Subramaniam, K. N. *Vimarisana Kalai.* (Tamil). (The Art of Criticism) (Chennai: Narmada Padippagam, 1984).

Tandon, Bishen, ed. *Jnanpith Puraskar: 1965–1990.* (Hindi). (Jnanpith Award: 1965–1990) (New Delhi: Bharatiya Jnanpith Prakashan, 1991).

Tharu, Susie and Lalitha, eds. *Women Writing in India*. 2 vols. (New Delhi: Oxford UP, 1991).

Tripathi, Ravindra. 'Hindi Mein Alochana: Ek Sandighdh Upastithi?' (Criticism in Hindi: A Doubtful Existence?). Paper presented at *The State of Literary Criticism: Trends, Texts and Issues* seminar. Sahitya Akademi Auditorium, Rabindra Bhavan, New Delhi, 21–23 Feb. 2002.

Varma. Nirmal. 'Nammul Uraiyum Kadal.' (The Raging Sea Within Us). Interview with B. A. Krishnan. *Kalachuvadu* 37(Sept–Oct 2001), 32–40.

# 3

# PATRONAGE AND PROMOTION OF LITERATURE

We saw in the previous chapter that literature and literary criticism are both dependent upon and are, by themselves, kinds of institutions. The relatively short discussion on Schedule VIII of the Indian Constitution and its implications for languages, recognised and not recognised, threw light on the state as one such institution of patronage. Within literary circles, certain awards foundations also function as a body of patronage; they select and confer cash prizes and mementoes to authors and / or works, thereby providing financial support. They also publicise their awards, opening opportunities for these authors to become better known in the national and international arena.

A number of literary awards are being given at international, national and regional levels. Of these, international awards are naturally the most attractive because they select winners from across a large number of countries. Perhaps the most coveted of such awards—in India and elsewhere—is the Nobel Prize for literature. Despite criticisms that the selection process is racist and elitist and in recent times politically motivated, the Nobel Prize remains one of the most respected. Among other international awards that are much esteemed in India are the Man Booker Prize and the Commonwealth Writers Award. Although 'international' in that they consider literatures from different countries, these two awards restrict themselves to literatures produced in English from the Commonwealth countries or the erstwhile colonies. This linguistic insistence on English in awards given to literatures published in the 'postcolonial' countries only serves to intensify the dissatisfaction that many critics and writers have felt with the postcolonial model for its monolingual bias. That this may cause many worthwhile books in other languages—the *bhashas* in India—to remain unnoticed has been discussed earlier. We may once again recall that Amitav Ghosh had refused the Commonwealth Writers' Prize primarily on linguistic grounds.

Many literary awards in India given by organisations runs by various state governments also consider only novels / authors of a particular linguistic group. Kerala has the credit of awarding the maximum number of literary awards, among them the Ezhuthachan Award (which is decided by a committee selected by the state government), Vallathol Prize, Muttathu Varkey Award etc. Various states also have their regional Sahitya Akademi awards which are given by the State Sahitya Akademi foundations (these have to be distinguished from the National Sahitya Akademi, which is an altogether different body). These are autonomous bodies committed to the encouragement of literature and research in the languages of the respective states. Since these foundations are self-avowedly dedicated to the promotion of literatures in their respective languages, their linguistic restriction in them becomes, in effect, an act of self-assertion. The awards given at these regional levels often render a text / author visible to a larger audience and make them available for consideration for national awards.

National awards committees are mainly characterised by a process of comparative study between various linguistic traditions, although the Sahitya Akademi Award desists from this. In considering texts/ authors across various languages, these awards foundations differ from both international and what may be called 'regional' awards. In taking into account texts from different *bhashas* and selecting one winner from them, these awards foundations also imply that literatures produced within the political entity called 'India' do have comparable features. Since the awards necessarily have to discuss a number of linguistic traditions before arriving at a 'winner', the further implication is that more or less similar criteria—critical paradigms—can be used in reading texts produced in various Indian languages. Hence, the 'national' character of these awards rests primarily on the fact that they consider texts written in Indian languages. It is here that a national awards foundation may be said to differ from, say, the Nobel Prize Foundation.

The following discussion will centre around three select national literary awards: a. the Bharatiya Jnanpith, b. the Saraswati Samman awarded by the K. K. Birla Foundation and c. The Sahitya Akademi. These awards have been selected as case studies and it is implicitly understood that other national literary awards such as the Bharatiya Bhasha Parishad from Kolkata also perform similar functions.

The selection processes of these awards, besides offering perspectives on the relationship between the literatures of various languages, also reflect many of the issues and concerns regarding national literature, the functions of literature and the role of criticism in the country today. The analysis of the selection process will try to probe the assumptions implied in such a process, in the context of the literary–cultural ethos of current day India.

## THE BHARATIYA JNANPITH (INDIA'S SEAT OF KNOWLEDGE AND WISDOM)

The Bharatiya Jnanpith (India's Seat of Knowledge and Wisdom) was instituted on 22 May 1961 by Sahu Shantiprasad Jain and his wife Rama Jain. The objective of the award was to identify and felicitate *the* best literary creation in India in any of the fifteen languages then recognised by Schedule VIII of the Indian Constitution (which now includes twenty two languages). The first award was given in 1965 to G. Shankara Kurup, a Malayalam poet, for his collection *Odakkuzhal*. The award money was then a lakh and a half. It is now five lakh. Along with this amount, a bronze statue of *Vagdevi* or Saraswati, the Goddess of Learning and Arts, is also given. From 1982 onwards, the award is being given for lifetime achievement rather than for a single work. According to the then Director Shri Dinesh Misra,[1] this was largely owing to the difficulty in selecting one book out of the extraordinary number of books that were being published.

The first step in the selection process for the Bharatiya Jnanpith is to send out proposal forms to what its office-bearers call 'lovers of literature', consisting of writers, academics, critics and others. Out of the many that are sent out, a few hundred are filled in and returned. These proposals ask for names of writers who can be considered for the award in that particular year. Once the proposal forms are filled in, the Bharatiya Jnanpith uses a two-tier system of selection to decide upon the winner. The first stage is that of the *bhasha samiti* (language committee) which consists of three members who may be writers, critics or academics. Each language that is to be considered for the award, that is, every language that is recognised by the Constitution, has a *bhasha samiti*. The filled-in proposal forms are sorted according to each language and sent to the respective *bhasha samiti*. These *bhasha samitis* meet and decide upon one, two or three authors who they think can be considered for the Jnanpith. Apart from the names given in the proposal forms, the members of the *bhasha samitis* are also asked to propose the name of any author of their choice whom they think deserves consideration. The *bhasha samitis* send supporting material, that is, available criticism on the author and her/his writings to justify their selections. Authors selected at this level will then go to the second stage of the selection process, which is that of the *pravar parishad* (Excellence Committee).

The number of names that come from the *bhasha samitis* may be around twenty-four or so. From these a few get automatically eliminated, the reason being that the language in which a writer who won the award one year will not be considered for the next two years. This means that around two to four languages (in case there have been joint awardees) will not be considered for the present year. Finally, around fourteen to eighteen names remain and these are discussed in the meeting of the *pravar parishad*.

Once the fourteen to eighteen names are decided upon, Bharatiya Jnanpith collects as many works as possible of that particular writer and sends them to each member of the *pravar parishad*. The *pravar parishad* consists of eleven members and is headed by a prominent public person. At the final meeting of the *pravar parishad*, the debates will include the reasons for selecting or rejecting all the books / authors whose names have come to this level.

If all the members of the *pravar parishad* agree on a particular winner, her / his name is immediately announced. If, however, a consensus cannot be reached, Bharatiya Jnanpith collects more material on the writers between whom there is a tie and sends these to the members of the jury. The members are given another month to go through this material after which the *parishad* meets again and decides on the winner.

Once the winner is announced, a date is fixed and a chief guest is announced who will give away the award. At the same function, a book by the winner is released for the first time. If all original books have already been released, then a translation into Hindi is released for the first time at the function.

The two-tier selection process places any author at once in more than one position. The *bhasha samiti* level of selection places the author within the relevant literary and linguistic tradition. The constitution of the *bhasha samiti*, consisting of native speakers, academics and writers of the language, makes sure that the author is critiqued by people well aware of the traditions and changing modes in the literature of that language. Supporting material given by the *bhasha samitis* to the *pravar parishad* is confined to selections of criticism. It does not, however, sum up the existing criticism of the author's works, which may place her / him in a particular sociocultural scenario.

The *pravar parishad* level of selection places the author in the larger context of national literature. At this stage, it becomes inevitable that the author's works are compared to other works in various other languages. That such a comparison can take place is itself an expression of the implicit understanding that literatures of various languages written from a single nation—India—do have commonalities and are therefore comparable. While any comparison can be scary, one between fourteen or so authors can be really formidable. The Bharatiya Jnanpith looks for what it calls substantial 'original' contribution to the entirety of Indian literature. This 'originality' is measured in terms of form, content, the newness of what is written as well as the relevance of the text to recent cultural and political conditions.

The Bharatiya Jnanpith remains one of the best-known literary awards within India. In recent times, it *has* made a considerable difference to the way a writer has been looked at. The winner of the 2001 award, the Assamese writer Indira Goswami, has been widely read, published, critiqued and interviewed after she won the award. Though already quite a major figure within Assam, the award has brought her a wider, national acclaim. In one of the various interviews she gave after she was declared winner, she said that the primary reason she accepted the award was that it would give her greater visibility over the country (*Deccan Herald,* 7 April 2002). And indeed, it has done so.

## The 'Saraswati Samman' Awarded by the K. K. Birla Foundation

The Saraswati Samman is a literary award given by the K. K. Birla Foundation. Like Bharatiya Jnanpith, it too gives away only *one* award—but for a text (rather than an author)—in any of the recognised languages in Schedule VIII of the Constitution of India. This award is being given from 1991 onwards and the first person to receive it was the Hindi poet Dr Harivanshrai Bachhan for his autobiography *Dashdwar se Sopan Tak* (From the Door to the Stairway, 1985).

The Saraswati Samman has a three-tier structure of selection that includes, in order, a. *the bhasha samiti* or language committee, b. *the kshetra samiti* or zonal committee and finally c. *the chayan parishad* or final selection committee.

Like the Bharatiya Jnanpith, here too, the process begins with sending out proposal forms to academics, writers and critics asking them to propose any book published within the last ten years which they think can be considered for the award. The completed proposal forms are then sent to the respective *bhasha samitis* which consist of three members who can again be writers, academics or critics in their respective languages. Each *bhasha samiti* sends one book which it considers most deserving. The convener of each *bhasha samiti* also has to send a three-part write-up consisting of

* the literary scene in that particular language in the last fifty years with special reference to the genre under consideration
* a brief sketch of the literary career of the writer and
* a brief analysis of the book recommended. Mostly, this looks at the theme, the historical significance and the technique employed.

The *bhasha samiti* also sends all available critical material on the book to the next level, that is, the *kshetra samiti* or zonal committee. There are four *kshetra samitis*; one for each zone, that is, east, west, north and south. The languages of each of these zones will come under the respective *kshetra samiti*. For example, Tamil, Kannada, Malayalam and Telugu (and now, Konkani) will come under the south zonal committee and so on. Sanskrit alone is considered by each zone in rotation.

The *kshetra samitis* are made up of the convenors of the *bhasha samitis* and each *kshetra samiti* meeting takes up all the books recommended by the language committees coming under its jurisdiction. Since all the members are given all the materials sent by each *bhasha samiti*, the argument becomes dialogic. Each zonal committee sends one book to the next level for consideration i.e. to the *chayan parishad*.

The *kshetra samiti* is perhaps the most important stage in the selection process because it acts as a forum for a comparative analysis of texts that are not linguistically very different from each other. This is based on the idea that a particular geographic region may have fewer differences between its constituents. For instance, the Southern languages Tamil, Malayalam, Kannada and Telugu, all belong to the Dravidian family of languages. The states also share very close histories – many parts of them have been ruled by the same dynasties and even the British tended to treat them as one presidency. All these similarities and shared legacies make a literary comparison between the states a fruitful exercise. The publication of anthologies of South Indian literatures in translation, mentioned earlier, may be recalled in this regard.

The recommendation of each of the *kshetra samities* is given to the final selection committee i.e. the *chayan parishad* which consists of twelve members and is headed by a retired Chief Justice of the Supreme Court. It is here that a second level comparative study takes place where each of the recommended works is seen as part of the totality of Indian literature and the award is announced, which consists of a prize money of five lakh rupees and a citation.

The most impressive feature about this selection process is the amount of strenuous work that goes in. To begin with, the *bhasha parishads'* reports, and especially the three-part write-up for each language, help place the particular text in the context of the literature of the regional language to which it belongs. In the past few years, the Foundation has also tried to get as much of the book under consideration as possible translated into Hindi and English and provide these along with the rest of the material to all the members. If a translation already exists, it is appended to the material. This ensures that all the members at every level of selection have first-hand knowledge of at least part of the book they are selecting or rejecting.

As in the case of the Bharatiya Jnanpith, the final award is given at a function organised by the K. K. Birla Foundation.

## THE SAHITYA AKADEMI: INDIA'S NATIONAL ACADEMY OF LETTERS

Among all the three awards discussed, the Sahitya Akademi is the only one that has the assistance of the Government of India. It is different in character from all the other awards mainly in that while both the Bharatiya Jnanpith and the K. K. Birla Foundation (Saraswati Samman) give one award every year—either for a book or for an author—the Sahitya Akademi gives no less than twenty-two awards every year; one for each language recognised by the Government of India and one for English. What it does not do, therefore, is engage in any comparative study between the literatures of the various languages.

It is also the only one among the awards discussed here that considers English *along* with the other *bhashas*. This makes it different in character from many other awards. International Awards like the Commonwealth Writers Prize etc. that consider English do not consider any other language. On the other hand, Indian national awards foundations like Bharatiya Jnanapith and K. K. Birla Foundation that consider the *bhashas* do not consider English. This practice reiterates the segregation between Indian writing in English and Indian writing in the *bhashas*. Sahitya Akademi, on the other hand, places these on the same plane and thereby assists in seeing them as part of a larger whole.

The award is given to one outstanding work published in each of the languages six years prior to the year of the award. For example, books published between 1995 and 2000 will be considered for the 2002 Sahitya Akademi Award.

The selection process begins with the preparation of a ground list of eligible works, which is usually entrusted to an expert in the language. Experts are chosen out of the names recommended by the Language Advisory Board which is the equivalent of the *bhasha samitis* in the other two awards. Along with the ground list, the previous year's ground list is also sent to the members of the Advisory Board and each member is asked to recommend two books, either from these names or any other name that they consider worthy.

The next level of selection is the Preliminary Panel, which consists of ten 'referees' and, as in the case of the language committees, there is one for each language. The recommendations of the language committee are sent to each referee and s/he is asked to recommend two books. Interestingly, to avoid influencing, one referee does not know what another sends. The language committees also do not send any secondary material along with the recommended books. The Akademi assumes that every member of every level of selection will deem it her/his duty towards literature to keep abreast of latest developments in their languages. Moreover, the Sahitya Akademi makes it necessary that a book be in circulation for at least two years before it is considered for the award. The Akademi likes to believe that this period will help the book go into circulation so that the selection committee members become acquainted with them. It is left to each member to search for secondary or supporting material for the books recommended.

The recommendations of the preliminary panel go to a three-member jury. At this stage the Akademi purchases all the books recommended by the preliminary panel and sends them to each of the jury members and to the convenor. The decision is finally taken by consensus or by majority.

## CRITIQUING THE SELECTION PROCESSES...

A closer look at the selection processes would reveal that many of the issues identified in the earlier two chapters operate at the level of basic assumptions here. The most obvious of them all is the concept of 'national literature'. Literary historiography has in recent times problematised the very idea of a 'national' literature. The debate has further heated up with the increasing awareness, production and consumption of streams like Dalit, folk and women's literature that rupture the ideal of a streamlined national literature. However, the basic assumption in all the awards is that despite the divergent languages in which literature is produced in India, they share certain qualities which makes it possible for foundations like the Bharatiya Jnanpith and the K. K. Birla Foundation to decide upon *one* winning text / author. The then Director-in-charge of Bharatiya Jnanpith Mr Dinesh Mishra acknowledged the difficulty of the task in metaphorical language in the interview he gave to this researcher:

> How does one compare the beauty of the rose with the fragrance of the Mogra (double jasmine) flower? One has a wonderful perfume and another looks beautiful. And this challenge is always there before the pravar parishad and they are aware of it. So we try, as far as is possible for an educated human being, to read all that is available to us and discuss them. A kind of consensus emerges from these discussions and from the material available to us. Then these are used as solid proofs. Obviously, all of them are great writers and outstanding in their own languages. To decide who is the best among these is a really tortuous process. (Interview dated 15 March 2002)

Yet, a comparison has to be made and the director himself pointed out what he (speaking for the Bharatiya Jnanpith) felt were the common features: 'In the decision, we take into account technique, completeness and their speciality and we look for some unique contribution by the author' (15 March 2002). He went on to note:

> So many languages, religions, food, clothes, but something, somewhere binds all this together. Nowadays, we see so many things out to sever things. But this, hopefully, is only a *tamasha*(joke or farce). The binding spirit is probably stronger. And I feel that all Indians—Hindus, Muslims, Sikhs, Northerners, Southerners—all have their hearts in the right places. And one thing that does bind Indian literature in all its shapes and sizes is the spirit of humanism that is at its core. This probably connects Indian literature with world literature. All kinds of literature – songs from Bengal or folk tales from Tamil Nadu – all are connected and the Human Being is at its centre. We have to keep this human being alive, give him strength. And if we have to kill this human being, why need literature? One sword is enough. Hit it on his head and he dies. But a writer gives strength to live and go ahead. (15 March 2002)

This may seem suspiciously like a paean to the same humanism that literary theory and ideological criticism in recent times are trying to repudiate as harbouring a hidden agenda. However, we should recognise that the speaking voice does not necessarily subsume cultural, ethnic and experiential differences under humanism, but sees humanism itself as a paradigm that encompasses and accepts the differences. The motto of 'Unity in Diversity' implies this ideal. The above remark also brings to the fore the ideas of 'world and national' literature as one that centres around the 'human being'. Animal rights activists and environmentalists may find this lopsided, but the importance of humanity and the necessity to respect the dignity of everybody—including the Other—is the kind of humanism that seems to be operating in the avowed policies of the awards institutions. Hence we find that in the texts / authors selected as winners or even discussed at various levels of the selection process, different voices and experiences are considered and given space. For instance, the Marathi Dalit text *Upara* by Lakshman Mane won the Sahitya Akademi Award in 1981 although it does not appear to have been considered specially as a 'Dalit text'. The Gujarati text *Angaliyat* received the Sahitya Akademi Award in 1988 while many women writers such as Qurratulain Hyder and Ismat Chugtai, dealing with various kinds of feminist / women's themes have won these awards, as have also writers such as Mahasweta Devi who focuses on themes such as tribal issues and problems of bonded prostitutes. Despite the awardee list being studded with these names, the overarching picture is one where Grand Narratives like nationalism, humanism etc. are valorised. A more complete analysis of the award-winning novels as well as the available criticism on them would be necessary to see how far the awards question or unquestioningly propagate certain ideas / ideologies and notions, a possible area for further research and analysis.

However, we may mention that as far as the Sahitya Akademi is concerned, the years immediately following Independence seem to have been marked by recognition to texts that encouraged nationalistic and humanistic sentiments. This was perhaps natural given the political and social climate of optimism during the Nehruvian era, the introduction of various development programmes and the unconscious need to sacralise the nationalist movement itself. Hence, one can find that texts such as Kalki's Tamil novel *Alai Osai* (The Sound of Waves) (Sahitya Akademi, 1956), Rajaji's rendering of the Ramayana in *Chakravarthi Tirumagan* (The Divine Prince) (Sahitya Akademi, 1958) (which reaffirmed the centrality of this primal epic for the nation), V. S. Khandekar's historical Marathi romance *Yayati* etc. were given the Sahitya Akademi award. However, from the mid-1960s and 1970s, texts questioning social norms and sometimes even presenting the nationalist movement in a different light came to be recognised, for example, Chaman Nahal's *Azadi* (Freedom) which won the Sahitya Akademi award for English in 1977. Jayakantan's *Sila Nerangalil Sila Manidargal* (Some Men at Some Moments) that won the Sahitya Akademi Award for Tamil in 1971 sensitively differs from mainstream sexual mores and boldly portrays a variant of matrimonial relationships. The feminist writer Rajam Krishnan's *Verukku Neer* (Water for the Roots) too was recognised with the award the next year for its depiction of woman's experiences. A definite focus on form can be seen in the later 1980s and 1990s; the Anglo-Indian epic *Trotter-Nama* won the award in 1991 at a time when ethnic communities were asserting their historical sense and presence through such chronicle novels. Ki. Rajanarayanan's *Gopallapurathu Makkal* (The People of Gopallapuram) which won the Tamil Sahitya Akademi in 1991 and *Jhadajhadati* (Punishment)—dealing not only with the contemporary history of a Maharashtrian village, but also critiquing state-sponsored irrigation projects—won the award for Marathi in 1992. Krishna Sobti's Hindi novel *Zindaginama Zinda*

*Rukh* (Chronicle of the Directions of a Life), which has a similar formal structure and deals similarly with history, had already won the award in 1980.

These notwithstanding, there have been definite parameters mentioned in the citations that place the winners within particular paradigms and foreground concerns such as interrogation of tradition, reinterpretation of history, voicing the struggles of depressed classes and so on. For instance, in one of the discussions recorded in the meetings of the East *Kshetra Samiti* of the K. K. Birla Foundation (held on 5 October 2001), there is an interesting debate on two texts selected by the Bengali *Bhasha Samiti*. Of the two, Sunil Gangopadhyay's *Pratham Alo* (*First Light*) was selected for its 'different' treatment of the Bengal renaissance whereas Maitreya Ghatak's novel was rejected for its conventional treatment of the Karna episode from the Mahabharata. The rising importance of critiquing received tradition as a parameter can be seen also in the selections of texts such as Indira Parthasarathy's Tamil play *Ramanujar* (Saraswati Samman, 1999) that depicted the contemporaneity of life and teachings of the Acharya Ramanujar and Vijay Tendulkar's Marathi play *Kanyadaan* (Saraswati Samman, 1993) for its focus on the Dalit movement. Manubhai Pancholi Darshak's Gujarati novel *Kurukshetra* (Saraswati Samman, 1997) is interesting for its different depiction of a marginal episode from the Mahabharata; a critical write-up on it in the souvenir and the citation mention that the novel upholds the value of racial harmony in India.

In other words, we see that the paradigms used in the comparison of various literary traditions presume certain concepts and values essential to literature and stress their role in India today. Yet, the very process of comparison between various traditions may seem too onerous a task and in this context, we need to take a closer look at the multi-tiered selection which takes place in the three awards. Both the Saraswati Samman and the Bharatiya Jnanapith have more than one level of selection wherein a text is placed primarily in the context of its language. The Saraswati Samman also places it in the context of its region. All the three awards place the selected text in its national context. The three levels of selection correspond roughly to the different paradigms used in the categorisation of texts. Yet again we see the importance of language—not necessarily as the final deciding criterion, but as a convenient point from which to begin. However, the centrality of language can be gauged by the dictum in the Bharatiya Jnanapith to disqualify automatically texts of languages which have won the awards for the last two years. This is, however, offset by the rule that a particular duration of time should have elapsed before a text is considered.

The very idea of language committees or *bhasha samitis* is based on the institutionalisation of language and its study since the committee is made up of a group of 'scholars', writers and academicians from that particular language. Despite this, there is the stress on native speakers, for only they can form part of any such committee. A native Tamil speaker who is also a scholar of Hindi cannot form part of the Hindi language committee and insofar as this is concerned, one can see the insistence on what we had earlier identified as the 'insider' factor, if not syndrome. In this case, it implies that in order to respond most sensitively to a language, mere scholarship, however comprehensive and deep, is not a sufficient condition. One can hear faint echoes of what Bhalchandra Nemade had said in the context of English (quoted in the first chapter). A look at the various language committees will reveal that most of the members, apart from being native speakers of a given language, are also academicians in these respective language departments and in this position have access to academic critical tools. Academicians from English departments seem to be the only ones allowed across languages. The importance of Schedule VIII of the Indian Constitution again comes into play here as only those languages recognised by this Schedule can be considered for the awards. Indeed, it would otherwise be impractical as there would hardly be academicians or literary / language scholars in unrecognised languages. Since these cannot be taught at schools or colleges, no language committee can be constituted in their case. To overcome this, Sahitya Akademi, through various special issues in its journal *Indian Literature*, lobbies for government recognition for the other languages.

We also need to note that the founding rules and principles governing the Bharatiya Jnanpith and the Saraswati Samman consciously (and politically) preclude English texts being considered for these awards. Apart from the fact that English is not one of the languages recognised by Schedule VIII of the Indian Constitution, there is also the implicit understanding that English literature from India is getting enough recognition (as Dinesh Misra stated in his interview) to the detriment of literatures from other languages. The practice in the Saraswati Samman of translating the text as well as the critical material into English and/or Hindi is reassuring in the context of the demands made by critics like G. N. Devy and Aijaz Ahmed to make literatures from various Indian *bhashas* available to the general public in India and to readers and academicians in other countries. The practice in Saraswati Samman of translating the text as well as the critical material into English and / or Hindi makes it further possible for critical readings of these texts to be included in the debates. In this context, the presence of academicians in the selection committee makes it more probable and possible that these texts will be taught at college and university levels and that researches will be conducted on them.

In the awards mentioned above, publishing houses and the awards foundations do not have much to do with each other. General readers, critics, and academics—all of whom are clubbed under the heading of 'lovers of literature'—send in their nominations to the language committees. On the other hand, in the case of awards such as the Man Booker Prize or the Commonwealth Writers Award, it is the publisher who sends selected publications for consideration. The Man Booker Prize for instance, restricts the number of entries to one or two per imprint for each publisher (Roy <http://www.biblio-india.com/archives>). Amitav Ghosh's refusal letter to the jury of the Commonwealth Writers Award reiterates this relationship between the publishing houses and awards foundations. It ends thus:

> Finally, on a note of apology I would like to reiterate that this situation would not have arisen if I had known that my publishers were intending to submit *The Glass Palace* for the Commonwealth Prize. It is too late unfortunately to amend that oversight; fortunately, it is not too late for you to make other arrangements for the final competition. (www.amitavghosh.com)

This is despite the fact that the Commonwealth Writers Award specifically states that publishers must obtain the author's consent before submitting the book.

This connection may also lead us to consider the financial implications of these awards as the addition of tags such as 'Winner of Commonwealth Writers Award', or 'Nominated for Booker Prize' means a substantial increase in sales to an extent that does not work with national awards. The constitution of the jury of many of these international awards is also telling. The Man Booker jury consists of five members: a publisher, an academic, a journalist or writer, a general reader and the chairperson. These jurists are asked to desist from reading critical material on the selected books and therefore work with the text alone; they operate primarily with the jury's first-hand awareness with the book (www.bookerprize.co.uk). In the case of the Commonwealth Writers Award, the book to be considered should have been in public circulation for only a year. This naturally reduces chances of availability of serious criticism on it, again forcing the jury to rely on their first-hand knowledge of the book. Since these international awards work primarily with one language, the prospect of all the members of the jury reading the text could be very high. Yet, the selection process of the Indian awards discussed above helps both in judging a book and in creating awareness regarding the literary and cultural ethos in which the book is produced and consumed. [2] Not only do these awards draw upon existing criticism and critical paradigms, they also construct their own criticism, especially the Saraswati Samman.

The relationship between publishing houses/ the publishing activity and these awards is not restricted to merely sending the texts for consideration. Among the three awards mentioned above, the K. K. Birla Foundation is the only one that does not have a publication division of its own. Both Sahitya Akademi and Bharatiya Jnanpith have their respective publication sections that not only publish the works that win awards, but also bring out their journals. Sahitya Akademi sponsors translations of all its winning books into all other languages recognised by Schedule VIII besides other significant works. This massive project can play a considerable role in bringing together the various languages of India, but the quality of translations leaves a lot to be desired, feel sensitive readers. There appears to be little consensus regarding the use / glossing of Indian words; parenthetical translation is almost indiscriminately used and very few translations have a useful critical introduction. The decision concerning *which* book is to be translated is made by an advisory committee. Invariably, the book has to be a 'classic' and therefore should already be famous. The target language advisory committee then appoints the translator(s). However, it is only recently that these translations have been made available in bookstores other than the Sahitya Akademi outlets themselves, making them more visible to the book-buyer. Besides these, Sahitya Akademi has other publication projects, among them being the series 'Makers of Indian Literature', which is a series of monographs on writers down the ages in all the Indian languages and the five-volume *Encyclopaedia of Indian Literature* that contains detailed entries on authors of all languages, generic developments in all languages and other issues related to literary studies.

Besides its publications, the Sahitya Akademi periodically organises seminars and 'authors meets'. These seminars serve as a forum for active interaction between the various Indian languages on issues identified as important – the role of criticism and narrative to name a couple. The proceedings of the seminars and the papers presented are published in the form of books and are thereby made available for further discussion and research. Some of the important and interesting examples of such publications are *Narrative: A Seminar* edited by Amiya Dev and *Nativism: Essays in Criticism* edited by Makarand Paranjape.

The Sahitya Akademi does not perceive of or project itself only as an award-giving institution; rather it sees itself as one that is committed to the promotion of literature in the various Indian languages. It is called 'India's National Academy of Letters' and is part of an Institution that also contains the Lalit Kala Akademi (dedicated to the fine arts) and Sangeet Natak Akademi (dedicated to music, dance and drama). Avowedly, publication is the main task of the Sahitya Akademi, but it desists from projecting publications of the winning books as the only one deserving attention. Apart from these, the Sahitya Akademi also has four regional boards—one each for each zone: east, west, north and south—which promote intra-regional and comparative studies. Among their important duties are the preparation of bibliographies of inter-language translation, conducting seminars and publication of dictionaries.

Bharatiya Jnanapith publishes translations primarily into Hindi although by March 2002, they did have plans of publishing not only the winning books, but also the two other books which get short-listed for the award, into English and Hindi. It is notable and praiseworthy that Bharatiya Jnanpith publishes not only the books which have won the awards, but also other books considered to be important landmarks in various languages. Among the latter are books such as T. Janakiraman's Tamil novel *Mohamul* (The Thorn of Passion) and Padma Sachdev's *Bhatko Nahin Dhananjay* (Dhananjay, Do Not Lose Yourself). So far, however, only Hindi translations of books have been made available.

Apart from these, both the Sahitya Akademi and the Bharatiya Jnanpith have their own journals. The Sahitya Akademi brings out *Indian Literature* in English and *Samakaleen Bharatiya Sahitya* (Contemporary Indian Literature) in Hindi. Both these journals carry translations from all the Schedule VIII languages into respectively English and Hindi besides publishing original works in these two languages. *Indian Literature* also declares that 'in keeping with the policy of Sahitya Akademi of extending recognition to living literatures in languages that have yet to get constitutional recognition, the journal is now including materials from minority and tribal languages like Maithili, Bhojpuri, Tulu, Kodava, Khagpuri, etc.' (http://www.sahitya-akademi.org) (After the website was last updated, Maithili has been recognised by Schedule VIII). The journal includes reviews of books and discussions on various issues. Recently, it has been publishing special numbers on different linguistic traditions and generic classes.

The Bharatiya Jnanpith has only recently restarted the publication of its Hindi journal now called *Naya Jnanoday*, literally, the New Rise of Knowledge (it was earlier called *Jnanoday*). The journal contains a main article dealing with important national events. One such event that appears to have many main stories is the project to unify the rivers of India and the evacuation of villages due to the Narmada Dam project. Although a literary journal (it is subtitled: *The Monthly Literary Journal of the Bharatiya Jnanpith*), it does not restrict itself only to reviews, creative writing and criticism. On the other hand, by including essays on such diverse cultural, social and political issues, the journal attempts in a way to align literature and literary interests with such 'aliterary' areas. The journal also contains reviews of books, interviews with authors and creative writing in Hindi. Apart from this, Bharatiya Jnanpith also has *Jnanpith Pathak Puraskar*(Jnanpith Readers' Family), an association that sends periodic newsletters and lists of publications and for which the members get a discount. The tendency of Bharatiya Jnanpith to incline heavily towards Hindi in translations, its journal and newsletter, however, tends to keep it at a distance from the southern states where Hindi is actively and politically opposed.

Both the K. K. Birla Foundation and the Sahitya Akademi also give other awards based on other criteria. The Birla Foundation gives away the Bihari Puraskar 'for the Hindi writers of Rajasthan' (Souvenir 1999–2000) and the Vachaspati Puraskar 'to honour a writer for his work in Sanskrit published during the last ten years' (Souvenir 1999–2000). The guidelines provided by the Foundation for these two awards are interesting with regard to the role of language and positionality. The notion of the location of the author comes into play in the Bihari Puraskar, but 'the definition of a resident of Rajasthan is quite liberal. In addition to the original residents of Rajasthan (they may be residing anywhere) a person who has been living in Rajasthan for more than seven years is also eligible for the Puraskar' (Souvenir 1999–2000). It is not made clear in the souvenirs if the award implies that Hindi writing from different places will be vastly different enough to give a separate award for Rajasthan or if this award is to promote writing from this state. Nevertheless, what *is* clear is that the author's location—here within a *linguistic* and political framework—is brought to figure in this special award. In the case of Vachaspati Puraskar, the Foundation sees it as an attempt at overcoming the pitfalls of the inadequate discussion of Sanskrit works in the Saraswati Samman: 'Literary works in Sanskrit are also eligible for consideration for the Saraswati Samman. But a comparative assessment of these works with those of the other modern Indian languages presents various difficulties' (Souvenir 1999–2000). What is also interesting here is that the only deciding factor is language: 'Thus this Puraskar is somewhat different from the literary awards. It is not confined to a literary work, other works in Sanskrit and even a translated book into Sanskrit are eligible for consideration' (Souvenir 1999–2000). This also implies that the award looks at all of Sanskrit writing as one entity while also acknowledging that the role of Sanskrit as an unspoken and purely intellectual one today places it at a somewhat different level from other *bhashas*.

The Sahitya Akademi, projecting itself as 'India's National Akademi of Letters' as it does, gives a separate award for translation besides awarding fellowships to scholars.

As awards institutions, all the three foundations considered in this chapter are required to publish their annual souvenirs when the award is formally presented. The souvenirs in the case of the Saraswati Samman and the Bharatiya Jnanpith carry in them, the citations given to the winners as well as a detailed description of the processes of selection while also providing a complete list of the jurists at various levels. The Sahitya Akademi souvenir, possibly because of the number of languages it has to deal with at any given time, restricts itself to a very short critical note on the winners. Interestingly, all the souvenirs carry the entries both in English and Hindi. It would be interesting to speculate on the assumptions behind this. Are we to assume that most educated people in India with an interest in literature *should* or *would* know one of these two languages? Or are we to assume that all the awards look upon

Hindi as the representative 'Indian' language while English is the communicative link? For after all, it *is* difficult to gainsay the role of Hindi as the one language spoken by a vast majority of the country's people. If neither of these, what is the alternative? For to publish all entries in all languages would be unthinkable. Possibly, the use of another *bhasha*—the winning *bhasha*—would make the entries definitely readable (although they might of course, end up looking like signboards giving names of the towns in railway stations).

Apart from the souvenirs, all the three awards institutions discussed above have each published a compendium that includes a detailed account of the institution, a critique of the works of the winners so far, along with a printed copy of the citation given to them, followed by a list of the members of the jury at various levels. These perform the necessary function of informing the readers of their awards and most importantly of providing a critical reading of the writers who have won these awards; they add to the available critical material on these writers, throwing more light on the role they played as producers and products of a cultural ethos.

However, we also need to ask the important question regarding the role that these awards play in society at large. Quite expectedly, the institutions themselves are sure that the awards confer some kind of immortality on the writer, although the general reader and critic may think otherwise. For instance, in the same interview quoted earlier, Chandra Chari, editor of *The Book Review,* felt absolutely the contrary. It is true that the amount of publicity given to international awards such as the Man Booker Prize, the Commonwealth Writers Award etc. has not been given to the home-grown awards until recently. In the last three to four years, however, the situation has changed. Perhaps in a bid to understand more of our own literary culture, Indian literary awards are publicised so that they have begun to receive more critical attention in the media. Even competitive examinations at the national level such as the UGC–NET and quiz programmes such as 'Mastermind India' and 'University Challenge' include questions on the winners of these awards, making knowledge about them part of general knowledge more than before. Still, these awards have to go some way in terms of their public relations. In an age when websites have tended to replace libraries as the main source of information, few of the Indian awards have well-documented or periodically updated websites. The Saraswati Samman does not intend to go 'public' as it fears the controversies that might erupt; the Bharatiya Jnanpith had, by 2002, plans of starting a website whereas the existing website of the Sahitya Akademi is far from updated and complete. The lack of interest shown by newspapers and other magazines towards the winners is probably again part of a social ethos where the three 'f's—films, food and fashion—rule the world of journalism and literature is thereby relegated to monthly or fortnightly supplements. The offices of the awards themselves complain that the newspapers and news channels are more interested in covering any controversy concerning the foundations or surrounding the awards rather than the awards themselves. Mr M. H. Venkateswaran, Officer on Special Duty at Sahitya Akademi mentioned in the interview given to me regarding the coverage of the controversy over the award of the Maithili award rather than the award ceremony itself in 2001.[3] Similarly, the controversy over the election of its president in 2003 was covered because of the bitter contest between the writer Mahasweta Devi and the critic Gopichand Narang. The Sahitya Akademi also mentioned in the same interview the demand by Doordarshan to find sponsors for telecasting the series of documentaries on its winners.

It is also to be noted that despite any avowals, the awards are given to the author, even in the case of the Saraswati Samman where a particular text is mentioned. Nowhere is this brought out more forcefully than in the stipulation in the rules governing all the awards that the same author is not to be considered again for the award. This is quite in contrast to many international awards such as the Man Booker Prize where a writer (J. M. Coetzee is an example) can win the award more than once. In fact, although the Booker restricts the entry to two books per publisher, if an author has already won the award, he is automatically considered despite the restriction.

## Publishing Houses

In spite of this apparently bleak picture, the patronage given by publishing houses themselves to translations and English works from India is indeed encouraging. The period from the 1980s also saw a boom in publishing in India that could have been part of the reason for the rise of so many writers and so many experimentations with form, language and technique. The rise of myriad publishing houses which are taking an active interest in bringing out new and different writers as well as translations, is one of the important features of the Indian literary scene since the 1980s. The first of the new publishing houses to make news was Penguin India in 1986, a joint venture between Ananda Bazaar Patrika and Penguin. Ravi Dayal Publishers followed up almost immediately while HarperCollins India, a tie up between Rupa and HarperCollins came five years later. Needless to say, almost all of them are literary-cum-business ventures, chiefly business. These firms, along with Oxford University Press and Macmillan India are some of the largest publishers of English books in India. Almost all of them publish translations into English from various Indian languages; the Macmillan series, Modern Indian Novels in Translation, was for some time one of the leading forums that could provide readers with the best of literature written in the *bhashas*. The publications of Katha, an organisation dedicated to translation projects, are yet another series that bridges the yawning gap between languages. The rise of publishing houses such as Dalit Media Studies, Cre-A (Tamil) and the further blooming of already existing publishing firms such as Alliance in Tamil and Rajkamal in Hindi are proof enough of the growing roles played by this sector. Many of these publishing houses, one should not fail to note, are ideologically committed – Kali for Women and Stree have already been mentioned as publishing houses that are self-avowedly committed to women's studies. They not only publish new women writers, but as noted before, also sponsor translations into English of works by women writers from across the country besides rescuing older writers from near-anonymity. They also publish studies in humanities and social sciences, especially interdisciplinary studies about women. Similarly, Dalit Media Studies is an institution devoted to studies on Dalit issues and also the publishing of Dalit texts. It has a website too.

In the last few years, publishing houses have played a far more critical role in the production, dissemination and reception of books than ever before. They not only publish books, but also market them and see them through the media in their initial stages. Although this is a role they have been playing for years, there is a keener critical awareness in the way they do so today. Publishing firms like Kali for Women, Stree and Dalit Media Studies are themselves institutions that are governed by certain principles and ideologies. The phenomenon of the rise of such publishing institutions is itself a reflection of the growing critical interest in 'marginal' literatures and the tendency to recognise the differences and similarities in the writings by women across languages. It is also an appreciation of the need to create a corpus of texts that could serve as a forum where the voices of women, dalits and other suppressed classes can be heard. At the same time, the publication of these texts would help create a new set of critical responses or lead to the modification of already existing ones, while also willy-nilly creating new critical categories that would necessitate a new aesthetics. In effect, these publishing houses point to the process of formation of such categories at the point of publication itself rather than at the point of reception. A similar case can be made for the Macmillan Modern Indian Novels in Translation series where the publishing firm itself started offering the division of the texts into various categories – one for each language and finally, one for Dalit Literature in Translation. They point to the use of certain categories in which literature is placed at the time of its production. First language and then issues has been almost the favourite mode of classification. It is possible that with the publication of more books by and about Dalits, Dalit literature in translation would itself be further subdivided into Dalit Kannada literature in translation or Dalit Marathi literature in translation. There is already a collection of Dalit poetry in Gujarati. Such categorisations also make the act of publishing itself more a critical rather than a mechanical activity. The possible dialogue between such different categories and the importance of such a dialogue has already been dealt with.

The proliferation of translations of short stories and novels from the southern states in recent times cannot be ignored. Titles like *Routes: Depiction of the West in Southern Short Fiction* (2000) place fiction of all the four southern languages (they do not, however include the Konkani language) in one category. In many ways, this is a reflection of the feeling that these four states and their traditions are somehow different and unique from that of the rest of the nation. Analysis of the kind that Meenakshi Mukherjee has made in *Realism and Reality* wherein novels from all four zones are analysed as one entity may give this the lie. At the same time, the feeling that these four states have been largely ignored by nationalist discourses may also have had a hand in their self-projection. It is felt that anthologies of translations tend to leave the best of the Southern writers out. Amit Chaudhuri's much acclaimed *The Picador Book of Modern Indian Literature*, although admirable in many respects, lumps all south Indian literatures into one mass of 'south'. Almost as a reaction, not only are earlier South Indian writers such as Madhavaiah and

Rajam Iyer resurrected through translations, but the newer crop of writers is also being rendered into English quite soon after their publication. Imayam's *Koveruk Kazhudaigal* (Mules) published by Cre-A in 1994 has been translated into English as *Beasts of Burden* by Lakshmi Holmström in 2001 by East-West Publications. The publication and translation of *Karukku* too did not have a great gap. As already mentioned, many of these translations are also considered for awards—like the Sahitya Akademi translation award—thereby providing greater impetus for the activity itself.

One important aspect that needs to be reiterated here is the publication, recognition and translation of criticism. This is still in a relatively embryonic stage: very few critical essays get translated across the *bhashas*, thereby making it difficult for a fruitful dialogue to emerge on criticism as a discipline across them. Even the Little Magazine culture, as was already noted, restricted itself to translations of essays from British and European critics; they included the acceptance speeches of winners of the Nobel Prize for Literature, but seem to have been relatively uninterested in translating across *bhashas*. Even a critical introduction to a translation is a new essay written by a scholar of the source language for the specific purpose of this publication and need not necessarily involve a dialogue with critical modes and methods in the literary tradition of the source language. Awards institutions *do* consider and even select critical works, but there appears to be little scope for incorporating these critical ideas into a critical dialogue across languages. A look at some of the critical works which have won awards is revealing. Shamsur Rahman Faruqi's *Sher-e-Shorangez* (An Anthology of *Sher*) (Saraswati Samman, 1996) is a reappraisal and rehistoricisation of the Urdu ghazal tradition and a reanthologisation of the poems of Mir Taqi Mir. G. N. Devy's *After Amnesia: Tradition and Change in Literary Criticism in India* (Sahitya Akademi for English, 1993) is another important and path-breaking book that was recognised through an award. Most of the other winners appear to be attempts at reclaiming classical poetics or reappraisal of earlier writers: for example, Thirunavukkarasu's *Thirukkural Needhi Ilakkiyam* (Ethical Literature of Thirukkural) (Sahitya Akademi for Tamil 1974), A. S. Gnanasambandam's *Kamban: Pudiya Paarvai* (Kamban: A New Look) (Sahitya Akademi for Tamil 1985), Vasudevarasan Agrawal's *Padmavat Sanjivani Vyakhya* (An Explanation of *Padmavat*)[4] (Sahitya Akademi for Hindi 1956), Nagendra's *Rasa Siddhanta* (Theory of

Rasa) (Sahitya Akademi for Hindi 1965). However, attempts to theorise and rehistoricise recent trends have also been occasionally recognised in such instances as Vallikannan's *Pudukkavithaiyin Thotramum Valarchiyum* (The Origin and Development of New Poetry) (Sahitya Akademi for Tamil 1978), M. Ramalingam's *Pudiya Urai Nadai* (New Prose) (Sahitya Akademi for Tamil 1981) and Namwar Singh's *Kavita ke Naye Pratiman* (New Characteristics of Poetry) (Sahitya Akademi for Hindi 1981). Still, the lacuna in the awareness of critics and critical thoughts across *bhashas* is often debilitating for researchers. Even recent publications of anthologies of criticisms that claim to contain representative samples of current criticism in India appear to fight shy of publishing translations of pieces by recent critics of various *bhashas*. For example, the anthology edited by G. N. Devy, who was among the first to point to the absence of a native critical tradition in the *bhashas*, inclines heavily to classical concepts of criticism. This is not to deride the value of classical criticism entirely for being located at a particular historical, literary moment, but to point to the necessity of perhaps a series of publications in making critics of one *bhasha* better known to others; and thereby making a generative dialogue between them possible. The complaint that there is no critical tradition in the *bhashas* can perhaps be better understood or the lacuna rectified by such publications which would also make research into critical traditions easier and not so forbidding a task as it appears to be now.

Establishments such as journals, publishing houses and awards foundations play an important role in constructing and critiquing a literary and cultural ethos. These establishments are not only products of such an ethos, but they also critique them and reshape them in their own ways. The ways in which these—especially criticism—interact with creative literature will form the bulk of the rest of this work.

## Notes

1. All of Mr Dinesh Mishra's statements quoted here were made during a personal interview conducted on 15 March 2002 at the Bharatiya Jnanpith office on Lodhi Road, New Delhi. This was his last day as Director-in-Charge of Bharatiya Jnanpith. The interview itself was conducted in Hindi and then translated by the researcher into English.

2. The Nobel Prize selection too follows a similarly stringent method. Unlike the Commonwealth Writers' Award and the Booker Prize, the publishers play no role in nominating the book. Nor does it require a book to be available in English before it can be considered. Here, a selected group of people alone can nominate. These include members of the Swedish Academy (or other academies that are similar in purpose and construction), professors of literature and linguistics at universities and university colleges, nobel laureates or presidents of societies of authors that are representative of the literary production in their countries. However, information about nominations and other proceedings is to be kept confidential for a period of fifty years. (www.nobelprize.org/litt/)
3. Most information about the Sahitya Akademi was procured at a personal meeting with Mr M. H. Venkateswaran, Officer on Special Duty (P) at the Sahitya Akademi Office at Rabindra Bhavan, New Delhi on 16 March 2002.
4. *Vyakhya* is a specific method of criticism identified in classic Sanskrit tradition and followed in many classical languages and in Hindi. It refers to a detailed explanation and interpretation of the text. *Padmavat* is a long poem written by Mallik Mohammad Jayasi and its position as a classic has been the topic of much debate in Hindi literary studies.

## References

Chaudhuri, Amit. Introduction. *The Picador Book of Modern Indian Literature*. Ed. Amit Chaudhuri (London: Picador, 2001).

Dev, Amiya, ed. *Narrative: A Seminar* (New Delhi: Sahitya Akademi, 1994).

Dinesh Mishra. Director in-charge, Bharatiya Jnanpith. Personal Interview, 15 Mar. 2002.

Ghosh, Amitav. 'Ghosh Letter to Administrators of Commonwealth Writers Prize' (18 Mar. 2001). 23 Nov. 2001. *http://www.amitavghosh.com*

Imayam. *Koveruk Kazhudaigal*. Beasts of Burden. Translated from the Tamil by Lakshmi Holmstrom (Chennai: East West Publishers, 2001).

Mukherjee, Meenakshi. *Realism and Reality: the Novel and Society in India* (New Delhi: Oxford UP, 1985).

Paranjape, Makarand, ed. *Nativism: Essays in Criticism* (New Delhi: Sahitya Akademi, 1997).

*Saraswati Samman Souvenir, 1999–2000.*

Vishwanatha, Vanamala et al. *Routes: Representation of the West in Short Fiction from South India* (Chennai: Macmillan India Ltd. and the British Council, 2000).

# PART TWO

## Fiction as Discursive Space

# A BRIEF INTERLUDE

Literature and literary criticism are sites where cultural, social and political issues jostle, blurring disciplinary and discursive boundaries. If aspects related to many such issues are being embedded in criticism, fiction itself is fast becoming a discursive space which engages with these issues in multifarious ways.

The next two chapters will attempt to place fiction in India since the 1980s along the same plane as the discursive literature dealt with so far. Novels may either give a different perspective to the ideas and issues that criticism throws up or they may merely reiterate the concerns. For instance, if *The Memory of Elephants* has been regarded by critics as a 'diasporic' text, the novel itself may question this assumption. If feminist lawyers like Zoya Hasan demand a gendered reading of the issues relating to the Uniform Civil Code, we may read a novel like *Breaking Ties* as fictionalising such a demand. If criticism is becoming increasingly conscious of race, caste and gender as matrices of identity, novels like *The Memory of Elephants* and The Gopallapuram Chronicles use fictional space to inscribe the histories of their communities. If criticism is becoming increasingly inter-disciplinary and is drawing from various seemingly unconnected discourses, novels like *Jhadajhadati* bring in issues related to development projects and the ways in which they are executed into the very fabric of the text.

The very act of 'reading a novel' needs to take on more expansive meanings. One needs to see not merely the novel qua novel, but also take note of its critical reception and the ways in which such a critical reception has impinged upon our understanding of the novel itself. Therefore, it becomes necessary to see how a novel like *Red Earth and Pouring Rain* has been seen as exclusively 'Indian' based on its narrative and how a different kind of narrative in the Gopallapuram Chronicles offers a different kind of community identity. We need to also see, for instance, how the consideration of a novel like *Jhadajhadati* for the Saraswati Samman Award or the presentation of the Sahitya Akademi Award to *Angaliyat* or the Bharatiya Jnanpith to Indira Goswami has affected these texts / writers.

It becomes equally necessary for us to see the implications of reading texts from different linguistic and discursive traditions together. We need, for instance, to study texts such as *Red Earth and Pouring Rain* on the one hand and *The Memory of Elephants* and The Gopallapuram Chronicles on the other together to come to a fuller understanding of how the opposing discourses of nationalism and regionalism operate within the fictional space.

We need perhaps to also move out of viewing translations as necessarily 'inferior' to the 'original.' A more practical approach would be to accept the fact that it is only through translations that a number of texts from across India are made available to us. It is therefore inevitable that our understanding of India's literary culture is heavily mediated by translation – and this need not be such a bad thing, after all!

# 4

# THE NATION, HISTORY AND IDENTITIES: *THE MEMORY OF ELEPHANTS, GOPALLA GRAMAM, GOPALLAPURATHU MAKKAL* AND *RED EARTH AND POURING RAIN*

It is a critical commonplace that the novel form and the construction of nation are closely connected to each other. In the case of India, the statement holds true both for *bhasha* literatures and for Indian writing in English. We will see in this chapter how three novels—two written in English and one set of two novels in Tamil—deal with seemingly opposing discourses of regionalism and nationalism and address questions related to individual and community identity from this perspective. In the process, the long-standing accusation that English writing from India tends to overlook or gloss over ethnic peculiarities and subtleties will also be automatically addressed.

Each of the novels examined in this chapter defines identity in different terms. Boman Desai's *The Memory of Elephants* (1988) is a novel about the Parsi community in India and appears to have been written with the specific purpose of making the Parsi way of life better-known to Parsis as well as to others. Ki. Rajanarayanan's Tamil novels *Gopalla Gramam* (1976)[1] and *Gopallapurathu Makkal* (1993) inscribe the history of a Telugu migrant community within Tamil Nadu – a community whose distinctness may be under threat as much as is that of the Parsis'. Vikram Chandra's *Red Earth and Pouring Rain* (1995) rewrites and reinterprets a vital period of Indian nationalist history – the 1857 War of Independence. The difference between them is obvious – and crucial. The pan-Indian and 'nationalist' strain of Chandra's novel is offset by the stress on ethnicity in the other two novels. It is very often thought that the use of English almost naturally allows for this kind of a pan-Indian and nationalist world view in the texts. To a certain extent, this *is* true. In her essay 'The Anxiety of Indianness: Our Novels in English', critic Meenakshi Mukherjee points out that one of the important criteria for the construction of the nation is the erasure of internal and ethnic differences and that, by virtue of its social position, the English language succeeds in securing this (78). Yet, a novel like *The Memory of Elephants* may belie such a claim, for the use of English over Gujarati, the language of most Parsis in India, seems to stress the ability of English to include an increasing number of registers. It may not seem so strange either that the Tamil used in the Gopallapuram chronicles can take in the dialectal variations and reinscribe the marginalised history of the Telugu migrant community.

All the three novels rewrite and in a sense reinterpret history. But the history they so reinterpret is each different. Furthermore, each of the novels deals with the issue in different narrative moulds. *Red Earth and Pouring Rain*, given its affinities with the postmodernist, postcolonial New Indian Novel in English, would see itself as 'writing back' to the colonial centre and telling the story from an 'Indian' perspective. This shift in perspective, in turn, arises out of the now common understanding that colonialism is a discourse that effectively mutilated the history of the colonised. The dichotomy between the coloniser and the colonised therefore acts as the basic principle of structure that can be seen as the *raison d'être* for the thematic as well as the structural peculiarity of this novel. *The Memory of Elephants*, on the other hand, works not within any obvious dichotomy, but emphasises the need to assert and define the ethnic identity of the minority Parsi community. In contrast to the pan-Indianness of Chandra's novel, this assertion in *The Memory of Elephants* can itself be seen as a political 'answering back' to the nationalist discourse. The Gopallapuram chronicles can be read as a different *avatar* of the Parsi novel, and as thematically and structurally questioning nationalist discourses as well as the methodology of academic and mainstream history writing.

The rise of novels using fictional space to reconstruct and in a sense reinterpret nationalist ideologies and history is a phenomenon of the late twentieth-century Indian novel in English and in the *bhashas*. However, such trends can be traced even in the late 1970s. Part of the reason for this can be seen in the increasing importance given in politics and culture to ethnicity, race and language as markers of identity as well as to the awareness that nationalist and pan-Indian discourses often tend to homogenise, essentialise and thereby marginalise or erase smaller identity matrices. This, of course, does not mean that Grand Narratives such as nationalism or 'national history' are no longer being constructed; *Red Earth and Pouring Rain* can be read as constructing precisely such a narrative. Yet, all these discourses need to be taken in conjunction with each other to get a clearer picture of contemporary India; for under certain circumstances, Grand Narratives do play an important role. The only point for them is to realise their own ideological limitations and not pretend to a universality.

The recent trends in culture studies and criticism, with their vehement opposition of elitist and hegemonic positions, have projected alternate modes of historiography as a highly fertile ground for creative and critical literature to explore. The three novels chosen for study here represent different kinds of such alternate writings. Both Boman Desai's novel and the Gopallapuram chronicles are located within certain communities and ethnic groups and rewrite history from that vantage point. The Gopallapuram chronicles also show the seamier side of nationalist history. In fact, the very form of the novel can be seen as offering an alternative to it. *Red Earth and Pouring Rain*, however, positions itself as a binary opposite of colonial historiography. As the analysis in this chapter hopes to show, each of the novels addresses history in terms of private lives and/or individual communities. The interactions between various levels of identity become important and the ways in which these identities are negotiated take on great significance.

## Counter Memory: *The Memory of Elephants*

Boman Desai's English novel *The Memory of Elephants* is a Parsi novel and it is impossible to miss its ethnic and racial specificity. The Parsi novel is a genre that has been academically and critically christened and analysed in recent years. The period from the 1980s is seen as the period of the second generation of Parsi writers. The first generation included Cornelia Sorabji, Behram Malbari etc. in whose writings no acute awareness of their Parsi heritage or identity can be traced. They are termed 'Parsi' purely because of the ethnic background to which the authors belong and not because of any textual features. The second generation of Parsi writers, however, are deeply aware of and bring to the surface their Parsi-ness with the effect that the novel becomes a space where the Parsis' identity, their ethnic and racial history get inscribed. Among the important Parsi writers today are Dina Mehta, Boman Desai, Rohinton Mistry and Bapsi Sidhwa, all of whose novels, in some way or another, are deeply influenced by the Parsi way of life. The title 'Parsi Novel', therefore, often becomes a label that describes the ethnic and racial identity of the text as well as that of the author.

Critically, this ethnic label has been used to see how the attitudes and world view of Zoroastrianism have been translated into the novel form – how, for instance, do the Parsi writers view their position as expatriates in India from pre-colonial times, how do they relate to notions of religious strife and how do they relate themselves to the larger body of 'India' – these have been some of the important critical coordinates in the analysis of novels written by Parsis.

Boman Desai's *The Memory of Elephants*, in this regard, is eminently a Parsi novel for it self-consciously sets out to define and problematise Parsi identity. At the same time, its importance lies also in its position as a chronicle—an ethnic and race saga—and as a novel that is part of, yet questions, the new postcolonial Indian novel in English.

Many critics of the Parsi novel such as Nilufer Bharucha and Novy Kapadia speculate on the sudden rise of the new Parsi writer in the 1980s. Among the possibilities offered is the growing awareness of their ethnicity among the Parsis themselves. This, in turn, is perhaps due to the fact that the Parsi community is fast diminishing in number, thereby giving rise to the need for self-assertion and self-preservation. The fear of losing their religious and racial identity in the face of increasing migration and assimilation into Western cultures has also been identified as a factor that could have caused the sudden interest and even anxiety among the Parsis about their ethnic identity.

Faced with these issues, the need to stress and rediscover the meaning of Parsiness, however problematic, becomes a task of sheer survival. This again is a common enough trope in recent fiction, especially English fiction from India. Protagonists seem to take recourse to narration to escape from death and often, this narration often takes the form of reinterpreted history. Saleem Sinai of *Midnight's Children*'s fame and Sanjay in *Red Earth and Pouring Rain* are two striking examples. Homi's case in *The Memory of Elephants* is much the same, although he does not so much narrate his history as it is narrated to him. In this context, the reclamation and narration of ethnic and racial history—as is done in *The Memory of Elephants* and in *Red Earth and Pouring Rain*—takes on multiple meanings. To have a history and to have it told / narrated is to ensure that one's communal identity is safeguarded. To have it written down is to ensure its longevity. History, which is collective memory, is essential for the communal identity of a people. It ensures feelings of solidarity within the community besides maintaining its difference from others. In *The Memory of Elephants* Homi's essential problem of coming to terms with and accepting his present condition necessitates his knowledge and awareness of his historical past, and in this quest, it is his paternal grandmother who helps him.

This personal and almost spiritual reclamation of history is not, however, without its political counterpart. To tell *one's own* history is to tell it best. While this may seem like a privileging of the 'insider' position, we need to remember that in an unequal power relationship, the powerful do have the means to misrepresent the history of the less powerful. This will act as an important factor in a novel like *Red Earth and Pouring Rain*. On the other hand, even when power relations are not all that unequal or at least not overtly unequal, there still remains the danger of a minority history being effaced and thereby an entire ethnic identity getting lost. It is this that operates in *The Memory of Elephants*. It is interesting and important that in the ethnic sagas selected here—and indeed in ethnic sagas in general—the author belongs to the community whose history or way of life is being described and, in this sense, s/he becomes almost a raconteur like the oral historians. To take the analogy a little further, the novel form itself becomes not merely a space for telling stories, but a site where an entire community can be reconstructed and where its identity can be permanently inscribed. This same function was performed earlier by minstrels and *bhagavatars* who acted both as historians and storytellers. By taking on this function today, the ethnographic novelist renders his narrative a repertoire of the collective memory of his community. Hence, his membership within his community takes on special significance.

Novy Kapadia sees the rise and growth of the Parsi novel as questioning the homogenising tendencies of postcolonial criticism and the postcolonial Indian novel in English. She points out the by now more or less clichéd idea that postcolonial criticism privileges only the coloniser–colonised dichotomy, whereas very few, if any, of the second-generation Parsi writers choose to deal with it in such simplistic terms. The emphasis here is, by and large, on the ethnic identity of the protagonists and its implications. The staples of postcolonial criticism such as imposition of the culture and language of the coloniser over the colonised and the identity crisis resulting from such a political hegemony cannot be simplistically read into Parsi novels. In fact, *The Memory of Elephants* does address some of these issues, but appears to do so in ways that actually foreground its *difference* from postcolonial fiction and criticism.

Why an assertion of Parsi identity at all? *The Memory of Elephants* is very definitely and centrally a Parsi novel. Although many critics, including Novy Kapadia and Nilufer Bharucha, have focused on the allegorical content of the novel, this is not a text where the Parsi community can be taken as standing for 'any displaced community'. In fact, it is quite possible to read the novel as questioning the assumption that the Parsi family this novel depicts even feels 'displaced' in way we have come to view or describe displacement. The Parsi identity of the novel is made evident right at the beginning – in the very first paragraph where the protagonist Homi's grandmother admonishes him, 'You are a bawaji, Hormusji . . . but you yourself do not know what it means to be a bawaji. You should be ashamed' (*Memory*, 1). The word 'bawaji' is the common term for a Parsi and the admonition is meant not only for Homi, but also for all young Parsis who, due to a variety of reasons, are losing touch with their culture and heritage. The 'visions' in Homi's memoscan which follow are, in fact, a means of restoring his cultural moorings.

The need to know and understand one's heritage is absolutely essential and becomes an act of sheer survival as the Parsi community is one of the fast diminishing ones in the world – almost an endangered community. It is this that makes any *writing* of Parsi history and cosmogony a means of ensuring that future generations would know of their religion and heritage and that it would not pass into obscurity. This reclamation of history is vastly different from many postcolonial reclamations that are essentially exercises in reversing the hierarchy implicit in the binaries of powerful and powerless, coloniser and colonised, the one with the control of systems of knowledge and the one without it. Although these issues *are* present in *The Memory of Elephants* too, the novel form as a means of preserving the cultural heritage of the Parsis is a factor that calls for study.

The author has very deftly linked up the racial heritage, the memoscan and Homi's condition so that the novel as a whole is able to act partly as a postmodern novel and partly as traditional chronicle fiction. Homi's aborted affair with Candace and his subsequent failed attempt to continually relive his moment of sexual union with her through his memoscan become the fictional means by which Homi is allowed to enter into the realm of the collective racial past with the help of his Bapaiji. The memoscan therefore, acts as the science fiction avatar of the magic realist mode and makes credible Homi's forays into Parsi history, their life in Persia, their migration thence, their arrival at Sanjan and their subsequent rise to affluence.

What Homi first sees through his memoscan are accurate accounts of the history of the Parsi community in India, accounts that should be part of the memory of all Parsis. The arrival of Muslims in Persia, the confrontations between the two religions, the fleeing of the Parsis and their reception in India – these appear from all accounts to be well-known facts. Historical accounts and critical appraisals on the community draw these events mostly from *Kissa-e-Sanjan*, a Persian text of the tenth century.

If we look at the novel as chronicle fiction, the first section—titled 'Prelude'—acts as the origin myth of the community. The role and importance of origin myths for communities and therefore for novels dealing with histories of communities *as chronicle fiction does* cannot be understated, for they provide the basis for the collective identity of the group. The 'Prelude' offers the historical, cultural and political reasons for the Parsis' presence in India. Yet, as origin myth, 'Prelude' shows differences from its kind.

Most origin myths incorporate history and myth in a seamless manner; they offer a view of history without the precision of dates and places and with an almost improbable amount of divine intervention in human affairs. The Old Testament, the Hindu *puranas* etc. are classic examples of this. These stories follow what has academically been termed the religio-mythical model of history as against the Enlightenment model (with its emphasis on rationality and empirically verifiable facts), which had become almost universal since European colonial intervention. Origin myths are the stuff of folklore and anthropology; they are 'studied' by disciplines other than history, for history looks askance at, say, Abraham of the Old Testament living on for more than a hundred years and the Red Sea parting, or *Purusha*, the Primeval Being of *Purusha Sukta* 'giving birth' to humankind from parts of his body. Moreover, most origin myths contain elements of self-aggrandisement. The community spoken about is made to feel that it is the Chosen One in many ways. Hence, the Old Testament for example, takes pains to prove that God greatly favoured the Israelites.

Peculiarly, the 'Prelude' has none of the above features. It contains precise dates and names of kings; it carries accurate descriptions of the cities and villages in which the Zoroastrians lived, and perhaps most importantly, does not contain any references to the sanctity of 'homeland'. This last feature is responsible for many of the differences between the postcolonial reclamation of history and the kind of reclamation in *The Memory of Elephants*. Homi needs to understand his past in order to understand and accept his present, not necessarily to feel any kind of superiority over other cultures. He needs his history for a personal and almost spiritual reason as perhaps do many Parsis who have moved away from Zoroastrianism due to a variety of reasons. At the same time, the use of history in this way can be seen as a tacit indictment of academic, political as well as literary use of history as a means of 'giving it back' to the enemy or as an excuse for furthering enmity in the present day by reversing earlier hierarchies.

In fact, throughout the novel, we find characters evincing a spirit of non-violence and acceptance of the other rather than a blind denial of all other points of view. The first we hear of this vindication of what we may call *ahimsa* is from Bapaiji's own lips as she 'tells' Homi about the tolerance of the Zoroastrian religion. The picture that emerges is nothing short of a benevolent, multicultural Persia:

> The Persians were known for their humanity; vanquished kings were dealt with honourably, enemy towns left unmolested, their ranks welcomed into the services of Persia, and land given them to administrate; Zoroastrianism was the religion of the royal house of Persia, but Judaism, Christianity and even paganism were tolerated with equanimity. (*Memory*, 6)

One also needs to remember that the facts presented in 'Prelude' are historically validated and are not an attempt by the author to re-interpret Zoroastrian exodus from Muslim Persia; in other words, this is *writing* of history in a novel, not necessarily a re-writing. The attitude of tolerance is reiterated much more strongly a little later in the novel by Bahman's mother. Her response to Bahman's brutal killing of the Muslim who had killed his father is a classic rejection of the use of history—personal or political—as an excuse to perpetuate age-old enmities:

> Is it right to kill the man who kills your father? to kill the father of the man who kills your father? Does that give him the right to kill you? to kill your sons? First it is sweet, yes, revenge; but then it begins to justify all forms of corruption – mutilation, murder, assassination; it becomes your master and it becomes your own enemy. There is more honour in death than in such a life. (*Memory*, 16)

The constant references to Zoroastrian prayers also serve to reinforce this idea. One that is oft repeated is the common prayer of 'Ashem Vastu':

| | |
|---|---|
| *Ashem Vohu* | Blessed Is Virtue |
| *Vahistem Asti* | The Highest Good |
| *Ushat Asti* | The Greatest Happiness |
| *Ushta Ahmai* | He Who Loves Virtue |
| *Hyat Ashai* | For Its Own Sake |
| *Vahishta Ashem* | Will Find Virtue Is Bliss Untold (*Memory*, 21) |

A closer look at the prayer will reveal that it exalts the value of virtue and individual behaviour without openly referring to a god. The repetition of this prayer appears to reinforce the idea of a religious view not based on imperialist tendencies of expansion.

Another prayer, mentioned by Homi to the 'single-religioned' Julie is very similar: 'In one of the Zoroastrian prayers,' he tells her, 'there is a phrase: Manasni, Gavasni, Kunasni. Roughly translated, it means good thoughts, good words, good deeds' (*Memory*, 107). Such an open religious attitude of the Zoroastrians accounts for much of the psychological drama of the novel – Homi's refusal to give up one religion for another, Bapaiji being selected to settle a Hindu–Muslim dispute etc.

Related closely to these factors is the discourse of courage and bravery often used today to 'answer back' to a historical error. Githa Hariharan's *In Times of Siege* (2003) tells the story of a history professor whose sedate life is turned upside down by the *'Itihas*

*Suraksha Parishad*' (History Protection Committee) that chooses to take objection to his depiction of the life of Saint Basava. Most of the arguments link 'Hindu courage' to answering back to older historians. The novel beautifully deploys recent discourses that link up religious nationalism to questions of 'bravery'. Set against this discourse, the attitude of the Parsis to other religions and to their own history may seem suspiciously like cowardliness. Yet, the novel stresses quite strongly upon the necessity of such a tolerance and open-mindedness. One of the best illustrations of this is given by J. P. Cama when he talks about his visit to Jerusalem in what is the only long speech given him:

> . . . I was impressed by the sight of some nails, reputedly the nails with which Christ had been crucified, embedded in a stone some twelve inches thick. The nails did not make a Christian of me, but deepened my respect for Christianity and, as a consequence, made me a better Zoroastrian . . . . watching the nails, I realised that variations are also a form of exploration and development; Christianity became relevant to me as a variation of Zoroastrianism; each of them was profound by itself, but their conjunction provided a breadth which neither possessed alone; the many religions of the world reveal the world in all its variety like the variations of a theme. (*Memory*, 144)

This broadmindedness can also be seen in the way the Parsis relate to their history. 'Prelude' is the story of the violent uprooting of a people from their native land, yet, there is no malice towards those who forced this exodus nor is there any vengeful attempt to recover their lost land. This, the text seems to imply, is made possible because of a religious world view that does not lay parental claim to land or to truth, but glorifies values such as virtue and good deeds. In a world torn apart by attempts to regain the lost land, where history is used as an excuse for violent 'corrections' of past wrongs and where literature and criticism are also a part of such discourses, *The Memory of Elephants* comes as a refreshing relief where the values of human life and dignity are cherished.

The image of the elephant in the title is notable in this regard. The elephant is traditionally conceived of as possessing a very long memory, but a vindictive one. Most of us would recall the story about the elephant that remembered the tailor sticking a needle up its trunk and taking revenge years later. By calling the novel *The Memory of Elephants*, Desai has made an ironic use of this image, for there is little vindictiveness in the recounting of the racial history of the Parsis. At the same time, by invoking the very idea of memory in a historical novel, Desai has also conjured up the very Indian idea that memory constitutes history, thereby underlining the Indianness of the Parsi community.

The vast exodus of the Parsis to India would make them eternal expatriates like the Biblical Cain. In fact, critics like Nilufer Bharucha have seen the Parsis as just this – expatriates in precolonial times as well as now. Yet, one needs to read the text a little more carefully before applying the nomenclature of expatriates to the Parsis of India.

One of the important features of the diaspora is the sense of nostalgia and fond memory of the motherland and of the past. This is surprisingly absent in this text. To read the text—and thereby the Parsi condition—as 'postcolonial' is again problematic. The relationship between the Parsis and India has been one of trust and benevolence. In fact, the five conditions that Jadhav Rana, the King of Sanjan (now Gujarat) puts down (again well-documented facts) are still followed by the community to a large extent. For instance, the king categorically states that they should not interfere in the religion(s) of India. Even today, Indian Parsis do not accept any kind of conversion to their religion. In adherence to the dictates of Jadhav Rana, the wedding processions of the Parsis continue to take place at nightfall. In *The Memory of Elephants* Bapaiji has taken Gujarati to heart as her mother tongue so much that she refuses to speak to her grandchildren in any other language. In fact, Bapaiji has been justifiably seen by critics like Anjana Basu as representing the continued respect for the Parsis' covenant with Jadhav Rana: 'She is symbolic of those first Parsis who made a pact with Jadav Rana of Gujarat to embrace the Gujarati language, dress and customs,' says Basu (<http://www.gowanusbooks.com>). Moreover, although 'Prelude' takes pains to describe the architecture, pottery, dress and way of life of the Zoroastrians in Persia, there is no mention made of the language spoken. Throughout the novel, Persia is evoked as a memory, without nostalgia or vengeance. In *Representations of the Intellectual* (1994), Edward Said has this to say of diasporas and expatriates, in other words, exiles: 'The exile, therefore, exists in a median state, neither completely at home in the new setting nor fully disencumbered of the old, beset with half involvements and half detachments, nostalgic and sentimental on one level, an adept mimic or a secret outcaste on another' (36). In the light of this statement, which seems to aptly describe fictional and critical representations of the exile, the community in *The Memory of Elephants* does not figure even remotely as exile or diaspora. Yet, a critic like Nilufer Bharucha sees the Parsis in India as occupying different kinds of diasporic positions. On the one hand, as expatriates from Persia they are, she says, 'an Indian diaspora' ('Reflections in Broken Mirrors: Diverse Diasporas in Recent Parsi Fiction', 32); as privileged elite in colonial India, she sees them as being 'in psychological diaspora' and as migrants to England and North America, as 'Western diaspora' ('Reflections in Broken Mirrors: Diverse Diasporas in Recent Parsi Fiction', 32). She then goes on to point to the sense of loss evident in *garbas* (or folk dances) and the *Kissah-e-Sanjan*. Yet, this seems to be belied by *The Memory of Elephants*. Two aspects can be taken up for clarification. One is the case of language and the other the famous statement made by Homi in the novel: 'Home? Where? Aquihana or Bombay?' (*Memory,* 22).

The case of language has already been touched upon; Bapaiji's insistence on talking to her grandchildren only in Gujarati is part of the mental make-up of the kind of Parsi who has made India fully her home and has internalised the covenant between her Dastur (Parsi priest) and Jadhav Rana. However, Homi and Rusi know little or no Gujarati and this creates comical interventions in the novel until Homi makes Bapaiji realise that 'two weeks a year is not enough to learn a language' (*Memory,* 28; two weeks was how long Homi spent with his grandmother every year). Homi's distance from his language—Gujarati, not Persian—is an instance of diasporic or postcolonial or even modern Indian consciousness; for many Indians today are linguistic orphans, cut off from their mother tongue. Yet, *The Memory of Elephants* being a Parsi novel, forces us to see this within the coordinates of Parsi history and identity.

This issue has to do with the way in which we relate to our mother-tongue. Postcolonial criticism has talked much about the cultural cringe which colonialism creates in the colonised subject. G. N. Devy in *After Amnesia* called it cultural amnesia and defined it as a state where one feels a sense of shame regarding one's own culture and slowly erases its memories. Lack of knowledge or familiarity with one's mother tongue is often seen as the typical expressions of this. The condition of Homi and Rusi, therefore, is not very different from that of many other Indians. Yet, as *The Memory of Elephants* is concerned specifically with the Parsi community, this feature becomes a definite characteristic of that ethnic community and its distance from its culture. Lack of knowledge of Gujarati (the language that was partly forced upon them by Jadhav Rana) and not Persian (their 'original' language) is at the centre of the issue of this cultural amnesia.

In the place of Gujarati, English is used as the preferred language and this takes us again into the realm of postcolonialism. English was a language 'imposed' by the British even as Gujarati was 'partly imposed' by Jadhav Rana. That the Parsis take easily to both these imposed languages may be read in different ways. They may be seen as easily 'giving in' to hegemony while at the same time, the fact that they are able to retain their ethnic identity despite all the political changes may open our eyes to a different mode of resistance. We may refer here to Ziauddin Sardar's introduction to Ashis Nandy's *Return from Exile* which mentions how consent to power often acts as a means of subtle resistance, allowing the consenting community to retain its distinctiveness and at times even change the culture that they have been forced to accept (Sardar, *Introduction*, 21).

Nilufer Bharucha mentions that writings of early Parsis such as Behram Malbari and Cornelia Sorabji 'detail the ambivalent feelings Parsis have towards the land of their adoption, i.e. India and the attraction felt towards England' (Bharucha, 'Reflections in Broken Mirrors', 32). Other critics and historians have pointed out that the Parsis were a community which was among the first to welcome English education and had more or less an ambivalent attitude towards the British notwithstanding Parsi nationalist leaders such as Dadabhai Naoroji. In *The Memory of Elephants*, the true-to-Gujarati Bapaiji and the anglicised granny can be seen as two opposite kinds of middle-class people who emerged during the British rule. The fiercely nationalist Indian and the babu smitten by the West were the two prototypical Indians who appeared during the heyday of the nationalist movement in India. However, the focus on Parsiness in this novel leads us to see them as specifically representing two kinds of *Parsis*. What can otherwise be seen as a national phenomenon becomes, in a culture-specific text, an instance of asserting cultural and ethnic identity. Homi's distance from Gujarati, therefore, is part of his maternal heritage, the same heritage that makes him want to go to Aquihana for his education. However, this cannot be branded as anglophilia. For Homi, English is perhaps the only choice open as he gets precious little time to learn Gujarati. It is his Granny's anglophilia—literally her love for all things British or American—that causes this condition to become almost 'natural' in Homi and Rusi. We also need to remember that the distance is from Gujarati, a language half-adopted and half-imposed. If we were to read this aspect as pointing to the distantiation of Parsis from their culture, then, we would also need to stress that Gujarati, the language of the land of their adoption, has indeed become an integral part of their own culture. This would further lead us to question readings of the text that see it as exclusively diasporic, for the implication in the novel is that the Parsis have well integrated into the land that was once alien. They definitely do not face the problem of not being able to call any place their own which is the fate of exiles. This distance from Gujarati, therefore, makes Homi and his brother more Indian than merely Parsi – one of the instances where racial, ethnic identity and the national identity meet.

Another aspect that has often been used to show Homi's rootlessness—and thereby the exiled condition of the Parsis—is Homi's question quoted above: 'Home? Where? Aquihana or Bombay?' (*The Memory of Elephants,* 22). This has been read by critics such as Anjana Basu as depicting 'the concerns of modern Parsis – the identity crisis of a race which doesn't know where it really belongs' (<http://www.gowanusbooks.com>). Homi's question, however, opens itself out to more than such an interpretation. On the one hand, even if it does depict the kind of homelessness that Anjana Basu affirms, it is a homelessness that is part of the modern world with its mass migrations; not the homelessness of the Parsis in particular. For what are juxtaposed are Bombay and Aquihana, not Persia and Bombay. This is the crisis also of Abhay in *Red Earth and Pouring Rain* as we shall see later on, and of many other Indians who have chosen to go abroad for further studies or career prospects. Read in this way, the sentence can be seen as yet another instance where the Parsi identity and the 'Indian' one become inseparable. This kind of 'mis-belonging' is borne out by the fact that Homi feels uncomfortable with the American way of life that he is exposed to, as represented by the two women he meets – the religious fundamentalism of Julie Clooney and the sexual licentiousness of Candace. Interestingly, although Parsis are considered to be one of the most Westernised communities in India, both the women repel parts of Homi perhaps because of his religion and 'Indian' upbringing. Although not a devout Zoroastrian (after all, he does not even know what it is to be a bawaji), he is still loath to convert to Christianity. His natural Zoroastrian broadmindedness allows him to accept both religions, but not give up one for the other. In the second case, the elitism and Westernisation of the Parsis do not extend to include the licentiousness of Candace which almost devastates Homi. Such an attitude to sexual life that asserts itself here is very typical of the standard middle-class 'Indian' (irrespective of religion). Yet again we find that despite the stress on ethnicity, the larger picture of 'Indian'ness and the Indian identity of the Parsi Everyman comes to the surface.

The sentence also opens itself out to another, quite different reading. Given the Parsi ability to adapt themselves to new circumstances, Homi's question can well be taken to mean that he considers both Bombay and Aquihana his homes. For although he does not feel comfortable with either Julie or Candace, there is little in the text itself to suggest that Homi feels 'unrooted' both in America and India because of his Parsi heritage. Perhaps Boman Desai's own domicile in America and the tempting story of the Parsi exodus has made criticisms on the novel see it as an expression of loss and homelessness. But taken by itself, the novel seems to explore how different levels of identity—ethnicity, race, nation, and to a certain extent gender too—interact with each other, in particular historical and political conditions.

The interaction between racial and national identity appears as the subtext of many chronicle novels. By definition, the chronicle novel takes up a particular geographical area, community or race and delineates its history over a period of time. The chronicle mode can operate either as a method or as a genre. For instance, all the novels discussed in this section use it as a genre: they are all concerned with history and its various sub-textual levels such as identity, the formation of a community and the concept of the nation. A novel like *Jhadajhadati*, on the other hand, uses the chronicle as a mode—with its 'vastness', its epic scope etc.—but employs it to address different kinds of issues altogether. In *The Memory of Elephants*, the intersections between ethnic identity and national identity make for very interesting insights. This naturally leads us on to the intractable question of what constitutes a nation and a people.

Benedict Anderson's by-now famous assertion that a nation is an 'imagined community of people' and Ernest Renan's earlier definition of the nation as an elusive 'spiritual principle' ('What is a Nation', 18) seem to place the nation and the various races and ethnicities that it comprises, in a peculiar relationship. Ernest Renan had categorically and systematically discarded the many arguments set forth to demonstrate the sanctity of the notion of a nation. Anthropological discoveries may provide races with different ancestors, different nations may speak the same language while the same nation may speak different languages; finally geographical boundaries are highly fluid and hence, none of them can be definitive. In a nation like India, made up of so many ethnicities, the assumption in the present times is that ethnic / racial identities and national identities are at odds with each other. In effect, the two sometimes act as binaries. While 'nation' was the glorified term in nationalist discourses, 'regionalist' discourses (like that of the Dravidian movement) may have tried to reverse the hierarchy. But these discourses themselves have often been seen in negative terms in subsequent reappraisals. What chronicle novels, especially *The Memory of Elephants*, offer us, is the possibility of the simultaneous existence of both these identities. A simple way of looking at this is to see how, when and where the novel brings out the 'Indian-ness' of the Parsis. In other words, if we say, as we do, that the Seervai family is representative of the Parsi community, does the Parsi community at any point become representative of the Indian nation? If so, how and if not, why not?

There are certainly a few overt instances where national and ethnic identities intersect, and in most cases, this occurs when the Parsi characters come in contact with non-Indians. For instance, Rusi's experience in America marks him off definitely as an Indian immigrant, and more generally as a South Asian. His being called a 'scab' by Jan 'because [he] take[s] jobs from people who need them' (*Memory*, 262) is a typical response faced by many Asian and Third World immigrants to the United States. The other instance is the way in which Candace constructs Homi – 'an exotic, a scientist, a cripple, someone – something – *different*, nothing more' (32; italics mine) as Bapaiji tells him. This is a prototypical construction of the Orient – only here, the gender roles are interestingly reversed, leading us to a peculiar position of the so-long oppressed female gaze colluding with the oppressing colonial one. The other such experience occurs to J. P. Cama when he is asked by a British official to vacate his seat at an aeroplane display:

> Within the select enclosure of chairs an altercation was taking place; a tall, gangly uniformed English official was trying to remove a chair 'for one of the english ladies who just arrived' he explained, while a young Parsi in dagla, white pants and Paghri was trying to restrain him. 'I'm sorry,' the Parsi said, 'but this chair is reserved. My friend will be back in a moment.' The Parsi was smaller, but with the thick density, the quick strength, of a dwarf in his body. He spoke politely,

> but his face was stern. 'In fact, here he is now,' he said without turning away, as his friend came up beside him.
>
> . . . . .
> The Englishman looked nervously from the Parsi to his friend and back. 'Who are you to speak to me like this?'
> 'We know our rights,' said the Parsi with the same politeness, the same unwavering gaze. . . . .
> 'I could have you confined for the night.'
> 'That is a risk I will have to take.' (*Memory*, 118–19)

Here too, J. P. Cama is seen merely as an Indian, with no emphasis whatsoever on his ethnic, racial identity. In all these instances, it is overtly *either* the nation *or* the race that is asserted as the matrix of identity. However, when Homi is asked to define and explain his religion to his friends in Aquihana, his national and ethnic identities work together. He is seen as an Indian, but this Indianness does not relegate the Parsi in Homi to the background; rather, his Parsiness reinforces his Indianness. The discussions on Zoroastrianism and how an average American who had heard of the prophet Zoroaster saw Parsis ('a black-hatted, black-caped, black-garbed figure' (289–90)) help define Homi as an Indian as well.

This kind of simultaneity runs throughout the novel. The ethnic identity is rarely completely divorced from the national one. Although Bapaiji's overt reason for telling the 'tale' is to make Homi aware of what it means to be a Bawaji, it is evident through the novel that as far as Bapaiji is concerned, being a Bawaji also necessitates being an Indian, if only to respect the covenant made between the Dastur and Jadhav Rana.

The question that arises at this point is, what is it that makes *The Memory of Elephants* a Parsi chronicle? At a very basic level, the Parsiness of the novel is asserted by extra-textual factors such as the ethnic identity of the author. Boman Desai is a Parsi writing about the history of his community. This provides an 'insider' perspective which is held in high regard today. Moreover, as was already mentioned, the novel has also to be read against the backdrop of the many debates taking place over the diminishing numbers of the Parsi community, in which case, the novel becomes a means of safeguarding the history—at least of the *written* history—of the Parsis. This last point might make us want to rethink postcolonial laments about the loss of oral histories. While orality is hailed in postcolonial criticism as a 'true,' 'native' form of recording history, novels like *The Memory of Elephants* stress that orality and the written form have to coexist as modes of historiography.

Within the novel, substantial space is taken up in explaining the history of the Parsis in India and in describing their customs and traditions, like the *Navjote*, the marriages, death rites, as well as their cosmogony. To reiterate a point made earlier, these are not only for the benefit of Homi, but for all the Parsis who find themselves removed from their ethnic origins.

What Desai has in effect achieved then, is to recast the history of one community by collating it with that of a nation and narrating it in a form very different from that of academic history. And here we introduce yet another important feature of the chronicle novel, one that will often be invoked in the discussions that follow. The chronicle novel tells or re-tells a history – often a history that has been erased or misrepresented. It seeks to preserve this history, this version of history to be more precise. By doing it in the form of a novel, it allows for perspectives that may, in fact, work from between the binaries or assumptions of academic histories. For instance, the histories of minority communities (in the case of, say, tribals) are often relegated to the disciplines of anthropological or ethnographic studies. Chronicle novels construct these histories in a different form. It is here that the form of the novel plays an important part and one can best take recourse to Edward Said for an apt description. In the essay 'Arabic Prose and Fiction after 1948,' in *Reflections on Exile and Other Literary and Cultural Essays* (2001), he points out that the main difference between history *of* the novel and history *in* the novel 'is the history of the type of narrative incorporated within the narrative' (43). Referring to Marx's *The Class Struggles in France* and Flaubert's *L'education Sentimentale*, he makes this difference clear:

> Marx's (narrative) belongs eccentrically to a tradition of analysis and polemic taken in part from journalism; Flaubert's, no less eccentric in its own way, no less polemic, stands squarely within an institutional tradition, the novel's, whose language, pressures, and audience Flaubert assumes . . . as Marx cannot assume for his work. (*Reflections*, 43)

It is then, the *form* of the novel that is changed and metamorphosed in order that the purposes of history, anthropology and ethnography are incorporated; it is as a *novel* that the text is published, marketed and critiqued. This makes it necessary for critics to redefine and re-mark the boundaries of the novel and rethink about the relationship between the novel form and national form. For a novel like *The Memory of Elephants* which uses a minority ethnic position—one that is uncontroversial—also redefines the notion of a simple, unified India in which regional, ethnic or racial identities are often negated in order that a national one be reinforced, or re-enforced. This jostling at the boundaries of the novel form also leads, therefore, to a reshaping of the form of the nation which is compelled to accept a variety of voices which have just begun to speak.

*The Memory of Elephants* in which disciplinary boundaries between narratives are blurred exemplifies one of the characteristic features of the post-1980s Indian novel, an aspect not much taken note of by criticism. This post-modernist fluidity of the novel form reflects a similar fluidity existing in our everyday lives where revered and not-so-revered boundaries are becoming more and more blurred by the day and the very form of the nation and national discourse is being continually redefined and reshaped. The use of actual historical and ethnographic data within the space of the novel thereby transforms it into something that is immediately related and relevant to the world outside and the community of the novel in particular. This close relationship between the text and the world and the ways in which the postmodern novel has worked it out can be taken as one of the important features of the novels coming out from India in the late twentieth century. As we shall see, language is no constraint and in the novels dealt with here, it is all the more not so.

## Everyday Historiography: the Gopallapuram Chronicles

If *The Memory of Elephants* is a novel where the binaries of nation and ethnicity are seen from an in-between position (the minority status of the Parsis allowing this), the Gopallapuram chronicles describe the long and complicated processes by which communities and eventually a nation are formed. In so doing, they inscribe—not necessarily re-inscribe—the history of a small ethnic community.

The Telugu migrant community of Kommavars forms one of the many small, diasporic communities within the Tamil country and the Gopallapuram chronicles narrate the political, historical and cultural happenings that determine the construction of such communities. This would force us to reconsider the notion of diaspora and expatriatism. Both *The Memory of Elephants* and the Gopallapuram chronicles deal with historical events that occurred quite many years ago and hence assert the antiquity and the globality of the diaspora.

Interestingly, both the Parsis and the Kommavars are forced out of their native land due to Muslim 'oppression' (any political reason for choosing these novels is here disclaimed) although the particulars and the narration vary greatly. The Parsis flee Persia mostly in order to escape forceful conversion and to safeguard their religion. The story of the Kommavars is different and raises numerous interesting questions regarding identity. This is not to ignore the fear of conversion which is one of the reasons for the fleeing of the community. These aspects have to be taken into consideration along with the mode / form in which this history is narrated.

The 'Prelude' in *The Memory of Elephants* which is a variant of origin myth narrates the advent of the Parsis thereby relating the present to the past. Such a function is performed in the Gopallapuram chronicles by the story narrated by Mangathayaru, another grandmother. But unlike Bapaiji's story, this is narrated in a very different mode – precisely the religio-mythical model of history that 'Prelude' seems to so easily move out of.

Mangathayaru's story is full of supernatural interventions and miraculous happenings—what classical European poetics calls *deus ex machina*—giving the natural impression that the Kommavars' migration from Andhra to Tamil Nadu was not only divinely ordained but also blessed. This dramatic story, however, is so choreographed in the novel that it can neither be fully 'believed' nor dismissed as fable. Mangathayaru, unlike Bapaiji, is not narrating from collective memory. What she narrates later *becomes* collective memory. The 'validity' of the people's history she narrates primarily comes from the fact that she was a participant in the events that she describes. Yet, when she recalls the events, she is almost senile and cannot even remember the days of the week. Akkayya, for example, finds it impossible to believe her story: 'although all the men, women and children of the family used to listen to Mangathayaru's story with a degree of respect, Akkayya used to think that it was highly exaggerated' (73). Herein, we can find the germs of a different model of historiography emerging – one that questions the then existing notions of divine intervention and miraculous happenings. Although Akkayya does not fully disbelieve her story (he only finds it exaggerated), his scepticism does point to the existence of such a different perception of history much before the introduction of British education.

By placing this scepticism in a period prior to the establishment of the East India Company and before the English way of thinking became familiar to Indians, the novel problematises the relationship between pre-modern and the modern. For long, the Enlightenment model of historiography has been perceived as 'modern' and usually associated with colonialism. Even postcolonial re-readings of history and historiography have regarded this model as a colonial import and imposition on an Indian/oral historiographic tradition and have therefore sought to valorise its opposite. *Gopalla Gramam* discounts, although unconsciously, the importance of colonialism in this regard and in effect suggests that all 'modern' ways of thinking need not be traced back to its advent. On the other hand, it shows how scepticism regarding the older models could emerge from within the community itself.

Mangathayaru's history is so structured as to stress the close relationship between the human and the divine. The divine interventions recalled by her render the exodus of the Kommavars in a supernatural light. Hence, the miraculous way in which the tree falls and makes a bridge for them to cross the river, the way in which an *amman* (female tribal deity) makes them invisible to their Muslim pursuers etc. convince them of their righteousness. Such a story is often not the stuff studied in history per se, but in anthropological and ethnographic studies. Much like *The Memory of Elephants*, the Gopallapuram chronicles in the first part draw upon various disciplines and weave a different kind of history in the novel, thereby forcing the novel itself to undergo formal changes. As in *The Memory of Elephants*, here too, the novel is made to bear the burden of the collective memory of the Kommavar community and to create a space where the original identity and the expanding contours of its migrant identity matrices can be inscribed.

Various aspects of Mangathayaru's story make their presence felt very subtly later in the novel. The most important of such re-appearances is the image of the cow. When the 'Muslim king' (he is left unnamed; as though his importance is nothing more than the original reason for the migration) demands Chennadevi as his bride, the initial horror gives way to acquiescence. But what decides the community against the marriage is the sight of the severed head of a calf in the dining area of the marriage hall. The Kommavars are not vegetarians, but they hold the cow sacred. It is not so much a difference in religion that causes them to flee, but a definitive difference in customs that makes the Muslims their Other. The cow remains an important image throughout the novel: the first animal they see on arriving at 'their' place is a cow and the British are 'bad' as they eat beef. The novel even carries a brief folkloristic story that describes why and how the cow came to be sacred.[2] This story becomes almost a mythical metanarrative within the novel as we can trace many attitudes of the Kommavars to it which mostly surround the cow as a semiotic symbol. Even the name which they give to the newly created village—Gopallapuram—reflects the holiness attached to the cow ('*go*' meaning 'cow' in Sanskrit and many Indian languages) while at the same time conveying their gratitude to the first cow, although wild, which became their source of sustenance and the symbol of their first attempt to turn wilderness into civilisation. By incorporating a story that would fall neither within the discipline of academic history, anthropology or ethnography, but the realm of folklore, the Gopallapuram chronicles virtually redefine all that goes into characterising a people and a community. In many ways, the community is defined through the novel, and many folk stories, orally transmitted tales and even gossip, form part of the definition of this people.

Another important, more defining moment of such a relationship between this 'origin myth' and later events occurs when the British come to the Kommavars' area. When asked if the Kommavars would accept the British as their overlords, Mangathayaru's first question is whether the British are known to misbehave with the women of 'India'. When she hears a favourable report of the Britishers' behaviour, the community is directed to accept the offer. This decisive shift from self-sufficiency to dependence upon an alien people who eventually emerge as an imperial power, is caused by a peculiar event in the saga of their exile and settlement and this leads in turn, to the 'modern' era of the community.

The narrative method of the novel and the history that it narrates are closely connected to each other. *The Memory of Elephants*, in spite of using a large number of stories, was still 'limited' and restricted to the family that was taken as its centre. The stories it told were the stories of the people of that family and to that extent the family became representative of the Parsi community as such. In the Gopallapuram chronicles, on the other hand, the reference point is the entire community and the novels do not take the option of making a family 'represent' that community. The alternative is to evoke the sense of community as a community and to do this would require that connecting and controlling strategies be redefined and reorganised. Homi's memoscan acted in *The Memory of Elephants* as a convenient device—a scientific magic-realist device—that would make it 'natural' for Homi to listen to his story. In the Gopallapuram chronicles, on the other hand, there is no such device. The 'narrative' has to be clever and deft enough in bringing out the 'sense of the community'.

This is done mainly by employing an omniscient narrative voice. Although this is a feature that may seem unfashionable today, it is extremely useful in chronicles of this kind (*Kayar* is another example) where the cultural canvas of the novel is quite vast and potentially infinite. Moreover, this is a floating voice – one that slips from one part of the village to another part and therefore from one story to another. This apparent formlessness of the novel—a feature that can easily be associated with the post-modern form—is nevertheless intrinsic to the story. If, as in *The Memory of Elephants*, the Gopallapuram chronicles are also concerned with evocation of the history of one community, and this community is a regionally rooted one (unlike the Parsis who are spread out), then such an evocation requires a narrative that is apparently disrupted. This disruption has not much to do with the post-modern disruption of temporality, but rather with a more realistic understanding of how a community lives and functions.

This gives the novel a highly amorphous form. The swift weaving in and out of stories makes it appear that the novel has no controlling narrative whatsoever, but this very method also mimes the way a community is fashioned. One of the useful aspects mentioned in Benedict Anderson's *Imagined Communities* is that the concept of a community is such that although *all* the people involved will never meet each other, they do *feel* a sense of community because of the rituals, practices, festivals and perhaps most of all (to conflate Ernest Renan with Anderson), the sense of a shared misfortune. When this community is narrativised in the novel, the novel takes on a shape that seems extremely disjointed; the stories of various people involved seem to have nothing to do with each other, but each is an essential part of the narrative of the community and can, therefore, not be dispensed with. Within the space of the text, though, there *is* a structural attempt at connectivity – the final part of one section leads on to the first part of the next and so on. For instance, the cow is the connecting principle between two sections of chapter two, the school between chapters two and three etc. The effect is of an old woman narrating the story of the community and this use of association as the connecting principle has fetched accolades for the novel from critics such as Venkat Swaminathan, Ashokamitran, Nuhman and others for bringing oral narrative back into the Tamil novel.

One important difference between *The Memory of Elephants* and the Gopallapuram chronicles is that the former describes events which have already happened: it is set in an eternal past. In the latter on the other hand, the events are narrated as though they are happening in the present of the novel, although the grammatical tense used is the past. This effect is brought out largely by moving swiftly in and out of narratives and by casting most of the events as stories narrated by characters to each other. This is another feature of a village saga like the Gopallapuram chronicles. The focus of the novels is the village. It has been said of these novels, as also of Thakazhi's *Kayar*, that the protagonists in them are the villages and not any particular human being. This focus makes it impossible for the text to leave the village; any event occurring anywhere else—even the 'origin myth'—has to be narrated by a character who has seen it happen.

We have been stressing the point that the community is being '*narrated*' in the novel, and it would seem far-fetched to claim, as Prem and Ramesh have done, that the people of Gopallapuram find their existence *only* through and in the stories. It is true that the stories keep this community alive. But such a critical comment also implies a severance of the relationship between the text and the world outside it. The important thing about such a relationship in the context of chronicle fiction is precisely that the textual representation has to be faithful to the 'real' 'signified' that it purports to represent. There can be no sense of ambiguity about this relationship—*The Memory of Elephants* has to describe certain aspects of the Parsi community—their rituals, practices etc.—faithfully. It cannot afford to give ambiguous meanings to these representations. Similarly, the Gopallapuram chronicles have to represent the Telugu migrant community faithfully. Any kind of ambiguity may, in fact, work against the very 'functions' of these novels. Rushdie's *Shame* can act as a study in contrast. In his attempts to criticise certain forms of government, the novel represents Pakistan as the fictional country 'K' whose referent remains ambiguous throughout. Any accusation that the novel is anti-establishment can immediately be countered by the ambiguity inherent in such a representation. In *The Memory of Elephants* and the Gopallapuram chronicles, on the other hand, such an ambiguity of referentiality would call into question the very purpose of such a novel. To say the village of Gopallapuram need not refer to a Telugu migrant community and that its referents can be made ambiguous or that its history is 'merely' allegorical would also take away the value of this novel as a record of the history and culture of this particular group of people.

Although we have a raconteur in the person of Mangathayaru, there is another dimension to the oral ancestry of the novel. The disjointed form of the novel also serves to displace received and academic notions of history; for the novel is an amalgam of history and ethnography. C. T. Indra has pointed out that in keeping with ethnographic methodology, the novel offers 'thick description', (3) to use Clifford Geertz's monumental phrase, by which the geography and the environment as well as the cultural practices are made tangible. As she shows in her paper presented at an International Conference at Warwick University titled *Translation and Mediation* which foregrounded ethnography, the Madras Archives merely provides statistics of how the Telugu Kommavar community migrated from the Tungabhadra region of Andhra to the tip of the Southern peninsula somewhere in the late seventeenth or early eighteenth century. The novel, however, 'fleshes' this skeletal information with details of what caused their migration and the travails they underwent before creating their own village. She cites the notes in the archives that describe the Kommavar community as 'a very industrious and energetic section who exhibit great talent reclaiming wasteland' (2); the novel provides us with specific details regarding how they went about this task.

The stress in these novels is largely on the intimate relationship between the land and the people involved. The fact that the novels are structured as a village saga is not accidental. The Kommavars physically created (not merely constructed) their village out of woods and forests and lived consciously as a community there. This formation of a community is therefore seen simultaneously at many levels – as a self-conscious act of 'imagining' oneself as a community, as a product of past events (especially sufferings), as brought about by sharing cultural practices (an aspect that is splattered all over the book) and, perhaps most importantly, as united by land and its boundaries. At the same time, interactions between this village and others are also seen as a major force in constructions of newer and larger identities and in the changes that take place in the villages.

It is interesting to note that in this construction and later administration of Gopallam village, the role played by women is impressive. Most of the decisions in the early part of Mangathayaru's narration are taken by Chenna Devi's grandmother – the resolution to leave their land and migrate, the decision regarding the area / plot on which to construct their new village, the methods by which to burn the existing forest area and make it cultivable etc. are all decisions taken by an old and wise grandmother. Similarly, the important administrative decision regarding the acceptance of the offer of overlordship by the British is taken finally by Mangathayaru herself. This importance given to women in the construction and running of the village is heightened by the role played by goddesses rather than gods in their belief system. Given the rural nature of the novel, this feature becomes all the more important as most villages in Tamil Nadu (perhaps it is true of village life in India in general) have a goddess each as their guardian deity. These deities, called *sirudeivangal* (little deities) in Tamil become objects of devotion and propitiation. The processes by which these *ammans* get sacralised are examined in anthropological and ethnographic studies. The Gopallapuram chronicles illustrate at least two such processes – one portraying a historico-mythical process and the other a social one.

The first occurs during the exodus of the Kommavars from Andhra. It is a female deity, an *amman*, who helps them by making them invisible to their Muslim persecutors. This *amman* then becomes the deity to whom the entire village offers worship. In many ways, the story of the *amman* helping the fleeing community becomes part of its collective memory.

The other event occurs much later in the life of the village, although it forms the beginning of the novel *Gopalla Gramam*. A murdered woman and her punished murderer both get venerated as *sirudeivangal*. This process is a dramatisation and narrativisation of generally accepted notions of deification of such figures. The belief is that women whose lives are cut off before fruition of their wishes—especially women who are murdered—are deified as godheads in order to appease their spirits. This deification of women implicitly accepts the power inherent in women as well as the fact that this power has the potential to turn dangerous to the community itself. As already mentioned, the historical processes by which 'Little Deities' are formed and eventually become an integral part of the religious life of the village are also evocatively captured. This ethnographic detail, along with various stories that become folklore later on, is an important aspect of these novels. What is an 'event' in one part of the novel, becomes with the passage of time, part of the collective memory of that community. This transition plays an important part in the construction of 'community' and to this extent, we can say that the novel portrays this continuous transformation of tales and anecdotes in the process of telling and retelling, into myth–history–legend and now, we may include, novel.

It is often pointed out that although women in the rural areas face greater physical violence, it is also understood that they also enjoy greater freedom regarding their choices. Many stories in *Gopalla Gramam* testify to the choices that the women in the village have – the stories of Enthulu and of Naicker's wife who committed *sati* are just two of them. In both cases, what is stressed is the choice available to the women and the role that the women play in constructing the psyche of the village folk. Equally importantly in this novel, it is a woman's narration that brings the community into being within the text and gives it an identity; just as it was a woman (Chenna Devi) who was the 'original' cause of the coming together of this new community.

Once the village as a physical entity is constructed and basic agricultural activity is begun, conscious attempts are made by the villagers to welcome artisans and workers from nearby villages. In what may be seen as one of the best representations of community formation along Marxist ideas, once the means of production and the economic structures are made stable, the village takes efforts to improve other aspects which later affect this 'base'. The 'growth' of the village is seen in linguistic, caste and occupation-based interactive terms: 'Tamil-speaking Saiva Chettiars, Pillais called Vellalas, these had four-five houses. Along with Telungu Pattars, Tamil Pattars too began to do business' (*GG*, 95). The text goes on to describe the various other community-based occupations that entered Gopallapuram. How this bilingual society which was 'begun' by Telugu speakers, nonetheless, became part of a 'Tamil' society is illustrated by the language used in the text – a language that is a mixture of Tamil and Telugu. Direct speech often uses either Telugu words or is fully in Telugu: 'Emira Kasturi, *itta chesestive*' ('What, Kasturi, what are you doing?') (*GG*, 98) and '*Intihi ippindi; oorihi oorvindi*' ('Sour at home and tasty outside') (103). The figure of Sami Kannachari is yet another instance of just such a linguistic situation – he comes into the village as a Tamil teacher and his reaction is typical: 'what appalled him when he came to the village was the "Tamil" that the villagers spoke. He was equally dismayed by the Telungu[3] that the people spoke; they used to laugh at him even while he was close to them.' (*GG*, 21). The various jokes and quips about linguistic variations show how differences in terms of languages can exist and be 'joked' about without overt manifestations (or even an existence) of power hierarchies.

Interestingly, the Kommavar community in the initial stages of its formation and settlement is not shown to interact with any other community at all – they *physically* create their space and land. The village of Gopallapuram is *theirs* in a very physical sense and this closeness to land is often reiterated in the novel. Ki. Rajanarayan has been acclaimed as the chronicler of rural Tamil Nadu. And this is nowhere more evident than in the two novels that form the Gopallapuram chronicles which can also be read as country fiction. In terms of linguistic dialects, rituals described, various ethnographic and anthropological details, the two novels are supreme examples of the rural and regional chronicle. The traditional definition of the regional novel as depicting in detail the lifestyle and practices of one 'place' or region is, of course, valid here. However, it is not only the lifestyle that is evoked, but also the various changes to that lifestyle and the reasons for them, as well as the legends, folk tales and beliefs that go into the making of the collective unconscious of the people. At the same time, these novels turn into a space where the rise and formation of certain cultural aspects and practices of a rural community are chronicled. For instance, a substantial portion is taken up by the descriptions of various festivals and rituals that might be at odds with what are anthropologically called Great Tradition. The ritual of Lord Ayyanar—the rural deity in most villages—going out hunting and killing anyone who would come in His way is a common belief/ ritual in most villages, but remains relatively alien to the Greater Traditions. Similarly, the all-women's festival where men are not allowed, which causes numerous intriguing hypotheses about 'what happens inside' is another such. The liquor festival, common in many villages, offers itself for an interesting and humorous critique of the nationalist movement. In the face of Gandhian prohibition, the Congressmen are caught in the horns of a dilemma – how does one cope with a religious festival that necessitates drinking? At stake here is the discourse that sees alcoholism as necessarily evil and does not concede the validity of religious drinking where natural limits may be set.

Academic histories are what the subaltern studies group have been calling 'elite histories', histories that are acted out at a macro level. Rewritings of academic histories—as *Red Earth and Pouring Rain* does—often end up as reinterpretations of the same structure, but with an inversion of the hierarchy. Hence, we can find various rewritings of events from the perspectives of the victims and the losers. Village sagas like the Gopallapuram chronicles and *Kayar* go a step further. The focus here is shifted not only from the centre to the periphery, but also from leaders and events themselves to their impact on ordinary people. Simply put, the Gopallapuram chronicles narrate history as it is lived in the lives of the various people who make up the village of Gopallapuram and the Kommavar community. In the everyday lives of these people, none of whom is actively involved in politics or in policy or decision-making at the national level (the novel does not even allege that their 'national' role had been deliberately suppressed), the events occurring in the macro levels are reflected to a great extent. From something as small and 'inconsequential' as the introduction of tea as a drink or the coming of clocks and watches, to greater changes such as the introduction of the Western mode of education and 'thinking', the village and its people are affected by the politics of the nation at large. This is the vantage point from which history is seen and narrated. This kind of historiography—one that Felix Wilfred calls 'Everyday or Ordinary Historiographies' ('Whose Nation? Whose History?')—effectively displaces and reworks the notion of history as 'happening' in the metropolitan centres or even through revolutions and rebellions. History is seen as inhering in the changes that occur in the lives and worlds of the people described.

One of the effects of the process of this history is that identity matrices of people keep getting enlarged. This shift in identity matrices can be seen both in *The Memory of Elephants* and the Gopallapuram chronicles. While the Parsi novel showed how a particular family could be representative of an entire ethnic community, the Gopallapuram chronicles narrate how a community slowly becomes representative of larger communities and identity matrices. This shift in 'belonging' is very striking throughout the Tamil novel. As the novel begins, the Kommavar community represents only itself; its historical conditions and cultural coordinates mark it out as very specific. As people move out of Andhra and meet the other community whose story is strikingly similar to theirs, they become representative of all such communities which have been so treated and are put under such circumstances. When they settle in Gopallapuram and begin their lives and professions there, their belonging-ness to the Tamil society at large becomes stronger; one of the important markers for this being the importance given in the village (and therefore the text) to the rise and growth of the Dravidian movement in the early twentieth century. However, when the community accepts the British as their overlords because Queen Victoria had proclaimed herself as the Empress of India in 1857, they also willy-nilly become part of colonial India and their history from that point onwards can be seen as being linked to that of national history in general and Tamil Nadu history in particular. These changes in the various positions of belonging also point to how historical processes enlarge the identity of communities of people. One might even go so far as to conjecture that the 'design' in history that chronicle fiction identifies is this enlargement of identities without giving up the smaller identity matrices. Such a multiplicity of 'belongingness' is an aspect that was analysed earlier too in the analysis of *The Memory of Elephants*. This simultaneity implicitly raises questions regarding historiographies which look upon the nation and the region as mutually exclusive or opposed discourses / ideas. A history of the kind written in the Gopallapuram chronicles shows how the common people live in history and how changes in their modes of living are the actual site where 'history' is acted out.

Yet, the Gopallapuram chronicles do not merely reinterpret the 'notion' of history, but actively displace the Grand Narratives of the freedom movement. Towards the middle of *Gopallapurathu Makkal*, when Gopallapuram awakes to its sense of being part of the 'Indian' nation and the impact of Gandhiji comes to be felt, the novel slowly begins to move out of Gandhian nationalism to that of Subhash Chandra Bose, usually seen as Gandhi's antithesis. The critique of Gandhian nationalism also gives way to the rise of Dravidianism and Marxism as alternate ideologies. The Marxist belief that the Congress Party stood only for the elite of India and that the ensuing freedom would be freedom only for that community is an aspect dealt with also in other novels – an interesting and well-written one being Mukul Kesavan's *Looking Through Glass* (1995). However, the amount of space given to the nationalism and politics of Subhash Chandra Bose in the Gopallapuram Chronicles is quite unique. What is even more striking is the description of the moment of 'freedom.' The feeling that the novel acts partly as a strong indictment of Indian politics and

Indian freedom movement is nowhere brought out more strongly than in this. Most descriptions of the moment of freedom would normally focus upon the celebrations in the Red Fort and definitely mention Nehru's famous 'tryst with destiny'. Some re-writings would focus primarily or simultaneously on the riots that broke out in Kolkata and other cities in the wake of Partition which went with independence. The Gopallapuram chronicles, however, without openly highlighting either of these, bring out the sense of bafflement of the sailors of the Indian Navy who are asked by 'venerated' leaders such as Nehru and Rajaji to give up the mutiny with the promise of renewal of their jobs. The reality, as can be guessed, was far different. The deception lies not only in that the sailors lost their jobs, but also in that they lost their rightful place in the history of India's freedom movement. In nationalist historiographies, there was little place for any discourse that would paint leaders in a dubious light; just as they had little place for regionalist discourses of the kind that the Gopallapuram chronicles offer.

The novels, therefore, not only inscribe the history of the Kommavar community, but also portray how this community is continually in the making and is constantly forming and re-forming itself as part of larger groups. As times change, so do the ways in which the novel and the people *in* the novel tell this history. The overtly religious history of Mangathayaru slowly gives way to a more folkloristic mode of history where history is narrated through anecdotes that pass on to become 'history'. This gives way to the Enlightenment mode of narration followed in the telling of the freedom struggle with its specificity of figures and dates, and finally to the academic precision that characterises the history narrated by Mani towards the end.

The Gopallapuram chronicles can therefore be seen as ethnographic novels where the fictional space is used to rewrite the history of the formation and growth of a marginal community. Histories of the kind written in *Red Earth and Pouring Rain*, however, take on more pan-Indian overtones.

## Pauranic Historiography: *Red Earth and Pouring Rain*

First published in 1995, Vikram Chandra's novel forms part of what has academically been termed 'The New Indian Novel in

English' – a brand patented by Salman Rushdie and his *Midnight's Children* in 1981. The fourteen years separating *Red Earth and Pouring Rain* from *Midnight's Children* had witnessed a large number of shifts in perspective of the New Indian Novel in English itself. Some of the important features identified for this genre have been its use of 'english,' its re-writing of history and its use of Indian, non-Western oral narrative methods. The contentions *against* the New Indian Novel in English have largely been that the history that it rewrites is elite history and that its 'oral' narrative methods privilege, by implication, a caste, class and gendered India and thereby excludes ethnic communities and regional histories.

At a narratological level, the novel offers no small challenge. It proffers three main narratives into which are woven numerous smaller stories; a structure somewhat reminiscent of *The Memory of Elephants*. The use to which *Red Earth and Pouring Rain* puts this structure and the way in which it is developed is, however, very different from the Parsi novel. While Desai used a more or less science-fiction mode to elaborate on this technique, *Red Earth and Pouring Rain* takes us into the realm of rebirths, curses, curses that are working out and the use of storytelling as a means for *moksha*. These structural aspects impel us to trace the master narrative of this novel in the sacred Hindu texts of the *puranas*.

A short introduction to the structure and method used in the *puranas* will therefore not be out of place here. The *puranas* were possibly not the first to use this kind of narrative, but in the context of *Red Earth and Pouring Rain*, they mark the necessary starting point. At the same time, since criticism has often taken note of the Persian *Alif Laila wa Laila*, popularly called *The Arabian Nights*, as prototypical of the 'postmodern' narrative, the following discussion will also touch upon it.

The eighteen *mahapuranas* form an important part of the canon of Hindu religious literature and are traditionally seen as explanations of the Vedas. The narrative of the *puranas* is intricately connected to the underlying belief-systems in them – the concept of time as simultaneously cyclical and linear, the hierarchy in the material world and the various methods allowed for *moksha*. Structurally, all the eighteen *puranas* begin in the same way: a few sages under the leadership of Saunaka gather in Naimisharanya forest. Sage Suka, whose father was the legendary Veda Vyasa credited to have written the *puranas* at the behest of Sage Narada, comes their way. The sages then proceed to get doubts regarding moral and ethical issues cleared by the sage Suka. The answer comes in a motley of narrative modes – direct narration that tells us (and the sages) how the *puranas* came to be written, how the world was formed, deformed and re-formed (what are termed *sarga*, *pratisarga* etc. which are also different parts of the *purana*), explanations of philosophical concepts relating to time, the cosmos, morality etc., and further stories in which the basic situation of this story (sages asking for explanations and being answered with more stories) is recreated *ad infinitum*. The structure of the *puranas* then, can be said to be circular – the image generally associated with an 'Indian' notion of time.

Stories in the *puranas* also become a useful means of answering ethical and moral questions. This use of storytelling is certainly not peculiar to India. Buddha, Christ and many other spiritual and religious preceptors worldwide have used stories as an excellent tool / means for spreading moral values. What makes the *puranas* peculiar is the notion of time as simultaneously linear and cyclical and the attendant ideas on the temporality of human life.

In *Of Many Heroes*, G. N. Devy discusses the notion of time associated with generally the non-West and with India in particular. He argues, taking examples from philosophers like Bhartrihari, that traditional philosophy did not look upon time entirely as cyclical or linear, but saw it simultaneously as both. This, he says, is exemplified by the images of the road and the wheel to signify it. This simultaneity finds expression in many ways in the *puranas*. On the one hand, the *puranas* deal with cosmic history and this history is itself conceived of in terms of cycles of four *yugas* (aeons): *satya yuga*, *treta yuga*, *dwapara yuga* and *kali yuga*. While the yugas follow each other in a linear fashion, the end of *kali yuga* also signifies the beginning of the next such cycle. The importance of this can be gauged only by understanding that traditional thought placed each *yuga* below its previous one in terms of morality and goodness, thereby making the *kali yuga* the most depraved. The cyclical nature of the yugas promises renewal of morality and goodness. However, the 'fall' in morals in *kali yuga* is signified mainly in terms of the disruption of caste and gender hierarchies.

The cosmic cycle finds reflection in the human cycle of birth and rebirth. The concept of rebirth is one that is peculiar to many indigenous Indian religions like Hinduism, Buddhism and Sikhism. It believes that one's actions in any birth do not lead to a final 'end' in heaven or hell, but to a return to this world and its sufferings. Good deeds would lead to a 'better' birth while sins would lead to an 'inferior' birth. Implied in these are inherent beliefs in natural hierarchies among humans and animals, between castes and among the sexes. Implied in them also is the understanding that the material world is a place for suffering and that 'coming back' is not to be looked forward to. Liberation from this eternal cycle of birth, death and rebirth is *moksha* – a term quite untranslatable except loosely as 'absolute freedom'. One of the means for achieving this *moksha* is to tell and listen to the stories of God – which is what the *puranas* do.

A fuller understanding of the importance of the *puranas* would be possible only if we comprehend the manner in which they were deployed. They were not 'read' or sermonised about. They formed, rather, the central part of formal and oral storytelling sessions variously called *harikatha, katha kalakshepa* etc. These storytelling sessions were the basic means by which a community kept its history and identity alive – they invariably linked the stories in the *puranas* to contemporary situations and were also simultaneously a means of imparting religious and moral values. It was believed that the *bhagavatar* narrating the *purana* was taking on the role of the sage Suka and the locale of narration was a replication of Naimisharanya forest. The *puranas* were therefore continually rejuvenated. They became part of the collective memory of the people who were listening and so acted as a means of placing human history within the realm of cosmic and universal history. In the course of these narrations, the *pauranic* stories were invariably linked to contemporary political / social / cultural events / conditions, thereby asserting the constant relevance of the *puranas*. In many ways, such links made history a continued present, if not a point of reference.

In the context of postcolonial criticism, the British attitude to this kind of history has received much attention. The absence of precise dates and places and the practice of attributing every 'historical' event to a divine force had led many of the British commentators to make the infamous claim that Indians had no sense of history or time whatsoever. The coalescing of history, myth and legend in most 'Indian' narratives is perhaps best exemplified by the remark of Markline in *Red Earth and Pouring Rain*:

> I've read all your great books, all the great wisdom of the East. And such a greater mass of morass and darkness, confusion, necromancy, stupidity, avarice, I've never seen. Plots meander, veering from grief to burlesque in a minute. Unrelated narratives entwine and break

> into each other. Whole huge battles, millions of men a side, stop short so that some dying patriarch can give a speech about duty, a speech that goes on for fifties of pages. Metaphors that call attention to themselves, strings of similes that go from line to line. Characters fall in love or murder, only to have their actions explained away as the results of past births. Characters die, only to be reborn again. Beginnings are not really beginnings, middles are unendurably long and convoluted, nothing ever ends. (*Red Earth*, 283)

He could well have been talking about the very novel in which he is a character for this novel appears to have been written as an answer to Markline and the whole gamut of colonial attitude that he represented. This 'function' of the text as an 'answering back' to the colonial centre might well account for much of its features, chief among them being its meandering and apparently formless structure.

The unrelated narratives that 'entwine and break into each other' as Markline says (*Red Earth*, 283), are in reality part of a larger design that takes rebirth and *moksha* as its basic beliefs. No action in the *pauranic* narrative structure occurs exclusively in *this* birth or can be answered with reference only to the present. The 'past' in this structure stretches all the way back to the beginning of the universe and this connection between the past and the present makes it absolutely necessary that any action be explained with reference to such a 'past.' The endless stories, therefore, form part of a well-designed plan and do not reflect any formlessness.

The *pauranic* structure with all its religious implications has also been used in secular texts like *Kathasaritasagara* and *Kadambari* where the same deep structure of telling stories to attain *moksha* is used. It is this narrative structure that is used in *Red Earth and Pouring Rain*, although criticism has tended to focus much more on the *Arabian Nights* and the *Mahabharata* as master narratives. The Persian text has been used quite extensively in criticism to represent the 'postmodern' narrative structure and the importance of fictionalising. Scheherazade's predicament (or is it technique) of having to telling stories to save her life has been read as the prototypical human condition where we are all constantly making fictions of our lives in order to gives us our identities. At the same time, the infinitely looping structure of *The Arabian Nights* has made it a *tour de force* for narratologists who delight in the intricacies of diegetic and hyperdiegetic levels. Some of the criticism of *Red Earth and Pouring Rain* has suffered due to this – for example, Christopher

Rollason, while discussing intertextuality in the novel, deals at length with Western authors and *The Arabian Nights*, but completely misses out the 'Indian' context of the narrative. Many publishers' blurbs too talk about *The Arabian Nights* in a bid to entice the reading public into a maze of magic and 'unreal'.

However, if we are to see the text as an answering back to the colonial powers and their writing of Indian history, then the use of this particular narrative methodology within Sanjay's frame becomes a conscious and political choice. Here again, criticism has made vague references to the 'Indian' narrative tradition without overtly stressing what makes it 'Indian.' Reviewers such as Mukund Padmanabhan, Shobha Hiatt and Shashi Tharoor do mention that the narrative here is 'typically Indian' and also hint that it draws much of its 'strength' from being so. Perhaps the fact that much criticism on the novel has been in the form of reviews with very little scope to elaborate on details may explain this hiatus. However, criticism has used this narrative to slot the novel within the postmodern Indian novel tradition, although Amit Choudhary mentions certain inconsistencies in it – like the use of 'Arun'; a 'post-Tagorean' name – and sees these as making the novel more postmodern than 'traditionally Indian' ('Gods, Monkeys and Englishmen', 20). One lacuna that can be seen in most criticism on this novel is the total absence of any reference to Abhay's story or the connections between the three strands – Sanjay's story, Abhay's narrative and the Mishras' history. Perhaps this has again been fuelled by the fact that it is Sanjay's narration that falls into the critically popular 'Indian narrative tradition'. Yet, the connections between the three sections are important.

All the three major strands in the novel originate from the basic situation. Sanjay, the monkey, suddenly remembers his human consciousness and is faced with Yama, the God of Death and his deadly noose. In a replication of the Savitri[4] story, a deal is struck with Yama through the intervention of Hanuman – a deal that allows Sanjay to tell a story and keep at least one-fourth of his audience alive in return for his life. That Hanuman should enter the picture is not entirely a ploy to bring as many gods of the Hindu canon into the picture as possible. Hanuman is the *raison d'être* for many narrations of the Ramayana that form an integral part of everyday life among the Hindus. In fact, Hanuman proclaims that wherever the Ramayana is narrated, he will be present among the audience. *Red Earth and Pouring Rain* deftly turns this religious symbol of the ideal servant-bhakta into a witness to the telling–writing of another kind of history more contemporary but equally full of magic and divine intervention (and, we should add in the light of recent controversies, equally relevant). Sanjay's attempts to save his life through storytelling make him squarely a simian counterpart to Scheherazade, but the *pauranic* implications cannot be ignored. The story he narrates is, as his frame character says, history: 'but do not think that this story is untrue, because it is *itihasa*: thus it was; let this story appear among you, as it happened long ago, and it will clear your heart and cleanse your soul' (23), thereby skilfully bringing the historical into the realm of the religious. The text thus seems to be offering history instead of religious and moral stories as a means of cleansing the soul. But if this is true, why should our souls need cleansing at all? The text itself along with its context may provide an answer.

Many of the new Indian novels in English do not indulge in fantasia but deal primarily with history. This much-vaunted modernity has been fuelled by an understanding of the pitfalls of colonial versions of Indian history and culture which have for long misrepresented the Indian subject. In *Red Earth and Pouring Rain*, it is Janvi's death by *sati* that provides the suitable context. Her act of jumping into the pyre is an act of defiance of colonial as well as patriarchal rule over her. This supremely 'heroinic' act is, however, grossly misrepresented in Francis Sarthey's history:

> The captain desired to educate his daughters in accordance with the norms of civilised society, to deliver them from the dark pit of ignorance, but their mother, seeing in this the breach of the ancient sanctity of *purdah* a violation of her own overtly proud and sensitive Rajpoot [*sic*] honour, took her own life by immolation. Thus the interior darkness of India, that centuries old barbarism, took yet another life. (*Red Earth*, 287)

Sanjay's angry response to this is perhaps only typical – 'But it's not true . . . . What does it matter what we know? What they'll tell the world is this' (287–88). It is this kind of misrepresentation—a misrepresentation that even Indians believed—that needs to be rectified. And this novel, like Sanjay's code in the text, is the means of accomplishing it. This 'answering back' is therefore, done avowedly for the 'Rajpoot' princess, but inhering in the 'Rajpoots' are all Indians and all aspects of Indian history that need to be so corrected.

Operating along this binary of coloniser–colonised, *Red Earth and Pouring Rain* seeks, like many postcolonial texts, to subvert the hierarchy and place the colonised in a position of privilege. The act of writing the novel and in it, Sanjay's act of narrating his story becomes not only a means of survival and but also of settling scores. It is perhaps inevitable that the novel operate along contours that are not so clearly defined in terms of ethnicities and regional differences. The town in the novel is named as Lucknow, but this specificity does not really matter for what is dealt with is the history of a larger entity – India.

To say that this pan-Indianness is made possible mainly by the language of the text that itself has 'pan-Indian' overtones is however to take too simplistic a view of the matter. *The Memory of Elephants* was also written in English, but an 'english' that quite successfully blended the native Gujarati as well as the language of the sacred texts of the Parsis with the english of the text. This kind of trilingualism is represented typologically by placing religious prayers and their English translation in two columns as in:

| *Ashem Vohu* | Blessed Is Virtue |
|---|---|

*Red Earth and Pouring Rain* too, linguistically, does straddle more than one area. This is most evident in the various poems that are translated across the text – poems in the tradition of the Urdu *sher*. Yet, to attribute the 'national' nature of Chandra's novel to its 'english' is again to make a dubious statement and to forget that such pan-Indian discourses have been constructed even in *bhasha* texts such as Qurratulain Hyder's Urdu novel *Aag ka Dariya* and the Tamil novel *Alai Osai* by Kalki.

The 'writing back' implied in the novel is not however restricted to the content of the text; it spills over and finds better expression in the way in which the history is being told and it is here that we enter into the field of 'traditional Indian narratives'. Broadly the structure of Sanjay's narrative with its frame and inset narratives follows the pattern of the *puranas* – a pattern suggested by Hanuman himself as we noted: 'Straightforwardness is the curse of your age, Sanjay. Be wily, be twisty, be elaborate. Forsake grim shortness and hustle. Let us luxuriate in your curlicues. Besides, you need a frame story for its peace, its quiet' (20), Hanuman tells him, thereby elevating precisely that which Markline had denied value to. The story that Sanjay types therefore has a structure with the sage Sandeep narrating what he heard to a group of sages 'led' by Shanker. Like the standard *puranas*, this story contains in it if not the tale of its own creation, at least the story of how Sandeep came to hear it. As the telling continues, we also encounter various doubts and misgivings among the listeners. The following is one instance:

> 'Wait a minute,' one of the Sadhus said. 'Wait just a minute here.'
> 'You have a doubt?' Sandeep said.
> 'I do, I do. We can assume with certainty that at this point in his development, Sanjay doesn't speak English, no?'
> 'We don't have to assume. I asked my storyteller in the forest the same question and she said Sanjay knew no English.'
> 'Then how is it that he seems to know what Hercules is saying? Why is it that we hear what Hercules is saying?' (*Red Earth*, 184)

As can easily be seen, the moral and ethical doubts raised by the listeners in the *puranas* have given way to the more narrative and text-centred questions here, signifying perhaps a drastic shift in historiographical attitudes. Interestingly, although none of the listeners questions the value of the magical *laddoos* and their influence, smaller aspects of narrative seem to become questionable. Further, the narrative ends in a way typical of oral narratives: 'Thank you for listening to me. This was the story of Sikander and Sanjay, and those who listen to it attentively and with faith will be delivered from doubt, and after they have heard it they will be changed for ever, they will be something else' (489–90). We might reiterate that this reinforces the role of history as the means of achieving identity for a community, a role performed in the same mode by religious stories earlier.

By narrating their own history, communities assert their right to depict and represent themselves. In so doing, they might retrieve themselves from earlier misrepresentations. More importantly, such narration allows the community to remain alive in public memory and it is in this that the narration of history becomes an act of survival for the community. Yet, for Sanjay, this narration is not merely a fight with Yama; midway through his narration, it takes on cathartic implications as he finds that: 'But Yama is no longer my enemy. I must continue, not to keep his noose away, but simply to finish. We are almost finished, and we must finish so we can start again' (432) and Sanjay slowly becomes like the ancient mariner who *must* tell his story. This virtually spiritual tone accorded to the telling of history finally raises the novel itself to such levels: the story in the novel *must* be told and listened to for the survival of the narrators and the listeners depends upon it.

Sanjay's narration has its source in recorded extra-textual facts – the story of Benoit de Boigne has been drawn from archives and, like the Gopallapuram chronicles and *The Memory of Elephants*, *Red Earth and Pouring Rain* too blurs the boundaries between history and fiction. Yet it is important that the form in which this already narrated history is inscribed is part of the religio-mythical model of historiography which the colonial powers attributed to a 'less-developed' historical sense. Related to this was the inferior status attributed to 'orality' as a source of historical data. It is only very recently that oral stories and oral narrations have been accorded academic status. Yet, within the space of the novel, this distinction between orality and literacy is constantly blurred and eroded. Sanjay learns to write before he ever learns to talk and even the telling of history is actually a combination of writing and telling. Sanjay *types* his story and it is then narrated to the audience sitting outside. This bizarre situation merely reaffirms the existence of orality and writing as simultaneous and equally useful and necessary modes of recording history.

The *pauranic* structure of Sanjay's story is not, however, restricted to the outward structure alone. The underlying value system is the concept of rebirth and the working out of curses in various births, a system drawn directly from the *puranas*. Hence, we find that the stories Sanjay tells are the stories of his previous births and that the figures of Sandeep and Shanker act merely as agents of fictionalising. Sanjay's narrative falls quite squarely into the Sanskrit literary genre called the *sakalakatha* that narrates the various previous lives of the protagonist. This is the tradition to which other 'secular' Sanskrit narratives such as *Kadambari* belong. The *sakalakatha* is a form wherein, despite the various births and rebirths, the basic core of the human identity remains constant and unproblematic. In *Red Earth and Pouring Rain*, on the other hand, the overt form of the *sakalakatha* is used to problematise the notion of identity – the theme that connects the three frame narratives to each other.

The novel is not merely a rewriting of history from another perspective and in another mode; it also brings out the horrors of colonialism and of history in general to ordinary and common individuals such as Sanjay and Abhay. The effect of history—of clashes or contacts between cultures—is largely evoked by the sense of rootlessness and identity-crisis that it creates in people such as Sanjay and Abhay. Identity crisis is a much-used and abused term. It has been bandied about so much that its deeper and terrifying implications are often lost.

In a politically unequal power relationship such as that exemplified by colonialism, the offspring of the two cultures involved are often left in no-man's land. Contrary to more recent critical exaltation of the 'migrant' or hybrid position, at the moment of such a contact, this subject position can be absolutely frustrating. An article titled 'Neither on Either Side nor In-between: the Anglo-Indian in Post-colonial Indian Fiction in English' notes that this unrootedness can be traced to the distrust among Indians—especially Hindus—of any mixed heritage. This is the crisis of Sanjay, Sikander and Chotta Sikander, born of (others think) an Indian mother and a British father; they are trusted neither by the Indians nor by the British. In reality, of course, their identity is much more complicated. The same article mentioned above studies the implications of Sanjay, Sikander and Chota Sikander as Anglo-Indians: for while as children of the magical *laddoo*, they are the offspring of all those who touch them and their lineage is thereby vast, their position fits squarely within the official definition of an 'Anglo-Indian.' Moreover, they can trace their ancestry back to the Skinner family, one of the earliest and most notable Anglo-Indian families in India. The frustrations of this in-between position, being trusted neither by the Indians nor by the British are brought out in the letter that Sikander writes to Sanjay:

> while he did not doubt any of us individually, he said, it had been decided that those officers who were of partial English descent could not be wholly relied upon . . . . I stepped forward, and spoke: I am a Rajput, and my loyalty is unquestioned, you insult me . . . . I am a Rajput, I said again. Undoubtedly, he said, but you are also something else. (*Red Earth*, 395–96)

This exchange between an Indian officer and Sikander is the reason for Sikander fighting for the British and he himself is therefore unable to answer his question 'Was I betrayed, or did I betray?' (*Red Earth*, 396).

The situation that Sikander faces is reiterated implicitly in Sanjay's own story that deftly moves not only between different cultures and countries but also between different living forms. The form that Sanjay chooses for his narration, however, seems to reiterate his decision to take over his Rajput identity and place his British one under 'erasure.' This problematic of identity is not, however, a one-time affair. The novel seems to stress that it is reiterated every time there is a contact between cultures and there seems to have been no time without such a contact in Indian history. This is the theme that connects the three strands of the novel to each other.

If Sanjay's problems arise out of a politically unequal relationship between the British and the Indians, Abhay's problems develop out of a similar cultural relationship between India and America. Abhay belongs to that generation of youngsters who had left India for America in search of greener pastures, but not so well-rooted in Indian life to successfully adapt it there, nor comfortable enough with the American way of life to adopt it fully.

Abhay comes to represent the modern Indian and even the Third World migrant, a status that is unenviable despite critical and theoretical formulations glorifying this *trishanku* [5] position. A useful contrast can be drawn between Abhay and Homi. While culturally both are in similar conditions—expatriates from their homes in search of better academic opportunities in the same country,—Homi is far more rooted in his cultural life although 'he does not even know what it means to be a Bawaji' (1). Abhay's attitude, in fact, every word of his narrative and the action in it, is filled with ennui. So if both Abhay and Homi are alienated from their 'culture', what contributes to the difference in their attitude? We might say that by the time Homi comes to tell us his own story, he has had a solid grounding in Zoroastrian history, but the history that Abhay hears only confirms his sense of disillusionment with history itself. The story that Sanjay has just narrated and the 'academic history' that his parents—history teachers both—narrate is filled with wars, bloodshed and invasions. Sanjay's story has already told us what such invasions can lead to in individual lives. The kind of lifestyle Abhay witnesses in America only seems to stress the grossly sexual and commercial aspects of life, a life in which even human bodies are structured by market demands as exemplified by Amanda's mother who has had transplants of almost all external organs of her body.

*Red Earth and Pouring Rain* concentrates on a crucial point in Indian history – the 1857 War of Independence and it rewrites this war from the point of view of an Anglo-Indian who has chosen to retain his 'Indian' identity over the Anglo one. That Sanjay needs to discard this hybrid identity in favour of an unproblematic singular one forces us to reconsider the dubious social and cultural position of the racial hybrids of colonialism.

The pan-Indianness of this strand of the novel is offset by a similar condition faced by Abhay who reminds us of that certain kind of ennui and hopelessness which was believed to have characterised most of the youth of the early modern period. It is this kind of ennui that Jaidev christens 'culture of pastiche' in a critical book of the same name – a culture that he associates with an unthinking imitation of the modes of Western techniques of existentialist writings. Although Jaidev's book is more concerned with Hindi literature, its main concepts hold true for Indian literature in general. The strand in *Red Earth and Pouring Rain* dealing with Abhay's life may appear to be an instance of such a pastiche culture. We also need to point out that the brand of Abhays in the world does exist and that their existential angst and ennui does need to be recorded. The cultural rootlessness of the text cannot be blamed in any way for Abhay's condition, for Sanjay himself offers a study in contrast. Despite being a cultural hybrid in a political situation that is based on a hugely unequal power relationship, Sanjay's narrative shows a deep sense of faith and belief in a set of values. These may be values that he has chosen out of the two options available to him—Indian and British—but the choice allows him to negotiate the historical condition to his satisfaction. Abhay, on the other hand, seems absolutely unable to make a choice and in trying to inhabit the no-man's land of the cultural orphan (not hybrid), is left to feel sorry about his various losses. The failure of his relationship with Amanda only reflects a failure of the two cultures, their inability to meet and interact fruitfully on any ground, literal or metaphorical.

This is not to deny that the breakdown of the relationship of Abhay and Amanda also reflects the various failures of Sanjay as a lover and a husband (although Abhay's story is left technically open-ended, the overwhelming feeling is that the romance will end). Both Abhay and Sanjay are victims of history, histories into which they are born and over which they have no control. This is the Grand Narrative that Abhay's parents tell. Their stories, aptly titled 'what really happened', take the place of 'Prelude' in *The Memory of Elephants* and Mangathayaru's story in the Gopallapuram chronicles, offering the master narrative within which to place the stories of Abhay and Sanjay. It is a history of invasion, bloodshed and hegemony and, interestingly enough, touches upon the *pauranic* mode of explaining these while also seeing them as constructed narratives: 'this is what really happened, a remaking of the past, a reconstruction of the things that live on within us as they might have happened once upon a time' (*Red Earth*, 102). This is stressed time and again in phrases and terms like 'and a story was told' (104) and 'what really happened?' (102, 103), all underscoring the idea that the narrator has the privilege of ordering the past so as to convey his vision. What is also implied in the Mishras' history is that contacts between cultures are and have been an inevitable part of India's history. The notion that the Indian culture has always been a hybrid one and that 'pure' Indianness is a myth is best brought out in their narration:

> So the newcomers and the old ones collided and metamorphosed into a thing wholly new and unutterably old, fell into new orbits around new centres of gravity. In this anomie, the ones newly in power quickly created a perception that promised order . . . there was another perception . . . unity is diversity, diversity is unity. (*Red Earth*, 103)

Abhay and Sanjay have had the misfortune of living at the moment of this contact and they pay the price for it in different ways – Sanjay by losing his life and by the promise of memory after death given to him by Yama and Abhay by giving vent to the ennui that is liberally splattered in every word of his narration. All in all, notwithstanding the Mishras' assertion, the stories of Abhay and Sanjay and the 'now' of the novel seem to show history as a series of changes in which innocent lives are affected. The communal riot that breaks out in the present of the novel almost claims the innocent Saira as its victim, a riot that stresses Sanjay's concern over this new idea: 'there was one new thing, one new idea that overwhelmed everything else, and this was simply that there should be only one idea, one voice, one thing, one, one, one' (*Red Earth*, 518). The reluctance to admit plurality is, perhaps, at the heart of many political and historical problems of the day. It is also a problem with the criticism on the text that has chosen to ignore Abhay's and the Mishras' stories. The novel on the whole gives the lie to its own title which is drawn from a Tamil poem of the ancient Sangam period. The poem is quoted within the text by a prostitute:

> What could my mother be
> To yours? What kin is my father
> to yours anyway? And how
> did you and I meet ever?
> But in love
> our hearts have mingled
> like red earth and pouring rain. (*Red Earth*, 197)

It is a poem that celebrates love as a means of overcoming every kind of difference, but in the context of the novel, hybridity remains a curse for the victims of history. Love too is subject to history and its vagaries, an idea reiterated in a novel like *Aag ka Dariya* where characters constantly bemoan: 'I am not interested in [history makers]. Why must they drag me into their conflict?' (*Red Earth*, 39). Unfortunately, although ordinary people may not be 'dragged into' historical and political conflicts, *Red Earth and Pouring Rain* reminds us that human relationships and our identities depend to a large extent upon the historical circumstances in which people live. The tragedies of Abhay and Sanjay are divided by almost a century and if Sanjay's condition is political, Abhay's has more to do with the cultural politics of the contemporary world.

## Summing Up . . .

All the three novels discussed in this chapter approach history in very different ways and, interestingly enough, all of them deal with more than one identity level. We had earlier seen that discursive literature has tended to place the nation and region as mutually exclusive categories. However, while *The Memory of Elephants* and the Gopallapuram chronicles take a view which can be called an 'in-between' or an interstitial position, the very fabric of *Red Earth and Pouring Rain* rejects hybridity as a fruitful option at the moment of 'contact' between cultures; in fact, Chandra's novel seems to stress that at particular historical moments, only binaries are available to the individual and that as often as not, in times of political upheaval, one's identity and loyalty are thrust upon one – witness the letter written by Sikander to Sanjay. The double vision that Sanjay is given—a symbol of a hybrid point of view—is shown to be more of a nuisance. Symbolically it becomes single when Sanjay finally decides to abandon Markline and all that he represents, thereby stressing that particular historical moments demand that stands be taken. It is to be noted that the name 'Sanjay' intertextually takes us back to the Mahabharata. In that *itihasa*, the special vision or *dṛshti* that the divine charioteer Lord Krishna bestowed upon Sanjay spiritually elevated the human charioteer who was then able to witness the ongoings of the great Mahabharata war and report it to his blind king Dhŕtarashtra. This ironical reference to the Mahabharata reaffirms the difference between the two Sanjays as witnesses to historic wars. The Sanjay in *Red Earth and Pouring Rain*, being without clear political sympathies at the time of his dual vision, can only feel frustrated by it.

Of the three novels discussed above, it is the Gopallapuram chronicles which deal at length with the formation of a community. Although *Red Earth and Pouring Rain* deals with a history that is part of a nationalist discourse, it does not really bring out the mechanics of nation formation. Being in the tradition of the post colonial new Indian novel in English, it is more concerned with 'writing back' to the former colonial centre in a bid to correct faulty historical accounts. *The Memory of Elephants* is different from both in that it tries to bring out and make known the Parsi way of life to other Parsis and non-Parsis. Each of the novels, therefore, depicts how history can be used in myriad ways for a variety of purposes and how many versions and modes of such writings are available. Yet, all the three novels deal with 'Indian' history and form part of 'Indian' literature. By voicing and bringing to novelistic space the lives and histories of small communities of people, *The Memory of Elephants* and the Gopallapuram chronicles effectively redefine the concept of India as a nation and Indian history as monologic. To come to some kind of a realistic understanding of India, we need to take into account *both* national, pan-Indian narratives and regional, smaller narratives, in short, *grand recit* and *petit recit*. To deny value to everything that forms part of a grand narrative or a majoritarian discourse is to fall again into the danger of misrepresenting India. The federal form of government can perhaps give us the best image of this; such a government implies a simultaneous existence of the regional as well as the national interests, with particular situations deciding which will take precedence.

These novels, dealing with various kinds of histories, in a variety of ways therefore, effectively redefine the notion of the Indian novel. As these novels are written both in English and the *bhashas*, the language of the text need not necessarily decide the treatment of history. These are novels that are the products of certain social, cultural and political formulations in contemporary India. By effectively blurring the boundaries between fiction, history and ethnography, these novels also create almost a new form of the Indian novel in each case, where fiction and discourse interweave and fiction *in fact becomes a discursive space*.

## Notes

1. Although written before 1980, this novel forms a part of the Gopallapuram chronicles the second part of which was published in 1993. *Gopalla Gramam* has to be read along with the second novel. Hereafter cited in the text as *GG*.

2. The story goes that in return for the highly necessary milk, humans would dedicate one day every year for the cow, decorate her and worship her and most importantly, desist from eating her meat.

3. 'Telungu' is how Tamils colloquially call the language Telugu.

4. Savitri's story is one of those that are usually used to depict the ideal Hindu wife and also the gullibility of Yama. Determined to marry Satyavan despite being told that she would be widowed within a year, Savitri undertakes severe penance to save her husband. On his death, she strikes a deal with Yama and gains a boon for begetting a hundred sons, a boon that Yama unthinkingly grants. Thereafter, Savitri holds Yama to his word and asks back for her husband in order that she may beget the promised number of sons.

5. Wanting to reach heaven in his earthly body, a king asked Sage Vasishta to grant him his wish. Having been refused, he asks the sage's sons to fulfil his wishes. Angered at being asked to defy their father, the sons curse the king to become a *chandala*, a man belonging to the lowest caste in society. Frustrated, he asks Sage Vishwamitra, Sage Vasishta's rival, to take him to heaven. In a bid to get back at Vasishta, Vishwamitra agrees, but the *chandala* king is turned back at the gates of heaven. Angered, Vishwamitra, suspends him in mid-space and begins to build another heaven around him. Frightened, like any ruler, at the prospect of a rival, Indra beseeches Vishwamitra to desist from his building. Vishwamitra stops, but also completely forgets about the unfortunate king. Because he is unable to come down or go up, this king has been called *Trishanku*, and has become proverbial for an in-between position.

## References

Anderson, Benedict. *Imagined Communities: Reflections on the Origin and Spread of Nationalism*. 1983. Rev. ed. (London: Verso, 1991).

Basu, Anjana. 'The Asylum of Memory'. Review of *The Memory of Elephants*. *Gowanus*. Spring 2001 (11 Sept. 2002). <http://www.gowanusbooks.com>

Bhabha, Homi., ed. *Nation and Narration*. (1990; London: Routledge, 1991).

Bharucha, Nilufer. E. 'Reflections in Broken Mirrors: Diverse Diasporas in Recent Parsi Fiction'. *Wasafiri*, 21 (Spring 1995): 32–35.

Bharucha, Nilufer and Vilas Sarang, eds. *Indian–English Fiction: 1980–1990: An Assessment* (New Delhi: B. R. Publishing Corporation, 1994).

Chandra, Vikram. *Red Earth and Pouring Rain* (New Delhi: Penguin, 1995).

Chaudhuri, Amit. 'Gods, Monkeys and Englishmen'. Review of *Red Earth and Pouring Rain* by Vikram Chandra. *Times Literary Supplement*, 2 Jun 1995, 20.

Desai, Boman. *The Memory of Elephants*. 1988. (Kent: Sceptre, 1990). This is cited as *Memory* in the later references.

Devy, G. N. *After Amnesia: Tradition and Change in Indian Literary Criticism* (Bombay: Orient Longman, 1992).

———. *Of Many Heroes: An Indian Essay in Literary Historiography* (Mumbai: Orient Longman, 1998).

Hariharan, Githa. *In Times of Siege* (New Delhi: Penguin, 2003).

Hyder, Qurratulain. *River of Fire*. 1959. Trans. Qurratulain Hyder from Urdu into English (New Delhi: Kali for Women,1998).

Indra, C. T. 'People's Narrative as Alternate History: A Study of Ki. Rajanarayanan's *Gopalla Gramam* (Tamil).' Paper presented at *Translation and Mediation* International Conference. University of Warwick: 6–8 July 2001.

Jaidev. *The Culture of Pastiche: Existential Aestheticism in the Contemporary Hindi Novel* (Shimla: Indian Institute of Advanced Study, 1993).

Kapadia, Novy. *Parsi Fiction*. Vol. 1 (New Delhi: Prestige Books, 2001).

Kesavan, Mukul. *Looking Through Glass* (New Delhi: Ravi Dayal Publisher, 1995).

Padma, V. 'Neither on Either Side nor In-between: the Anglo-Indian and Post-Colonial Indian Fiction in English'. *Presentations of Postcolonialisms in English*. Ed. Jaydeep Sarangi ( New Delhi: Author Press, 2007), 127–44.

Padmanabhan, Mukund. 'Drenched in Déjà Vu'. Review of *Red Earth and Pouring Rain* by Vikram Chandra. *Indian Review of Books* 4, no. 8 (1995): 2–3.

Patil, Vishwas. *Jhadajhadati.* 1990. Trans. Gajanan Chauhan from the Marathi into Hindi (New Delhi: Vani Prakashan, 1995).

Pillai, Thakazhi Sivasankara. *Kayar. (Coir)* . Trans. N. Sreekantan Nair from Malayalam into English (New Delhi: Sahitya Akademi, 1997).

Prem and Ramesh. *Ki. Rajanarayanan: Ezhuthulagam.* (Tamil). (The World of Ki. Rajanarayan's Writing) (Chennai: Kalaignan Padippagam, 2000).

Rajanarayanan, Ki. *Gopalla Gramam.* (Tamil). (Sivagangai: Selma, 1976).

———. *Gopallapurathu Makkal.* 1990. 2nd Ed. (Tamil). (Sivagangai: Selma, 1993).

Renan, Ernest. 'What is a Nation?' *Nation and Narration*. Ed. Homi Bhaba. (1990; London: Routledge, rpt. 1991), 8–23.

Rollason, Christopher. 'Vikram Chandra's *Red Earth and Pouring Rain*: Entwining Narratives and Intertextuality'. *IndiaStar Review of Books*, 23 March 2001, http://www. indiastar.com

Rushdie, Salman. *Shame* (New Delhi: Rupa and Co., 1983).

Said, Edward. *Representations of the Intellectual: The 1993 Reith Lectures* (London: Vintage, 1994).

———. *Reflections on Exile and Other Literary and Cultural Essays* (New York: Penguin Books, 2001).

Sardar, Ziauddin. Introduction. Ashis Nandy, *Return from Exile* ( New Delhi: Oxford UP, 1998).

Wilfred, Felix. 'Whose Nation? Whose History?' *The Struggle for the Past: Historiography Today*. Eds. Felix Wilfred and Jose D. Maliekal. Chennai Department of Christian Studies, University of Madras: 2002, 71–99.

# 5

# DEVELOPMENT AND ITS DISCONTENTS: THE STATE AND PROGRAMMES OF DEVELOPMENT

## *JHADAJHADATI*, *ANGALIYAT*, *KARUKKU*, *BREAKING TIES* AND *THE MOTH-EATEN HOWDAH OF THE TUSKER*

The previous chapter showed how fiction was used to correct or rewrite the form and content of histories of marginalised communities. Simultaneously, fiction has also provided the necessary space for discussions on various social, cultural and political issues, notably those which have been pressing themselves upon India in the last couple of decades. Many of these concerns incorporate India's attempts after Independence to create as just and utopian a society as possible.

Nehru's famous 'tryst with destiny' conceived of an India that was young, vibrant, full of promise, and eager to make itself one of the major economic and industrial powers of the world. The large-scale industrialisation and modernisation that followed the years immediately after 1947 began the process of what has been called 'development' – a concept that has changed shape and taken on different connotations over the five decades since. As development itself changed, so did attitudes and approaches to it. And more than any other form of literature, fiction, with its ability to address many individual, communal and national issues, has offered itself as one space where the idea, processes and execution of development can be depicted, debated and critiqued.

The very idea of development implies progress. When seen in terms of the nation, it involves the 'growth' of the entire nation. However, the parameters that decide this growth have changed over the years. In recent times, these parameters are largely economic and financial. Two dictionary definitions may make this clear: *The Longman Dictionary of Contemporary English* (International Edition 2004) defines development thus: 'A developed country is one of the rich countries of the world with many industries, comfortable living for most people, and usually an elected government' (428) while the *New Penguin English Dictionary* (2000) identifies a developed country as one that has 'achieved a high economic level of industrialisation and a high standard of living' (381). While both these definitions base themselves largely on the financial status of a nation, the political philosophy of the nation too is partly taken into account.

The allure of the idea of development as defined above has been such that the world has become divided into categories of 'developed,' 'developing,' and 'under-developed'. The hierarchy implied in this division has constituted development as a competitive concept making it almost necessary for the countries falling into the last two categories to try and 'match up' to the standards of the developed countries. There often little or no debate regarding the necessity of such 'catching up'.

This competition to reach the ideal development standards creates a vicious cycle wherein the developing and underdeveloped countries require funds for their development from the very same countries whom they are trying to emulate. Their dependence upon international monetary agencies like the World Bank and the International Monetary Fund only renders their dependency upon these already developed nations[1] irreversible.

However, it is necessary to include issues of human rights and social justice also within the purview of development. Although we rarely see the degree of liberty given to the citizens of a nation as a marker of its 'developed' status, this aspect is implied in the *Penguin Dictionary's* definition of a developed country as one that usually has an 'elected government', and an 'elected government' implies political equality to the citizens. That the literacy percentage of a country should also be a marker of its level of development is yet another instance of defining development in terms of non-economic criteria. However, in recent years, there have been several studies of how this 'literacy' is gauged. If merely knowing to sign one's name is the standard of literacy, then the socially progressive role performed by education is invalidated by it. The question of who defines development and in whose terms—in other words, the perspective from which to view development—therefore becomes a contention.

The notion of 'perspective' in discussing development naturally revokes the idea that it is a universal and incontrovertible concept. In the specific case of India, we can easily discern such differential perspectives, both across time and especially in the contemporary social scene.

Our reading and understanding of earlier civilisations and cultures within the paradigm of development often reflect our own understanding of the idea. Hence, when we label the Indus valley civilisation as 'developed' because of its very advanced health services and other comfort levels, we also make a judgement on what we consider as the benchmarks of development. It has rarely been suggested that ancient civilisations or rulers of one region tried to 'catch up' with other civilisations or rulers elsewhere by providing these facilities. One of the other indices of 'development' is the position of women. Recent feminist criticisms have pointed to the flaws in the nationalist historiographies of India that painted a glorious pre-colonial and pre-Islamic world where women enjoyed great advantages and high positions. Their accusation that it was contact with the Islamic and non-Hindu world which caused the slow degradation of the position of women has been used to construct a religion-based nation and to assert the supremacy of Indian culture (*Themes*, x).

The colonial period, however, saw a change in the attitude towards development, mainly because it was linked by the colonial discourse to the idea of modernity. The British chose to justify their colonisation of India by projecting the value of, say, the railways, the telegraph, the system of English medicine, the legal system etc. as markers of modern civilisation. By making such connections and by stressing the role of the imperial regime in bringing them to India, the British attempted to rationalise their colonisation of India. This attempt however, met with stiff opposition. Mahatma Gandhi, in his *Hind Swaraj* (1938), systematically denied as modern each of the British indicators of comfort. For instance, he argued that the British legal system only brought in a set of middlemen and denied direct legal access to the common man. Similarly, he argued, citing the Indian spiritual ideal of self-control, that he need not travel any farther than where his feet would take him, thereby questioning the spiritual value of the railways. Although many of Gandhi's arguments may appear lopsided or even absurd, we must remember that he was writing at a time in history when the need was to assert national identity and attack the British in practical and discursive terms. Another critique of this colonial theory of modernity came from the Marxists who argued that even had the British not brought in the railways, the telegraph etc. they would nonetheless have come to India, perhaps a little later. They further argued that this 'delay' need not necessarily have had a negative impact on India.

Both the above arguments challenge the British definition of 'modernity;' but while Gandhiji questions the very definition of what is modern (and by extension, 'developed'), the second set of arguments denies centrality to the colonial powers as the agency for the change. We arrive therefore at two aspects which make up development – the definition (that is what *is* a 'developed country' and what are its markers) and the agency (who/ what brings in this change). To this, we may add two more elements – that of implementation (that is, how are these changes brought about through what modes of execution) and assumptions (what makes us see the above 'markers of development' as such). The last can be exemplified by a reference to the British benchmarks of modernity – the assumption there being that facilities of easier communication and faster travel are necessarily positive changes in a society.

With Independence, however, the scene changed in India. Given autonomy of governance, India could decide *what* and *how* to develop as well as consciously choose the model for development. The agency for any programmed changes was now the Indian government itself. Moreover, statistics regarding such programmed developmental interventions—both for economic uplift and for social justice or human rights—function as governmental data which is often used for self-projection. It is based on this data that India is classified among nations as 'developed' or not. Hence, the decision of where and how to intervene plays an important role in the definition of the nation.

The model that India chose for planned development was that of the five-year plans, which are basically a structured budgeting of money for the next five years, the period coinciding with one normal tenure of any government. According to the plan, certain sums of money are allotted to different sectors such as education, defence, agriculture and heavy industries. We are now (2008) nearing the end of the Eleventh Plan and a survey of the ten previous plans is quite revealing. The accent on heavy industries and agriculture in the first three to four plans slowly gave way in the Fifth Plan to the motto 'Growth *for* Social Justice' rather than 'Growth *with* Social Justice.' The present plan has 'Towards faster and more inclusive growth' as its central theme. In effect, this change in motto gave a different, more humanist meaning to the very idea of development and directly brought the issue of human rights issues within its purview. The greatest difference, however, can be seen from the Ninth Plan (1992–1997) when, based on the Common Minimum Programme, the following objectives were decided upon:

a. priority to agriculture and rural development; aiming at generating productive employment and eradication of poverty;
b. price stability and acceleration of growth rate;
c. *food and nutritional security for 'vulnerable section';*
d. *basic minimum services of safe water, health facilities, primary education etc.;*
e. containing growth rate of population;
f. *ensuring environmental sustainability of development programmes;*
g. *empowerment of women and socially disadvantaged groups;*
h. promoting development of Panchayati raj;
i. ensuring self-reliance.

(*Manorama Year Book*, 2001)

The specifically highlighted points show how issues pertaining to human rights have been shifted under the rubric of development.

Many human rights issues do need the intervention of the judiciary and legislature to make such rights prevail. Although these do not come under the five-year plans (that is, no money is separately allotted for them), they can legitimately be seen as part of the strategies employed by the government to provide equal rights and opportunities for different sections of society.

Well-meant and often well-thought-out though many of these plans are, they have been censured from a variety of perspectives for faulty execution and lopsided assumptions. For instance, environmentalists claim that many projects of industrialisation have led to the degradation of the environment by posing a threat to life forms. Witness the furore surrounding the Narmada Valley now and the Silent Valley in the early 1980s. Postcolonial critics like Akhil

Gupta question the long-term validity of major projects like the Green Revolution which, despite increasing agricultural production, led also to loss of natural fertility of the soil (5). Gender offers itself as yet another marginal position from which to critique many developmental interventions. Feminist economists claim that the economic reforms and privatisation have resulted in skilled labour being replaced by machinery, thereby rendering many women jobless. The underlying assumption that women are naturally machinery-illiterate only augments the problem. Simultaneously, the fact that women's work in the unorganised sector is not considered as a contribution to national income is also brought to light. Legal experts take issue with successive governments for failing to implement or even seriously consider the Uniform Civil Code (UCC). Lawyers such as Archana Parashar and Zoya Hasan contend that governments have regarded the issue as one pertaining solely to minority religious communities whereas a large part of Family and Personal Laws affect women and that therefore the UCC should at least partly be treated as a gender issue. Similarly, caste activists argue that despite the passing of laws and legal reforms in favour of depressed castes and classes, there has been little change in society's attitude towards them. In this, the fault is seen to lie largely in the ineffectual implementation of these laws and what is more distressing, the lack of awareness of the reforms among its beneficiaries.

Fiction has been telling the stories of development for long, both from the nationalist angle as well as from the perspective of its victims. A definite change, however, can be perceived in the way it has addressed the issue after 1980. The general trend of the fiction of the era, as already noted, has been towards a greater discursivity. Novels dealing with development too show a nuanced understanding of the issue. Unlike an earlier novel, such as Kamala Markandaya's *Nectar in a Sieve* (1954) where the struggle against development was seen in terms of the time-worn battle between tradition and modernity, recent novels take us into the very heart of development projects or legal reforms; they either directly or implicitly tell us of the pros and cons involved. Rather than merely representing the issue in terms of a struggle between tradition and modernity, these novels call for different models of development and reforms so that the harm done to communities and societies may be minimised. They act as a forum wherein issues of public interest may be debated and discussed. The range of positions from which such texts speak is as varied as there are concerns and debates. This chapter will discuss three such issues – the government's irrigation projects, the attempts to alleviate caste hierarchies through affirmative action and the endeavours to give greater rights to women through legal reforms. The analysis of selected novels hopes to show that reading them in the light of these projects and reforms will require us to reconsider formal features as well.

## *JHADAJHADATI* AND THE GOVERNMENT'S IRRIGATION PROGRAMMES

Set in the remote village of Jhambali in Maharashtra, *Jhadajhadati* [2] tells the saga of suffering that it has to undergo because of the large dam which is to be built over the river that flows through and irrigates it. It therefore becomes almost natural that we read the novel against the background not only of the aims of, but also the reasons for such irrigation projects and see how the text questions different dimensions of such projects.

Irrigation projects are primarily an attempt to provide one of the basic human needs, namely water, to all sections of society and to make this water easily available for purposes of agriculture. Since a large amount of national income is generated out of agriculture (statistically, agricultural products constitute the fourth largest income-generating items in India, amounting to a total of 14, 963 crore rupees in 1998–99 [*Manorama Year Book, 2001*]), providing water for this purpose becomes a matter of national concern. Moreover, such projects, as Jai Nimbkar mentions at the beginning of her review titled 'Disturbing and Depressing' in *Indian Review of Books*, help in overcoming the dependence of agriculture on erratic monsoons, making available electricity for rural areas and providing employment and basic health facilities (SS). We may note that the objectives address what is termed the 'practical needs' of a community. In the federal system of government, irrigation projects and water facilities come under the purview of the state governments, which however need to get the funds for these projects from the government at the centre. The entire process therefore requires a good deal of teamwork since a lot of planning and documentation is required. For this very reason, they are open to rampant misuse owing to human greed and avarice, especially given the power-mongering nature of rural India today.

*Jhadajhadati* is not against the idea of development itself—for such interventions *are* necessary to correct geographical inequalities—but is critical of the underlying assumptions and the implementation of such projects which show a total disregard for human beings.

Irrigation projects have been divided to mainly two kinds, medium and major irrigation projects. Medium irrigation projects have a Culturable Command Area (CCA) between 2,000 and 10,000 hectares and major irrigation projects a CCA of more than 10,000 hectares. By the end of the Ninth Plan, i.e. by 1997, there were a total of 402 irrigation projects (*Manorama Year Book 2001*). Most of these statistics are official and have usually been projected by the government and government agencies to highlight the achievements of planning and development charted out and followed by them. While they would have been quite unquestioningly accepted for a long time, today they are regarded with severe reservation, as it is understood that these projects—especially the major ones—are fulfilled with disastrous effects on the flora, fauna and the indigenous people living in the areas where a given dam is to be built. The rightful publicity given to the Narmada Bachao Andolan and earlier to the Silent Valley Rebellion in Kerala have made the common people all the more keenly aware of this condition. One such instance forms the central theme of *Jhadajhadati*.

The proposed Jhambali dam project would help irrigate around 18, 000 hectares of land. It forms therefore, definitely part of a major project. Such a large project needs for its implementation active participation by the beneficiaries as well as those adversely affected by it. The idea of needs-based participation is one of the cornerstones of development theories today. Anand Sarup, a civil servant who has worked for eighteen years in planning and Sulabha Brahme, an economist, have categorically stated that, 'before starting their work, planners must find out what different individuals and sections of the public in different parts of the country want for themselves' (*Planning for the Millions*, 11). The idea of people's participation foregrounds the democratic basis of any ideal development project besides making the project itself benefit the maximum number of people with minimum possible damage.

*Jhadajhadati* however, describes how the very idea of a participatory and needs-based project planning is nullified by the greed and selfishness of the local politicians. The Jhambali project is initiated so that the villages of Khairpur and Baghethan—neighbouring Jhambali—would get the water they had been denied for ages due to natural reasons: 'Ambepur was a district between Pune and Satara. Its Baghethan village had some geographical peculiarities. To its west lay the famous hills of Sahayadri. There is widespread rain there, but to the east, absolute drought. The people there have almost got used to living in the drought' (57).

The plan to build the dam, however, is initiated not as a goodwill gesture or as a genuine attempt to help the people of Baghethan; the dam is to be built so that the local MP—Shingade Patil—can provide his son with a sugar factory in Baghethan. The omniscient authorial voice in the novel, without once interrupting the flow of dialogue, manages to debunk the politicians who make a mockery of the idea of participatory planning, by merely reporting the dialogue between the MP and his son:

> Shingade Patil had put forth the plan for Jhambhali dam when he was quite young. After all, his hundred and fifty acres would get irrigated and so with him, the village would also prosper. He tried his best to get his proposal accepted, turned all possible stones, but could not succeed . . . . He had a huge godown of fertilisers. He was personally against alcoholism, but his two nephews had three country liquor shops in Ambepur. When these two have managed to stand on their own feet, why worry about all these small things? Apart from these, he also had a petrol pump in Ambepur and another in Baghethan. Somehow with all these he made both ends meet.
>
> He was quite convinced that the dam would not be built in his lifetime. For some years, he had also forgotten about it. But four years ago, his eldest progeny returned from Pune after completing a degree in law. The demand for Jhambali dam got renewed strength in Shingade's *haveli* after that. This, not without good reason. When his eldest offspring was studying at S. P. College, two of his classmates had become ministers in the state assembly. One's father had already got him a sugar mill under the cooperative scheme and then left the field open for the son. This was not something easily forgotten. On this, Shingade and his son had many arguments:
>
> 'Tell me, Aaba, what have you left for me?'
> 'Son, for our country's freedom, I have …'
> 'All that's old yarn. Talk about today.'
>
> Shingade understood that his son would not so easily be talked off. And after all, what had he asked? Only a sugar mill, that's all. So Shingade Patil decided: the factory would be built at any cost. His dear son's wishes have to be fulfilled. The development of the district was an

> added advantage; killing two birds with one stone. To get permission to open the factory was no big deal for Shingade Patil: he had enough influence in Delhi and Bombay. Father and son put pressure and soon had collected shares to the amount of a few lakhs . . . (57–58).

The irony implied in the statement, 'The development of the district was an added advantage; killing two birds with one stone' paints a sorry picture of how ideas initiated with best intentions can be made to go awry by human avarice. It is also important to note that so much stress is laid on sugar factories. Sugar is the political power base in rural Maharashtra and hence, establishing sugar factories is part of securing power and political uplift and power in these areas. That local leadership can effectively make use of its 'influence' in 'Delhi and Bombay' (the national and state capital) tells us how the supposed interaction between regional and national levels actually takes place. The picture of rural India which emerges from just this one interaction is a far cry from earlier portrayals of the village as an idyllic beauty that is sullied by the entry of industries and insignia of 'development'. The dialogue quoted above also brings out how nationalist discourses—and this includes the discourse of national development—often act as electoral strategies for political parties to seize power. Shingade Patil's imprisonment during the freedom struggle is summarily dismissed by his son as 'old yarn', but is used by his party in gaining the 'respect' of the people. Like many other exposé of current-day politics, this too is brought out with a tinge of irony: 'During the freedom movement, he had faced imprisonment for two months and thirteen days. From then on, he had great influence in the politics of his state' (57). Patil's greed, when placed against this, is a very telling comment on the inefficiency of the democratic system that still idolises freedom fighters irrespective of their activities today.

While the political and personal motive behind the project is one of the reasons for its failure, the novel also implicitly critiques the assumptions behind such development projects. Ecofeminist critics—especially Vandana Shiva—have pointed out that most development projects try to make maximum rather than optimum use of natural resources, thereby bringing untold misery upon various life forms. In *Staying Alive* Shiva relates this attitude to Western masculinity and therefore brands most theories of development as patriarchal. The verity of this claim can be best seen in *Jhadajhadati* when the leader of the agitation—Khairmode Master—suggests the alternative of building three small dams instead of one large one:

> Why are you removing these villages? Why do you want to destroy these settlements? Won't it be better to make three small dams instead of one big one? Then no village will need to be evacuated. The other region will also get water. These people will not need to be displaced and we won't have to bear the burden of leaving the village. And development there definitely will be (*Jhadajhadati*, 64).

It is the response that is significant: 'The leaders and officers could not understand this superior intellect of Masterji. Who does he think he is? The Chief Engineer? It's simple – bigger the dam, more the water; more the water, more the development' (64). It is precisely this assumption that is responsible for the numerous problems which arise in dam building and irrigation projects. It appears as though the projects have been introduced by the government merely to show statistics and figures, and huge figures do look good in the international scene and brighten the prospect of grants from international funding agencies.

The importance of statistical data for national projection cannot be overstated. The government often uses statistics to showcase the benchmarks of 'development' and to stress the large numbers of people who have benefited from various projects. For long taken as redoubtable, these statistics are today suspect; they may misrepresent figures or show only a lopsided picture of the situation, even completely underplay and erase the stories of victims of such projects. The interpretation given to these statistics too plays an important role in the government's self-projection. The adverse effects of these projects were seen as necessary attendant evils; when viewed against the largeness of the benefits, the few undesirable side effects were seen as negligible. Today, however, we take a different view of the matter. Without questioning the necessity of the project itself, we have come to realise that action needs to be taken to avoid or correct these undesirable fallouts. It is this concern that we find in *Jhadajhadati*.

Government statistics enters into the very text of the novel. In public meetings and official gatherings, different kinds of data regarding the dam are presented. Again, the narrative voice does not openly deny the validity of these statistics. However, the structure of the novel is such that these statistics (and the government's interpretation of them) are juxtaposed with the stories generally considered unimportant in the light of the benefits projected by the rest of the data. This juxtaposition gives the text a highly ironic tone that allows it to offer a different version of the same project. For instance in one of the earliest public meetings held to justify the dam project, the politician openly says:

> the dam will cause five villages to be fully and four to be partially destroyed. It will facilitate irrigation of 18,000 hectares of land. The government has decided to spend a sum of forty-five crore rupees to build this dam and forever remove drought from Baghethan. Once the dam is completed, so much can be produced from the land that the farmers will feel they have got hold of nothing less than diamonds and pearls (60).

It will be noticed that the speech does not deny the prospect of the destruction of villages; it merely sees this destruction as inevitable and necessary. This 'inevitability' is suggested by never mentioning the destruction again, and by focusing on the benefits using exaggerated metaphorical language. The same technique is employed by the author to subvert this interpretation; the novel does not question the benefits or the statistics, but tells the stories of the people affected by the project. The extent of damage done, something the government glosses over, is heightened by its formal structure.

Like the Gopallapuram chronicles, *Jhadajhadati* too tells a series of apparently unrelated stories of people belonging to a single village. Much like a chronicle novel, it describes a fairly long period in the recent history of Jhambali. However, the connecting link in the Marathi novel is not merely the village, but the way in which the village will be affected by the dam. In fact, the dam becomes the means of uniting the village itself. That the novel weaves in and out of the stories of various families in Jhambali reiterates the magnitude of the damage done by the dam. In contrast to a novel like say, *Nectar in a Sieve* where the process of industrialisation and pollution is presented from the perspective of a single woman, *Jhadajhadati* gives us varied stories of loss, suffering and homelessness. It is because the novel chronicles the sufferings of an entire village that it becomes a valuable counter document to government's reports on developmental projects.

An important feature that we noted in chronicle novels discussed in the last chapter was that these novels did not move out of the village/community/area in which they were set. This feature affirmed the centrality of the village/community over any individual in the text. *Jhadajhadati* varies from such chronicle novels in this important regard: the text does move, along with the entire village, into Baghethan. This is made necessary by the theme – that of evacuation and rehabilitation as a consequence of the dam. It is this that provides the core of the human drama to the novel. It is the inability of the government to mitigate if not avoid the adverse effects of the project that is most severely criticised. This criticism becomes all the more strong when we take into consideration the fact that the author himself was a rehabilitation officer who was once put in charge of relocating an entire project-affected village. Many of the stories forming part of *Jhadajhadati* are drawn from his personal experiences. The novel therefore, becomes in a special way, a first-hand critique of various facets of development projects.

Rehabilitation is a necessary correlative in any development project which causes complete or partial destruction of habitable areas or life forms. In the case of the Jhambali project, at least four to five villages will be partially submerged and alternative living arrangements for these villagers have to be made by the government. Evacuating and resituating an entire village, however, is a daunting task and various kinds of practical, documentational and emotional problems have to be faced. In its impersonal execution of the plans, the government machinery does not give any weight to the emotional attachment of a people to their land. At the same time, heavy stress is laid on documentary proof in order that an individual be considered for rehabilitation and compensation. The uneducated status of the villagers—especially women—and the red tape involved in getting the necessary documents create some very pathetic, at the same time absurd, situations that merely go to reiterate the inefficiency of the ways in which development projects are implemented.

Rehabilitation involves the shifting of an entire village to a new location; here the Jhambali villagers are moved to the nearby village of Baghethan, the village that will eventually be the beneficiary of the Jhambali dam project. However, the decision is taken by an impersonal machinery and villagers from both the villages are not consulted at all with any serious intent. The Jhambali villagers *are* taken to Baghethan to 'see' their new 'home', but their opinion for or against the programme is not given much importance. The villagers of Baghethan are shown to be quite hostile to the idea of admitting new entrants into their locale. It is here that the impersonality of the government machinery becomes a deterrent. The villagers of Baghethan belong to a caste higher than the inhabitants of Jhambali; they therefore actively resent being compelled to share their village with them. The fact that the Jhambali villagers have been forced to evacuate due to a project that benefits Baghethan does not soften the opposition and animosity. The irony is sharpest when we get to know that the villagers of Jhambali get neither places to stay in nor safe drinking water in their new village. That a project which was conceived to provide one of the basic minimum facilities for one village merely snatches the same facility from another village is a sharp indictment of the entire process of planning and execution of such large-scale development projects.

A lot of documentation inheres in the process of rehabilitation. For instance, an individual has to fall under the category of 'project-affected' to get the benefits of compensation for land taken over for the dam site. To prove that one indeed comes under this category, documentary proof is needed. In the absence of such proof—at times because many villagers in Jhambali took their ownership of their ancestral land for granted—compensation is denied. The stories of people who fall prey to this dependence upon written evidence interrupts the saga of Jhambali at various places, sometimes creating absurd situations. One villager, for instance, is denied compensation because although his land was submerged due to the dam, it did not come under the area that the government had marked out as being covered by the dam. Even the people who did get compensation got it at a six-year old rate because the plans for the rehabilitation and compensation were that old. While some youngsters like Gunavant and Haibati get 'government jobs' as part of their compensation, and these jobs are promised at a public meeting in attempts to pacify irate villagers and an agitated leader, letters making them permanent government employees never reach them. In the absence of such letters, the government is unable to give Gunavant's widow a job when he dies, thereby passing on the problems arising out of the project to future generations as well. For permanent jobs, as Gajju finds out, bribing is necessary. Even when compensation for land is being given, some amount is automatically deducted for the farmers' Small Savings Scheme, because the rehabilitation officer's wife is an agent for this scheme and needs her commission. It may be remembered that the Small Savings Scheme was introduced by the government to reduce the dependency of the farmers upon rich landowners. The distress of the farmers who are already grappling with practical and financial aspects of the evacuation is a sad comment on how even the best ideas may be twisted for personal benefits. Yet another, perhaps the most absurd, situation in the novel involves Bannu Kaaki and subtly questions the extent to which we need to rely on documentation and certification. Narrated, like most other incidents, as a simple dialogue, the incident takes on ludicrous overtones:

> 'What's your name?'
> 'Bannu – Bannu Sawleram Karbande.'
> 'Is the sarpanch your son?'
> 'Yes, my husband's other wife's son – he's my husband's son only.'
> The officer became a little calmer. Lazily, he said, 'Old lady, you won't get any money'.
> 'What? How will I not get any money?' Bannu Kaaki almost screamed.
> 'You are dead.'
> 'What? I am dead?' Twisting her face a little, Bannu Kaaki said, 'Saab, why are you joking with an old woman like me?'
> 'But that's what is written in the record, no?'
> 'What is that?'
> 'Your stepson has given a statement of your death and got your death certificate. He has taken both your shares of the money long back.'
> 'Saab, you yourself tell me, what am I to do?'
> 'Get a certificate to prove you are alive.'
> 'But, saab, you are seeing, no? I am very much alive,' Bannu Kaaki began to cry loudly.
> 'Old woman, crying won't help you in any way. You will have to get that certificate,' the officer said loudly.
> 'But, saab, I am alive . . .'
> 'We need written proof of that. Get a certificate like that.' (*Jhadajhadati*, 102)

Illiterate as she is and having no direct access to law, the long-winding legal procedures that follow make it ultimately impossible for Bannu Kaaki to get the money due to her.

Apart from the financial and practical aspects of rehabilitation, the entire process involves intense emotional trauma. The attachment to 'home' and 'native land' in the Indian context is fraught with passionate sentiments. One's native village is associated with one's ancestors and for many Indian families, a village or town is seeped in memories of several generations. It is almost natural that many people wish to die in their 'native' land and would like to perform the marriages of their children there. The natural beauties of the native village have been a source of inspiration (sometimes made romantic by nostalgia) for generations of poets.

Given this, evacuating a village that had existed peacefully for centuries is no mean task. Vishwas Patil in an interview titled 'A Man, Fair Enough to Understand their Grief' puts it perhaps in the best possible way:

> For most of us, the mere thought of moving, even temporarily from one city to another, is frightening. For the serpent that lives in one's backyard is a friend, the ghosts and spirits that haunt the neighbourhood are acquaintances. But those of a new place immediately become fearsome. To have to give up for ever, one's familiar surroundings, must be a traumatic experience. (SS, 2)

He further asserts that 'resettling a [people] means uprooting them from all that they have ever known. It is not a joke, not even for the government' (SS, 2).

Much of the emotional stress in the novel comes from the reluctance of the Jhambali villagers to move and the trauma they face in the process. We find, perhaps naturally, that women are most affected and are most vociferous in trying to stall the evacuation. One of the first to fight against the very idea of the dam is Aavadai, a woman who made Jhambali her home after her marriage to Govinda. Her first startling attempt to stop the project at the *bhumipujan* (consecration of the land) is a reflection of the emotional attachment that people—especially women—have to their homes. This protest takes place ten years before the present of the novel and is therefore set at a point much before Khairmode Master even thinks of organising the villagers against the project:

> A lot of people had come for the *bhoomipujan* – the minister, MP Shingade Patil and many people from the drought-ridden area had come. A huge ceremony had been organised.... Aavadai saw Jhambali through the leaves of the trees and shrubs. Her eyes widened. She felt that the village deity was being submerged in the water. Houses were floating away in it. Animals were gasping for breath. . . . Aavadai was screaming, 'Why are you bent upon destroying us? Only because you can live happily? Don't you have mothers and sisters? Don't you have a household?' At that time, there were only a few policemen there. The minister and the officers shrank back. The *bhumipujan* ceremony came to an abrupt end, scattered. Aavadai, Khairmode Masterji, Pandu Yetala and many others from the village were arrested. All of them spent six days in prison. (*Jhadajhadati*, 39)

This rebellion is repeated in the present of the text when again Aavadai tries her own simple way of practically stopping the destruction of her house – she simply lies down in the path of the approaching bulldozer.

That Aavadai is emphatic about her husband's hard work in the creation of the house may seem to smack of internalisation of patriarchy from certain feminist standpoints, but built into Aavadai's resistance and anger is the agony of being forced to remove not only herself, but also memories which had gathered over the years. Moreover, it is today widely recognised that it is women who face the most trouble both in the process of moving out of an old home as well as moving into a new one. Apart from the practical problems involved, there is also apprehension about the reception in the new village; the availability of items of basic needs like water, grocery and the accessibility of medical facilities is no small matter. In many cases, very real dangers like eve-teasing and rape are an issue to be considered. The woman's attachment to her 'home'—her marital home—is therefore not to be so contemptuously taken as an example of her acquiescence to patriarchal ideology that dictates that she forget her natal home after marriage; there is the practical aspect to the issue in the Indian context. It is only upon marriage that a woman has a position of power as the mistress of a household—she physically brings up the house and makes it live-able—planting trees, bringing up animals give her, perhaps, a natural attachment to it. The prospect of years of hard work and emotion invested going to waste is what makes projects like the Jhambali project so sinister to people like Aavadai. The attachment that her family has to the village is brought out in their anxiety over their son Haibati's wedding – not the wedding itself, but the question of *where* it will be celebrated.

Unexpected problems arise in the marriage due to the dam because no girl is willing to marry into a family that is 'dam-affected' (*'bāndh peedith'*).

This puts the very idea of 'project-affected'—in this case 'dam-affected'—at more personal and even religious levels. As the novel moves, we realise that being 'dam-affected' becomes equivalent to being punished. The very title of the novel reiterates this – 'jhadajhadati' in Marathi means undeserved punishment or being punished without knowing the reason for the punishment. The people of Jhambali village begin to feel like pawns in a greater game over which they have no control. Masterji initially tells one student, 'Son, you must definitely have committed some sin in your past life, that's why you have been born in the house of a dam-affected in this birth' (142). The idea gets stronger as the days go by. Worried about her heavily pregnant daughter-in-law, Aavadai is nevertheless forced to keep her in the open in their 'new' village. When Anu advises Aavadai, 'it is not right to keep a heavily pregnant woman in the open air,' Aavadai's replies stoically, 'We have left our homes and households because of the dam. What of us? Open air and indoors, all are the same' (221).

It is the government's inability and even refusal to understand these aspects of resettlement that makes the very idea of evacuation and rehabilitation so emotionally charged. By centring the novel around these stories, *Jhadajhadati* subtly demands better implementation of policies and asks for a more sensitive understanding of human problems and emotions while planning such large-scale projects.

Simultaneously, the novel also frowns upon the politicisation of rural India and throws into relief different kinds of leadership. Critical focus on this would bring back the idea of human agency into criticism itself, for novels like *Jhadajhadati* openly declare that since it is human beings who have to carry out plans and strategies, even the best ideas are vitiated by human frailties. In one way, the novel shows the heights of selfless service that certain leaders like Khairmode Master can reach. Characters like Khairmode Masterji remind us of real-life leaders like Baba Amte and Medha Patkar who have been helping the local populace to organise themselves into a moral force. It is to be recalled that Vishwas Patil wrote this novel much before the Narmada dam controversy became a household name.

The politicisation of the project is so bad, however, that gender issues enter here as well. Khairmode's daughter Shewanta is raped in order that her father may stop his agitation. This again is a common enough trope in reality and in fiction: violence inflicted upon women is often a stratagem to demoralise the male members of a community. Underlying these actions are socially conditioned notions of honour and chastity (mostly female chastity as a measure by which to gauge male honour). However, within the space of this novel, poetic justice is meted out as the boys of Shewanta's area teach her rapists a lesson.

Quite unlike Khairmode are the local politicians who stoop to anything to gain power. Leaders like Shingade Patil and Taya Kamble represent that side of rural leadership that makes the best of us question the value of democracy itself. Indeed, each of their actions denies many of the assumptions of democracy and human rights, including the right to live in any place of one's choice. Despite well-meaning leaders and officials from the Central Government signing documents to provide suitable compensation, the local leadership cleverly subverts everything to suit its self-interest. Even the land given to the Jhambali villagers in Baghethan is un-cultivable; and when at all something *is* grown, the local leadership snatches the benefits.

*Jhadajhadati* therefore also acts as a novel wherein the very process of democratic governance is questioned. The massive Jhambali dam project brings out both the best and the worst in politicians and leaders and therefore many of the characters in the novel are static. People are shown in various roles and capacities; but they remain good, evil or merely pathetic throughout. The tragedy in the novel is not that of a single human being as in many earlier novels like *Nectar in a Sieve*. By portraying the loss of spirit of an entire village, *Jhadajhadati* writes a kind of tragedy that is caused not by one's character but by the State machinery and the ways in which the democratic system has degenerated from its original ideal. It may be tempting to give the novel a 'universal' meaning of tragedy for at a basic level indeed, the novel *does* seem to call for a criticism that foregrounds issues of human greed and eccentricities. For instance, Sankar Sarda's note sent to the Saraswati Samman committee when the novel was being considered for the award centres on morality, goodness and immorality and greed. It further links the sufferings of the dam-affected people to the eternal sufferings of the characters of the Ramayana and the Mahabharata: 'but from one point of view, problems of rehabilitation of 12,000 dam-affected people is just the outward subject of the novel. The true struggle is eternal like the Mahabharata. It is originated from the eccentric greed of the human mind' (SS). This search for overarching patterns in the grand narratives of the epics does, of course, provide a strong universal tone to the novel, yet it runs the danger of denying the contextual specificity of the novel and its contemporaneity.

*Jhadajhadati* uses the fictional space to raise certain portentous issues confronting the Indian people today. Questions regarding the cost at which development takes place and the ways in which our system is vulnerable to abuse, all form part of the recent history of the Jhambali community. Even the organised protest under the leadership of Khairmode Master remains inadequate in the face of the communal tragedy, a tragedy that is caused ultimately by the modalities of the state in providing basic health, water and irrigation facilities to all sections of Indian society.

## Caste and Affirmative Action: *Karukku* and *Angaliyat*

While *Jhadajhadati* lays the blame for the Jhambali tragedy on the faulty planning and implementation of large-scale projects, the government's measures for providing social equality to weaker sections of society too have come under attack, at times by the beneficiaries of these plans themselves. Two such 'weak' or repressed sections of Indian society are the Dalits and women. In both the cases, the government claims to be taking 'affirmative actions' and enforcing constitutional and legal reforms in order to alter the existing social hierarchy. How many of these reforms or affirmative actions have actually helped in changing the social structure and transforming people's attitudes towards Dalits and women is a moot point. That the majority of beneficiaries of such reforms remain unaware of the legal and legislative privileges granted to them is another cause for worry. Critiques of such reforms and affirmative actions often demand a deeper understanding of the social conditions which engender the inequalities in the first place and also ask for greater publicity to be given to these reforms. The Sixth National Conference of Women's Movement (held in Ranchi in 1997), for instance, called for more meaningful debates of policy changes in public forums (*Themes* xii) and we can see how fiction from the 1980s has been increasingly performing this demanding task.

The rise and growth of Dalit literature in the last twenty years or so and its subsequent acceptance and even canonisation by the academia, the theoretical and publishing world has attracted much attention. Is Dalit literature merely 'fashionable' or does it offer a serious threat to orthodoxy in society as well as aesthetics? There is a school of thought that the translation and publication of Dalit texts—especially the autobiography—into English is orchestrated by a group of non-Dalits who prefer to choose only those texts which deal with experiences of poverty and oppression and none that actively pose a threat to caste-Hindu orthodoxy. Commentators and ideologues like S. Ravikumar and S. Anand are of the firm view that this is the culture within which Dalit texts in English translation are 'consumed'. In fact, Ravikumar puts it quite strongly when he says, 'In the Tamil Bhakti tradition, some poets referred to themselves as 'dog' vis-à-vis their gods. Today, several Dalit writers seem to be performing a similar role vis-à-vis non-Dalit readers' (*Touchable Tales*, 9). Such arguments arise from a feeling that the most read, translated and taught Dalit texts do not induce feelings of guilt among the oppressors as do, say texts of Black American writers.

Such positions are part of larger sociocultural and literary debates concerning the very identity of Dalit literature. That there is a literary counterpart to the sociocultural-political movement among the Dalits to seek and gain even basic human rights and dignity is not a feature to be ignored. Yet, as an aesthetic expression of such an ideologically committed movement, how do we look at Dalit literature and what do we look for in a Dalit text? Equally importantly, how does the rise and subsequent growth of Dalit literature relate to the Dalit movement as a sociocultural phenomenon?

The discussion of two Dalit texts in this chapter—Joseph Macwan's Gujarati novel *Angaliyat* and Bama's much-acclaimed Tamil autobiography *Karukku*—will be read in the context of certain government policies and legal amendments which have deeply affected the Dalits of India. In so doing, the reading will also try to see how the texts weave into themselves certain political criticisms of the very institutions which ought to ensure equity. In the process, the issue of gender will also be addressed. Although *Karukku*, despite being the autobiography of a woman, does not overtly deal with the gender issue, such an angle is inherently built into the narrative. *Angaliyat* seems to address the issue in some detail, especially in the way Dalit women are often made the targets of upper-caste attacks.

The word 'Dalit' is of Marathi origin, which is not surprising, as two of the earliest and best-known Dalit thinkers and activists came from Maharashtra: Jotibai Phule and Dr B. R. Ambedkar. Of the two, Ambedkar has become more or less the figurehead of the Dalit movement. The translation of his letters, speeches, lectures etc. into various languages has helped in the mass dissemination of his ideas. Moreover, his own life stands testimony to many themes and motifs which run through Dalit literature and which are at the core of the Dalit movement as well. At the same time, Ambedkar's trenchant critique of Hinduism has led to various questions regarding the religious identities of the Dalits many of whom refuse to identify themselves with a religion which has marginalised and demeaned them for centuries.

The other important aspect of Ambedkar's influence is his use of legal system and the Constitution as spaces from where the caste battle can be fought. The idea of gaining power through representation—in the legislature or assembly—runs not merely through politics, but various other spheres as well, even the formulation of our academic syllabi. Part of the fear articulated by people like Anand and Ravikumar about the non-confrontational nature of Dalit writing taught in colleges and universities is that the texts 'selected' for study operate merely as a means to fill the required 'quota' of non-upper caste works in the curriculum; witness the large number of questions asked in *Touchable Tales* to academicians regarding the status of Dalit studies as an 'optional' rather than a 'compulsory' paper.

Ambedkar has been revered as the figure who made the Dalits aware that they are being oppressed; he is venerated as the one person who made legal and constitutional rights possible for Dalits who were denied even basic human dignity, thereby providing them with a suitable platform to fight from. Yet, Ambedkar has also been much criticised, especially for his reproach of Gandhi and of the Congress ideology. Although Gandhi saw himself as a Dalit rights activist, his activism was largely what is today termed 'integrationist' in nature; he sought to change Hinduism from within, while Ambedkar sought to and succeeded in rejecting Hinduism altogether. While Gandhi saw untouchability as a historical tumour of what was originally a benign division of labour, Ambedkar saw it as essentially built into the very structure of Hinduism. This tussle between Gandhi and Ambedkar even today forms two of the most common attitudes to caste and rebellion. The sharp contours of this division are somewhat smoothed in the figure of Bhavaankaka in *Angaliyat* as he seems to straddle both the paths.

It would be interesting to interrogate the route that Dalit literature takes – is it integrationist as Gandhiji was or is it politically subversive as Ambedkar was? Anand and Ravikumar would seem to be of the opinion that most texts are more Gandhian in their approach to the issue than 'Ambedkarite'. Yet, we should hesitate before making such generalisations. One of the important features of Dalit literature is its ability to use the fictional/textual space to describe what it means to be a Dalit in India. It seeks to bring out the many instances of oppression and violence which the various Dalit communities have been subject to and the attendant utter poverty they live under. It is thus both confrontational as well as subversive—for it brings literature into a direct encounter with the issue of caste—something that had not been 'engaged' satisfactorily. Mulk Raj Anand's monumental *Untouchable* (1935) and *Coolie* (1935) which were for long seen as the quintessential Dalit texts have now been replaced by texts written *by* Dalits.

The very emergence of Dalit writing—that is literature *by* Dalits—can be attributed to factors not at all purely 'literary'. On the one hand, the very need felt—by Dalits and others—to bring Dalit experiences into the field of literature (and thereby implicate caste-Hindus) is part of the growing awareness that the oppression and suppression of Dalits is something that needs to be denounced and corrected. Secondly and more importantly, the Dalits' awareness and their potential—economic as well as aesthetic—for 'writing' – has been made possible largely because of the phenomenal increase in literacy levels among the Dalits. This in turn is owing to various petitions submitted to the government by the Dalits themselves and by certain specific affirmative actions taken by the government.

To explain this a bit further, we need to look at the various roles that law can play. Nobody can claim that merely passing a law changes the social conditions completely and removes all evils. However, as Archana Parashar says, the law can perform a symbolic function – by the very fact of making some action 'illegal', it can draw attention to that action, its widespread nature and can therefore lead to subsequent changes. This further implies—although Parashar does not make it explicit—that certain behaviour patterns will be non-essentialised and defamiliarised. For instance, the use of caste names as terms of abuse (such as *dhed* in Gujarati) was never questioned, yet, laws like The Untouchability Offences Act of 1955, Protection of Civil Rights Law of 1976 etc. necessitated that the common people rethink given and set notions of expression and change them. Hence the use of caste names reflecting attitudes, unconscious or conscious, societal behaviour has been forbidden and such a step has brought about a change in the metaphors used.

At the same time, we should also be aware that the government has little time or money to publicise these laws by itself and in today's context, needs to work in tandem with various media and media channels (with their ubiquitous chat-shows) to effectively project them and make the beneficiaries aware of its policies of 'development' or modernisation.Education, however, is and has been an important mode of social uplift. It was, we may remember, denied to many sections of society either scripturally or due to poverty. With the introduction of British education and the setting up of missionary schools across India, a small, but politically valuable number of Dalits gained access to formal education. The role of education here can never be overemphasised: it gives the subject a certain amount of self-confidence and the courage to question established notions of class and caste superiority. The literacy percentage of Dalits grew from 15 per cent in 1971 through 21 per cent in 1981 to 37 per cent in 1991 (Mendelsohn and Vicziany, *The Untouchables*, 34); especially for Dalit women this percentage shows a substantial increase in the same years, from 6 per cent in 1971 through 11 per cent in 1981 to 24 per cent in 1991 (Mendelsohn and Vicziany, 34).

Literacy and education are 'strategic needs' of society – needs that can be transformative and are potentially subversive. Novels like *Kayar* (1979) and recently *The House of Blue Mangoes* (2002) unravel the politics and ideological conditioning involved in the refusal to provide Dalits with necessary education.

The social uplift made possible by education is precisely the kind of benefit that caste-Hindus and the collaborating Christians do not want the Dalits to avail of, as is made evident in a novel like *Kayar* and it is for precisely these reasons that education becomes an important subject in many Dalit texts. It is especially true in *Karukku* where much of the narrative space is taken up by the unnamed protagonist in dealing with the fruits of education. Talking first about her elder brother, she says, 'Once when Annan was signing out his books, he added his title, M. A., on a sudden impulse. Immediately the attendant brought him a stool to sit on, and what's more, began addressing him as "Sir"' (15). This is soon followed by various other instances related to herself and she discovers that being educated and being good at studies helps her attain a social standing that defied her caste status: 'And I studied hard, with all my breath and being, in a frenzy almost. As Annan had urged, I stood first in my class. And because of that, many people became my friends, even though I am a Paraichi' (15). Again in high school, she recalls: 'I studied hard and got the best marks in my class. Because of this, all the children would speak to me and were friendly . . . . They asked me to help the children who were really backward in their lessons. I was overjoyed' (18). She finally asserts, 'because of my education alone I managed to survive among those who spoke the language of caste-difference and discrimination' (20).

This importance given to education can also be related to the life and influence of Ambedkar who may have himself owed part of his revolutionary status to the education he got in the army cantonment, the scholarship given by the Gaekwad of Baroda (which incidentally, he got *because* he was a Dalit), and his education in New York and London. Therefore, although *Karukku* does not make any overt statements regarding Ambedkar or his influence, the undercurrent of viewing education almost as a panacea can be traced to the life of Ambedkar that has become quite well-known among Dalits. It should be mentioned that the importance and transformative nature of education runs through many other Dalit autobiographies like Sharankumar Limbale's *Akkarmashi* (1984) as well where again, the protagonist finds that it is only through education and the policy of positive discrimination ('reservation') that he is able to overcome many of the hurdles placed in his path by his caste identity.

Yet, the system of education comes under severe attack in *Karukku*. The education system is ironically shown as merely one of the many institutions which perpetuate caste discrimination. This again needs to be seen in the context of assertions that although the policies of the government provide equal opportunities for Dalit children to gain access to schools, there is little control over the behaviour of other children or for that matter, the teachers in the schools. The attitudes of people who should, ideally speaking, help remove caste distinctions and promote egalitarianism are, alas, quite the reverse. In 'Reaching the Unreached: Enabling Dalit Girls to Get Schooling,' M. V. Sreedhar points out that despite entry into schools, Dalit children are victims of negative stereotyping and of the aspersions cast by teachers who have internalised these stereotypes. The protagonist in *Karukku* is such a victim and all these experiences become part of her autobiography which begins to occupy a space between an intensely personal experience and that of a community's.

The heroine in *Karukku*, hailing from the much maligned Parayar community, is typecast as dirty and 'naturally' prone to criminal activities. This typecasting follows her almost everywhere and she finds herself wrongfully accused of having stolen mangoes from the school tree. Hence, when the headmaster says, 'You have shown us your true nature as a Paraya' (16) or when the priest says, 'After all, you are from the cheri. You might have done it. You must have done it' (17), they are voicing the generally propagated opinion about the Parayar community. Similarly, the Principal's response to her request for leave to celebrate her siblings' First Holy Communion is one of derision: 'What celebration can there be in your caste, for a First Communion?' (19), he asks her. The protagonist increasingly finds that she can never be rid of the caste-tag even in the seemingly most egalitarian of institutions, especially the Church. The hesitation on the part of the Mother Superior to accept her—a 'harijan'—as a nun, the way in which the sisters spoke about the lower castes and the menial jobs the children of these castes were asked to do, all reinforce the continuation of the caste hierarchy within the clergy as well.

The indictment of the Church needs to be specially looked at here. In its initial stages of existence in colonial India, the Church offered to a large number of untouchables security from the degradation of caste, while also materially aiding them in times of famine. This supportive attitude of the Church—in general of religious institutions—can be sharply contrasted to the description in *Angaliyat* of the treatment meted out to the Vankars by the upper castes—executors of religious laws—in times of flood. When Valji upbraids Teeha for supporting Ranchhod Dehlavala, an upper caste man from their village, Teeha responds thus:

> He is not from our village, we are from his – at his mercy, the objects of his contempt and beatings. My father used to tell me that when the floods came and our *vas* was submerged, it didn't matter to anybody. When the waters finally receded, after some five days, everyone from there sought shelter on the Godia Tekra – in the midst of snakes. Your father was born there. Many little children were buried there. Then followed cholera. Half our community was destroyed; nobody was fortunate enough to get even a drop of medicine. This very Ranchhod gave out medicine, food and clothes to other people. Your grandfather, my grandfather, Dhana, Dhoola and the metar (elder) of the *vas* visited him to beg for help; but he remained unmoved. In the evening he asked them to clean the entire village and said he'd decide afterwards. They cleaned the muck and the mess; the cats and dogs that had lain dead for days and after all that, they got some leftovers. (10)

The role of the missionary Churches was initially in direct contrast to this: offering material help during famines, epidemics and floods. Clerics and missionaries such as Clough even arbitrated with judges on behalf of the lower castes as happened when Madigas of Andhra Pradesh were unjustly accused of having caused the death of cattle and the local people asked the British government to enforce the traditional order of caste hierarchy (Mendelsohn and Vicziany, 85). But the indictment of the Catholic Church in *Karukku* makes us reconsider our impression on this too. In fact, *Karukku* also records how, by the time the autobiography came to be written, there was an unedifying volte-face by the Church. The parish priest of the protagonist's Church, far from helping the Parayar community or interceding on their behalf with the police, actually gets a few people from their community arrested. At the time of the strife between the Parayar and Chaaliyar communities, the priest actually informs the police about the strategies of the wronged Parayar community. The conversation among the people brings out the callousness of the priest:

> 'It's that St. Anthony who brought us victory.'
> 'They thought our Paraya boys would be easy game. But Our Lady exposed that thought for the sham it is, didn't she?'
> 'We must have a sung Mass, a Pusai, in gratitude next Sunday.'
> 'Why must there be a sung Pusai, di? Did this priest ever help us, even with the dust of his feet? When our men who were hiding in the Church were caught and taken away, this priest was sitting at ease in his bungalow, his legs crossed, smoking his cigarette happily and watching it all.'
> 'And not only that, sister-in-law. We didn't have the money to attend the adjournment and asked the priest for a paltry loan of a few rupees, but he absolutely refused.' (29)

That the caste hierarchies have infiltrated even into the space of an institution which had begun as a means of overcoming the indignities of caste is a tragic comment on the selfish workings of the Church. Ambedkar was among the first to comment on the ways in which the Church in India was giving up its potential for social change and that it was fast submitting to the ideology of caste-Hindus in order to attract them. Many other social reformist leaders such as E. V. Ramaswamy Naicker, respectfully called Periyar in Tamil, too so critiqued the Church in India. *Karukku* tells us precisely how this affects the people whose initial attraction to Christianity was the liberation it promised from caste distinctions.

The critique of practised Catholic Christianity occurs in *Karukku* at two levels – one from the point of view of a young girl belonging to the religion and the other from the vantage point of a

Dalit nun. Both are interrelated in that as a young girl, the protagonist is *taught* the religion by the clergy that she later joins in the hope of using the Church as a platform for social work. However, the adult protagonist's recounting of her childhood experiences shows how a certain insensitivity to children's feelings marked the clergy that teaches her the religion.

It is the last part / section of the autobiography that recounts how the Church and Christianity were imbued into her young mind. Interestingly, we find a constant focus on sin and fear rather than the 'love' that Christ had professed. Even the experiences in the Church flout the notion of love and 'charity' underscoring the mercenary nature of the clergy. The protagonist's descriptions of her experiences as a child in the Church border almost on subversion. When asked to lock up the Church at night, for instance, she describes her feelings thus:

> I was frightened to go inside the Church by myself. I felt a bit braver if there was someone with me.
> If ever I had to stay alone in the Church, my insides would quake. Because just at those times I would remember the stories that the Sisters had told us in Scripture lessons about the Devil.
> . . . .
> I would die of fear then. But usually I forgot about it when I left the Church and came outside.
> The nuns never seemed to tell us any cheerful stories. (71–72)

The notion of the Church as a place where preternatural fears are overcome is neatly subverted here; and the blame is put squarely on the clergy who work through 'fear' rather than love and understanding. This is almost the same kind of fear that was instilled in the Dalits by the upper castes whenever they sought to cross the caste boundaries set by tradition. The role of the Church in changing the social order is clearly a pretension here. This 'teaching by fear' continues throughout the childhood of the protagonist in the stories she is taught, in the admonitions not to touch the host by teeth or fingers etc., all of which she finds to be false as an individual. This part of the autobiography, in fact, acts as a powerful personal memoir where the subject's search for a fruitful and 'emotional' response to her religion is chalked out. In fact she begins the section with a confessional sentence, 'When I look back upon all these years that have gone by, I realize that the Bhakti and belief I had in God has changed in a curious way. I am myself surprised at this' (70). It is this change that is the subject of the section. However, it acts also as a strong indictment of the ways and means used by the Church to educate its 'flock' in matters of religion, forgetting all the compassion and love which is at the centre of much of the actual teachings of the religion, but focusing rather on terror and fear. At a later date, the protagonist herself realises after reading the Old and New Testaments on her own:

> I learnt that God has always shown the greatest compassion for the oppressed. And Jesus too, associated himself mainly with the poor. Yet nobody stressed this nor pointed it out. All those people who had taught us, had taught us only that God is loving, kind, gentle, one who forgives sinners, patient, tender, humble, obedient. Nobody had ever insisted that God is just, righteous, is angered by injustices, opposes falsehood, never countenances inequality. There is a great deal of difference between this Jesus and the Jesus who is made known through daily pieties. The oppressed are not taught about him, but rather, are taught in an empty and meaningless way about humility, obedience, patience, gentleness. (90)

The above quotation carries within it some ideas of what has evolved and is still evolving as Dalit theology, a branch of Christianity that seeks in the figure of Jesus the epitome of the Dalit experience and seeks to use the Church as a platform for social reform.

The mercenary nature of the clergy becomes evident in the policies adopted in their institutions of 'charity'. The New Year's Day celebrations, for instance, end with a lament by one member from the community: 'I asked the priest for a calendar, smiling sweetly at him all the time. He actually asked me for money, Akka. He says he'll only sell them' (57). The Reverend Mother's response to request for holy pictures is very similar: 'Have you given me some money in order to buy you holy pictures? Very well, now, you may all go home quickly *without leaning on the walls or touching anything*' (58, *Karukku*, italics mine). One wonders whether the injunction is not to defile the Church by touch. The protagonist ruminates: 'They spoke so eloquently that we should love everyone, for we are all God's children. Yet the people they chose to talk to, those whom they admitted into their schools, those with whom they claimed relationships were all rich' (98).

This indictment of the Church and clergy works alongside a strong attack on the system of caste itself and its ubiquitous nature.

The autobiography skilfully brings out what it means to be a Dalit in Tamil Nadu. In the autobiography, the experiences of an entire community are brought out. It is in this that *Karukku* as a Dalit autobiography reworks the very genre it is a part of.

The form of autobiography has often been seen, like the novel, as a Western import. It is a form that necessitates the centrality of the subject in public life and is essentially a form that celebrates the self and its individuality. An autobiography, in other words, is written by a person already well-known so that her / his life-story can become a source for others to draw inspiration from. At times, as in the case of Gandhi, it also becomes a means of serious introspection. In the case of Dalit literature, the form of the autobiography takes on clear political overtones. It is said that one of the important features of Dalit writing is that the identity of the speaking subject is not merely individual; it is largely a community-based one. In other words, the Dalit writer writes primarily and often exclusively as a member of her / his community. This feature by itself unsettles some essential notions of an autobiography as more personal and a celebration of the ego. By placing the protagonist within her caste and village the text makes her a representative of the locale reinforcing this by keeping her unnamed, a rare thing in an autobiography. As a celebration of the ego, the autobiography *has to* deal with names because names essentially provide the individual identity. By eschewing this, *Karukku* effectively locates the individual firmly within the community and the village.

Moreover, as part of a larger collection of one kind of protest literature, Dalit autobiographies are historically situated, as are all Dalit texts (Digish Mehta qtd. by Rita Kothari in 'Short Story in Gujarati Dalit Literature') and as such defy notions of an essential, transnational–historical self which is the centre of a traditional autobiography. Since the Dalit subject's identity as belonging to a 'lower', 'unclean' caste is thrust upon her by others in *Karukku* much of her self-definition consists of asserting her sense of self-worth or in describing the processes by which this self-worth is proven. The experiences of oppression in schools and colleges that we hear of in *Karukku* as well as in other autobiographies such as *Akkarmashi* vindicate the attempt to use the autobiography as a means of describing the possibilities of overcoming the social, economic and cultural stigma of being a Dalit. In the case of *Karukku* this works also at the level of gender wherein the text becomes a space to articulate such means of resistance which are not organised or politicised and are therefore left largely undocumented by male and academic historians. In the process, it captures the everyday life and household activities of the women of the Parayar community and also the ways in which their religion forms an essential part of their lives.

The profound interconnectedness between the caste identity and the self of the speaking subject arises largely because of the oppressed position of the subject. She finds that even if as an individual, she would like to be rid of her caste identity, she is constantly reminded of it. Witness the various instances where she says, with increasing bitterness: 'But it was the same story at school, though. They always spoke in a bad way about people of our caste' (15); 'Anyway, I finished there and went to a different college in order to take a B. Ed degree. It was the same story there too' (21); 'Wherever you look, however much you study, whatever you take up, caste discrimination stalks us in every nook and corner and drives us into a frenzy' (23). Most of the experiences of the subject are those of pain, poverty and anger – experiences suffered *because* of her identity as a *paraichi*. In turn, it is these events that construct her Self, a Self that is socially, culturally and historically rooted. It is this which makes it impossible to separate the caste from the self.

Yet, we need here to face allegations that such experiences as presented in *Karukku* do not evoke feelings of guilt in the readers belonging to the upper castes; in the castes that are openly indicted in the narrative. These allegations need to be reconsidered in the face of many facts.

First, *Karukku* is formally not an uninterrupted life story. It is not, as has been observed even in the critical introduction, a life story told chronologically. It is interspersed with sections or sub-sections of direct attack or talk that overtly indicts upper castes and urges Dalits to resist the epistemological and physical violence inflicted upon their persons and community. Many of these sections read like direct polemic or even propaganda for Dalit activism. These sections play an important, almost choric role, for they locate the individual story of the subject within the larger context of the large number of untold and un-chronicled stories of the people—especially women—of her caste. In *Karukku*, these sections take the form of an indictment of the caste system itself, of various institutions that promote and sustain the system and of the ways in which economic oppression goes hand in hand with caste oppression. The use of a single textual space to tell one's life story *and* to discuss polemical and political issues concerning caste consciously blurs the boundary between creative writing and polemical encounters. In fact, this brings polemics and politics right *into* the sphere of creative writing and effectively erases the 'lalit-Dalit'[3] distinction which was so much at the heart of literary controversy in Gujarat.

The protagonist's own attitude towards caste in general and her caste in particular needs specific attention. Most analyses of the Dalit movement in India point to two broad phases. The first, from 1857 (marking the time when Queen Victoria 'took over' India from the East India Company) to around 1917 saw little criticism of Hinduism. The focus was largely on gaining acceptability and in overcoming those aspects of their culture that were largely cited by the upper castes to brand them as 'unclean' or 'uncivilised.' In retrospect, this phase was characterised by a sense of embarrassment at being a Dalit. In some ways, this embarrassment was re-enacted in the post-Mandal period that saw the rise of what Rita Kothari calls the 'Dalit middle-class'. One of the texts which best illustrates this point is Sharankumar Limbale's *Akkarmashi* where the author–protagonist's attitude towards his caste and even family undergoes a sea-change after his education and 'government' job. His attempts to give up eating meat, his sense of shame at traditional Mahar jobs, all point to this. In Bama's *Karukku*, however, such a feeling of shame and self-disgust is absent. On the contrary, in keeping with the spirit of the second phase of Dalit uprising, there is a sense of pride in her caste and the entire narrative is testimony to her sense of dignity in the various 'jobs' her community performs. Interestingly, this is narrated from the point of view of a woman and therefore, the 'jobs' which are described will question not only caste, but also gender hierarchy. Historically though, we should note that conversion to Christianity was a preferred mode of social uplift in the first phase. The second phase of Dalit uprising was characterised by a feeling that the Dalits need not change themselves to suit upper caste standards of morals or cleanliness and fostered a corresponding sense of pride in one's caste and the labour that went with it. So very often in *Karukku* we find the protagonist (and once her brother) answer the Naickers back with a strong assertion of their caste identity:

> He thought my Annan looked unfamiliar, and so he asked, 'Who are you, appa, what's your name?' Annan told him his name. Immediately the other man asked, 'Thambi, on which street do you

> live?' The point of this was that if he knew on which street we lived, he would know our caste too. Annan's reply was sharp, like a slap in the face, 'I am a Paraya from the Cheri street.' (15)

This bold and unashamed assertion was actually a rebuttal of traditional notions that lower-castes should be ashamed of their caste-identity. Needless to say, it provokes immense anger in the upper caste circle and Annan's grandmother to apologise for her grandson's behaviour. The same continues even into the protagonist's own experiences. When she tells her mother of the indignities she has to face because of her caste, her mother advises her to lie about it, but despite the pain and anguish, she retorts, 'But why should I pretend to these people that I'm from a different caste?' (18).

This refusal to deny one's caste identity is complemented by the sense of pride and dignity which the protagonist feels in the labours of the caste. The entire narrative stands testimony to this because significant amount of space is taken up in describing the various household as well as field tasks that the women of the Parayar community perform. Certainly there is no sense of self-pity or anguish at the poverty that the protagonist grew up in; rather the greatest strength of the novel lies in bringing out the energy and vivacity of the community. Again here, the form of the autobiography needs to be reconsidered. Apart from individual experiences of the protagonist, a large amount of space is taken up in describing the village, its natural bounties, its religious sites, its caste divisions, the work done by the women etc. Among these, the last includes everyday household work like grinding spices and cutting vegetables as well as work done in the fields of the Naickers. The songs sung in the process, the gossip that goes on among the women and indeed, the ways in which these activities regulate even their religious life are all brought out in almost loving detail. For instance, the description of the fights that take place at the site of the water pump make for hearty and funny reading, as does the description of the various nicknames given to children – nicknames that get stuck to them all through their lives (6, 7). The stories of Bondan and Kaaman are part of regional lore—not history or legend, but contemporary gossip-news-material—while the descriptions of the Chinnamali festival, the screening of the MGR[4] film etc. bring out the small-scale entertainments that are so much a part of the lives of the people.

It is not for nothing that so much space is taken up by the author in describing the village and its small and big events. Part of the reason for this lies in securely contextualising the narrative. The village, its small incidents, its stories, legends and festivals come alive before the reader and the loving detail and relative absence of pathos with which these are described serve to negate the commonly held view that the culture and labours of the Dalits are 'low' and 'mean.' Secondly, this technique also enables the protagonist to ensure that her identity is firmly fixed as belonging to a particular village and a community from that village. Hence we find that nowhere can we divorce her experiences from that of her community – these are experiences that have arisen *because of* her belonging to this particular community. The individual therefore, gains importance as a member of her community and it is in this that the oft-repeated point about Dalit literature—that it is firmly rooted in its community and its experiences—can be invoked again.

What is equally important here is that the assertion of the dignity and value of 'labour' is made from both the caste and gender perspectives. The everyday tasks of women have rarely been the subject for literary descriptions, those of Dalit women are even less so. Yet, in *Karukku*, it is these descriptions that make up the 'history' and the community. It has often been a complaint of feminists that the 'ordinary' lives and chores of women—chores that actually help in the smooth running of the family and make possible certain material acquisitions—have not found a place in literature so far. By placing them so centrally in *Karukku*, the protagonist offers a different, feminine view of community, its experiences and its history. The humorous tone in which many of these incidents are narrated shows the vivacity of living even within the confines of caste discrimination. This exuberance however, should not be taken as an excuse for not bringing in reforms, for one can often hear voices that assert that when the community seems to be happy enough doing their traditional jobs, there is little need to allow its members to move to other more lucrative jobs or to provide them with education. It is to avoid a recourse to this attitude that the polemical interventions stress constantly and strongly on the problems faced by Dalits. It is also for this reason that the polemical interludes form an integral part of the text.

One of the central descriptions in the text is the way the women in Cheri Street manage their houses as well as outside labour without men and even help the men escape the police in the face of the fight between the Parayar and Chaaliyar communities. The actual description of the violence takes up more than ten pages: from page 25 to page 39. But the highlight of the trouble was that:

> The police were furious that the women were smart enough to continue working and taking care of their children even without their men, and so they rounded up all the women workers, forced them into their lorries and dropped them off on the other side, in the village. The police were really riled when they heard that the women who went to work were actually taking food to the men who were hiding in the forest. (35)

The same happens when the women device a clever plan to help a man attend his son's funeral by disguising him as a woman and bringing him right under the nose of the police. These incidents point to a different kind of resistance to oppressive forces – a kind of resistance that requires a space like the autobiography novel to find utterance. These are modes of resistance that hinge on feminine modes of behaviour and female perseverance. They do not rely so much on violence or on political policies, but make use of simple, everyday strategies to defy oppressive forces like the police.

This kind of feminine resistance is also present in *Angaliyat* where Methi and Kanko save the men—especially Jeevan—from the police and the upper caste men (195–199). Here again, we find a form of resistance that is strategic, does not follow any 'prescribed' modes and is little documented. Part of the success of Dalit literature is to tell such stories and make them known.

Two points emerge here – one is the centrality of violence in Dalit life and the other is the role of the police. Both *Karukku* and *Angaliyat* give us useful insights into both.

Violence is almost a part of life in most Dalit communities. Mendelsohn and Vicziany point out that after the 1970s there appears to have been an increase in what are officially termed 'Harijan atrocities'. Whether more incidents are being reported (implying the earlier collaboration—conscious or otherwise—of the media with upper castes) or whether the incidents themselves have increased is a moot point. But indications are clear that uprisings by Dalits are more often than not followed by brutality against the Dalits. Violence here becomes a means of 'teaching a lesson' and is most openly articulated in *Angaliyat*. Teeha's rebellious attitude to the Patils who eve-teased Methi incurs the wrath of the upper castes and the entire *vas*—settlement—is the victim. This is the threatening note put up:

> *If you have anything to do with any of your community members in Ratnapur or let any of them enter here, that will be your end. You will be thrown out of the village, without even a drop of water from the lake.* (30; italics in original)

The above is an excellent example of the use of threat and brute force to keep the Dalits from being united and from getting organised. The Patils understand that once the Dalits become organised, they—the Patils—will lose power. One of the Patils tells the others: 'If they [the Vankars] were united, it would have been difficult for us to live in this village. The day they achieve self-recognition, the sun will set on us' (xx). Later in this novel as well as in *Karukku*, the police—a force that should ideally help in implementing pro-Dalit laws—becomes a further means of oppression. Jeevan's in *Angaliyat* is a case in point as is the attitude of the police towards the Parayar community in *Karukku*. In fact, the police themselves carry traditionally circulated notions of 'caste-behaviour'. In the fight between the Parayar and the Chaaliyar communities in *Karukku*, the entire Parayar community gets implicated legally. The failure of the police force in enforcing the laws to reduce violence against Dalits comes out very strongly here. *Angaliyat* takes this critique a step further by contrasting their activities before and after Independence. What emerges is the sad reality that prior to Swaraj, the police was far more respectful towards laws and justice, whereas in later years, they became mute machinery of the upper castes. This dual portrayal of the police force also acts as a means of scrutinising the notion of Independence and what it has meant for some of the most oppressed castes of India. The criticism that Congress's idea of Swaraj is not meant for everybody is sadly by Bhavaankaka who in this aspect appears to be more an Ambedkarite than a Gandhian.

In other words, the depiction of the machinery of the State and its inefficiency in helping the Dalits in any way are an important feature in Dalit literature. This anti-institutional stance of Dalit literature gives it a political angle which might be ignored by a mere thematic and structural reading of the texts. Hence, the complaint that very few translated Dalit texts openly engage with the politics or the politicisation of Dalit atrocities may be met adopting a critical method by which the Dalit texts may be read in the context of various institutional attempts to reduce atrocities and noting the degree of success or failure of these systems. The legal system, the police, legislatures providing access to and admission in schools etc.

prove quite ineffective in their final implementation as the people involved in executing these policies are often themselves full of preconceived notions of essentialised caste-related behaviour. For instance, the protagonist of *Karukku* finds that in her college, 'the government has arranged that Scheduled Caste students should get special tuition in the evenings' (19). The underlying belief that Dalit students are 'naturally' poor at studies and need special help makes the protagonist seethe with anger while the other students 'titter with contempt' (19). Even if the government prefers to call this 'positive discrimination' or 'affirmative action' the effect is to intensify certain set prejudices instead of removing them.

This is brought out even more strongly in the attitude towards women and is best represented in *Angaliyat*. Like *Karukku*, *Angaliyat* too does not openly or centrally deal with gender issues, but the fact that Dalit women are often the targets of physical, psychological and sexual abuse is borne out by the events in this Gujarati novel. Not only Methi's initial eve-teasing, but also the ways in which many people view the practice of widow remarriage affirm the working of the ideology. Upper-caste notions of feminine purity are associated with one-man-for-all-life policy whereby a woman is expected to remain loyal to her husband. In the Vankaṛ community, on the other hand, widows are not only allowed to, but are also encouraged to remarry. As Rita Kothari explains in her very illuminating introduction, this practice, defying the basic precepts of feminine chastity, was seen by the upper castes as a sign of the Vankars' degenerate morality. In the novel, Bhavaankaka explains the pragmatism of the practice (115). This discourse about the pragmatism of the custom that had given them the name of 'lowly' is followed also by a sharp criticism of the very standards according to which the Vankars are judged:

> 'In that case, how do widows in these high castes spend their lives?' Teeho could not help arguing.
> 'What happens in the nooks and corners of their houses does not travel through their walls, Teeha! Our caste is a foolish one and so announces these things from the rooftops. I can tell you, I have not seen fair crows even in Kashi!' (*Angaliyat*, 116)

This conversation between Teeha and Bhavaankaka acts almost as a fictionalisation of the struggle among Dalits between the move to integrate into the larger society by shunning the practices that were seen as 'lowly' and the confrontationist move that necessitates that Dalits show a sense of pride in their own peculiar customs and traditions. We already saw that *Karukku* did this by spending time and space in describing the everyday actions and labours of the Parayar women. *Angaliyat* does this in many ways. One is the use of polemic and argument, in most of which Bhavaankaka, as the 'saint' of the *vas* has the final word. The other is, as in *Karukku*, the description in great and loving detail the labours of the Vankar community.

In the first case, we come yet again to the figure of Bhavaankaka as a conflation of Gandhian and Ambedkarite attitudes towards the caste issue. While the spirituality and religiosity he brings into his discourses and his very involvement with Gandhi make for one part of his character, the other seems strongly aware of the shortcomings of the Congress ideology ('these are the signs of the so-called Swaraj for us' (199)).

It is the rebellious side of his character that surfaces in the conversation cited above with Teeha on page 53. He comes across as being more in favour of taking pride in the practicality of Vankar customs rather than of merely judging them by the standards set for and by others. Sociologists such as Sharmila Rege point out that these standards are the reason for the relatively abysmal action against the rapists of Dalit women. The upper caste attitude is largely that rape as 'dis*honour*' does not operate here as Dalit women are considered to have no 'honour' in the first place. This has been the reason why Dalit women have so often been easy sexual targets for upper caste men. Mendelsohn and Vicziany put it succinctly when they say: 'the Untouchable woman was never so degraded or ritually polluted as to be sexually unapproachable. Untouchability was always a curse, never a protection' (11). The central event in *Angaliyat*—Methi as the victim of eve-teasing—forms part of the much larger set of attitudes towards Dalit women and honour. *Karukku* manages to avoid the issue openly, but in the evocation of the life of the Parayar women, the strong sense of duty to family, community and religion is presented, effectively nullifying accusations of lack of culture or sense of honour.

The pride in 'labour' is an important aspect of Dalit uprising because by reiterating the social need for their labour, Dalits can successfully uphold their role in the very society that keeps them in the margins. We need to remember here that the hierarchy of labours went hand in hand with hierarchy of caste. The Parayar community is considered 'polluting' because of its associations with the beating of the *parai* or drum made of cowhide. Rita Kothari mentions that the Vankar community is a weaving community and possibly the only one in India to be seen and treated as Dalit. Her introduction traces their 'Dalit-ness' to their job of disposing of dead cattle. However, neither of the novels chosen for study here openly deals with these aspects of Dalit labour. One reason for this may be that very few of the communities continue their traditional labour. Secondly, a large section of the Parayar community today works as bonded labourers in villages and this is the cause of much of their troubles. Yet another novel like *Koveruk Kazhudaigal* (*Beasts of Burden*) by Imayam does deal with the role of some of the Dalit communities (the community of washermen and washerwomen) in funeral rites and other village customs. *Angaliyat* deals at great length with weaving, the traditional occupation of the Vankars, although the association with disposing of dead cattle is not touched upon—in fact need not be—as Rita Kothari points out that it is a fact lost in the mists of history. Its importance is largely as sociological detail.

*Angaliyat* raises weaving to a metaphysical phenomenon, almost a spiritual activity. The warp and woof of the weaving machine becomes in some sense the pattern of the novel itself and at many places, characters take refuge in weaving, as does Teeha when Methi becomes unavailable to him forever. The patterns and riots of colours that begin to characterise Teeha's weaving become a means of artistically giving vent to his feelings. Very interestingly, the novel does not make the obvious connection between weaving and Gandhian ideology. It might be remembered that for Gandhi, weaving was a quintessential 'Indian' labour and he too raised it to a metaphysical level while making it a means of attacking British methods of economic exploitation of India. Looking at the novel as a critique of Congress ideology, therefore, we seem to be peculiarly placed. On the one hand, there is a strong criticism of Congress and its notion of Swaraj as well as its modes of operation. On the other hand there is the elevation of the 'labour' of weaving to a mystical phenomenon which seems to us in hindsight, a celebration of Gandhi. Within the text itself, however, Gandhi and the Congress are not so comfortable in each other's company. Where even the congress fails, Bhavaankaka and others take recourse to Gandhi. Indeed, at a point, dissatisfied with Congress ideology and its modes of operation, Bhavaankaka goes to Sabarmati. His reaction on Dehlavala getting a letter from the Congress thereafter is pregnant:

'The sun of Gandhiji Bapu is still warm in this country, Dehlavala' (201). This separation of Gandhiji from the Congress raises the former to greater heights especially as we are constantly reminded of the Congress's failure to provide a suitable 'Swaraj'. The two sentiments reach their peak in one sentence when Bhavaankaka says: 'Gandhism disappeared with Gandhiji' (227). This marks an interesting use of Gandhiji within the Dalit context. Equally interestingly, there is little such mention made of Ambedkar although Ambedkar's role in raising the consciousness of the Dalits can never be overstated. This absence is as puzzling.

While both *Karukku* and *Angaliyat* focus on Dalit experiences, the Tamil text makes explicit connections between economic and caste hierarchies. In *Dalit Sahitya: Srujan ke Sandarbh*, (Dalit Literature: the Context of its Creation), many of the essays deal with two kinds of definitions of the term 'Dalit' – a 'broad' one that may include *all* kinds of oppressed people (including class) and a 'narrower' one that is caste-specific. The essays also mention that economic status cannot be considered as a basis for 'Dalit' status because the foundation of social hierarchy is not economic status, but caste. However, at various points, *Karukku* makes some important connections between caste and economic uplift. The downtrodden condition of the Parayars is so maintained by consciously closing down all avenues of economic uplift. The intense struggle that many Dalit children have to face to gain education is part of this process because education will open the gates for better jobs; jobs that the government's policies of 'reservation' or positive discrimination and affirmative action have made available. This economic uplift will in its turn reverse or throw into chaos the existing caste hierarchy and may even make the upper castes economically 'lower' than the Dalits. One only has to recall a novel like *Kayar* which shows how, as part of the emerging Kuttanad, Dalits, thanks to education and newer employment policies slowly begin to upturn the existing social order. Yet, economic exploitation—in the form of forced, bonded labour, exploitation and discrimination *in* the workplace etc.—helps in maintaining the caste hierarchy. This is best brought out in *Karukku* in the many polemical interventions in the protagonist's life story:

> How did the upper castes become so elevated? How is it that we have been denigrated? They possess money; we do not. If we were wealthy too, wouldn't we learn more, and make more progress than they do? But when it comes to it, even if we are as good as they are,

> or even better, because of this one issue of caste alone, we are forced to suffer pain and humiliation. (23)

It is in a way reinforced by the story of Nallathangal (recounted, seemingly unconnectedly, in pages 9 to 11 of the text). The name of the woman Nallathangal in Tamil country has become synonymous with poverty. The story serves not merely to reinforce the forced poverty of the Dalits, but also performs the important function of providing the *sthalapurana*[5] of the village temples nearby, reinforcing the centrality of space and location in the autobiography. The long descriptions of the hard physical labour put in by the community—especially by the women of the community—too bear out the economic conditions under which they live. Yet, there is no trace of anguish or shame at such physical hardships or even poverty. The descriptions are so given as to induce a sense of wonder at the capability of the community while also evoking the sharp sense of injustice that such a community—so hardworking and so necessary for the village—has been literally on the fringes of society and their work belittled. Reflecting upon this state of her community, she says:

> Even though they worked so hard and suffered bodily pain, our people laughed and were cheerful. This is a community that was born to work. And however hard they toil, it is the same kuuzh everyday. The same broken-grain gruel. The same watery dried-fish curry. It seems they never even reflect upon their own terrible state of affairs. But do they have any time to think? You have to wonder how the upper castes would survive without these people. (47)

The notion of caste and gender hierarchy is so ingrained in the people that even the games children play reinforce them – the master (Naicker) scolding the worker or the husband beating the wife are all faithfully reproduced by the children in their games. In their inimitably imitative way, these games provide an index to the general attitudes towards caste, gender and violence prevalent in the community.

Such a reworking of the form occurs differently in *Angaliyat* wherein the structure of well-known love-stories like *Heer Ranjha, Shireen Farhad* and *Laila Majnun* is exploited. These are legendary love-stories following the pattern where two members from traditionally warring families fall in love. Almost as a rule, these stories end in tragedies – with the lovers being killed or committing suicide. The plot has been a favourite with many cultural forms including the ubiquitous cinema that has for long survived on it. *Angaliyat* makes use of the same plot, but brings into it elements of caste and *paragna* (area / village) thereby providing an altogether different dimension to the love story itself. At times, however, the novel does smack of melodrama, especially in Methi's self-sacrifice to 'build' her home with her husband Chuntia which is nearly of the kind portrayed in the film 'Mother India'.[6] Again, Methi's attempts at suicide and Teeha's rescue are also quite cinematic and melodramatic. However, rather than reducing the force of the novel, these formal changes can be seen as an attempt to include caste issues in motifs already found successful, but which have so far been used to muffling the caste dimension. Rita Kothari points out in her introduction that Gujarati criticism has been more or less devoid of any element of Marxism despite the almost pan-Indian and national nature of the Progressive Writers' Movement. This conservatism has been well met by the use of such 'popular' formulaic tropes and by injecting the caste element in them.

An important aspect in any novel is the language used in the text. Like the issues of aesthetics, behavioural patterns, customs etc., this too has ideological implications. A significant contribution of Dalit literature has been to unsettle existing notions of literary language, just as it redefines the existing notions of literary experience. The language generally used in literature has been the 'standard form', a form associated with particular castes and classes of people. Most protest and minority literatures therefore consciously use dialectal forms of language to stress the importance and validity of the culture, oppressed and suppressed. *Karukku* has won much acclaim precisely for the use of such a dialectal version right within the narration rather than just in reported speech. In fact, Bama herself mentions this as the important feature of her writings and sees this as keeping her distinct from other Dalit writers who use such a dialectal quality only in reported speech (http://www.outlookindia.com). *Angaliyat* too, Rita Kothari mentions in her introduction, redefines the notions of literary language in the context of the 'Lalit-Dalit' debate. Yet, dealing as we are with translations, these varieties which might be so unsettling to a reader of the original text, may not affect others as strongly.

Yet, as translations of minority literatures written in dialectal language, these texts offer sufficient opportunity for experimentation in English as well. It has often been said of English in India that it has no dialectal variations or at least 'english' literature has not sufficiently captured these variations. These translations can venture into such a possibility – an opportunity that does not appear to have been much utilised. The language of the translations of both the texts chosen here is in no way subversive or even vaguely dialectal. The language of the translation of *Karukku* is, of course, far simpler than the language in most 'literature' written in regular English, with short sentences and a racy pace. Yet, it demands no special effort on the part of the reader as does, say, another translated text such as Bhalchandra Nemade's *Kosla*, translated as *Cocoon* by Sudhakar Marathe and published, like *Karukku*, by Macmillan Modern Novels in Translation. The language of *Angaliyat* similarly makes for quite easy and unhindered reading. Critics like Ravikumar might lay the blame on the fact that neither the translator nor the publisher is a Dalit, thereby introducing issues of situatedness of not only the author, but also the translator, publisher as well as the reader.

As in the case of most minority literature, one question haunts the critics and scholars of Dalit literature: who can write Dalit literature? Can non-Dalits too write what is called 'Dalit literature?' This question relates directly to the position of the author's subjectivity as a criterion in the categorisation of texts. This further implicates us in the dichotomy of the insider-outsider positions and the consequent valorisation of the former in discourses today. The issue relates to the very definition of a category: is a text categorised based on the theme or on the position of the author? In the case of most protest and / or minority literatures, it is the author's position which often decides the placement of a text. This is perhaps necessitated by a fear of 'outside' positions—especially of writers belonging to the group/s identified as the oppressors—which makes us look upon any text written from a non-insider position with suspicion. This suspicion stems from the fear that writings from such positions may use the fictional / discursive space to recreate and even perpetuate the same hierarchy that such protest literatures are disputing. Hence, literatures about Dalits (or Dalit issues) by non-Dalits are regarded with suspicion; they are often read as having some 'hidden agenda' that could run contrary to the interests of Dalits.

On the other hand, there is a school of thought which looks upon textual categorisation as being decided by the theme/s and treatments *within* the text, irrespective of the position of the author. This would then necessitate a Dalit text to be so characterised because it describes the plight of being a Dalit in this world. Such a characterisation of Dalit literature however, is much debated by activists, writers and spokespersons. Anand, for instance in *Touchable Tales*, says categorically at one point during his interview with Arundathi Roy: 'I hope you agree that nondalits cannot claim to produce "Dalit literature"' (*Touchable Tales*, 17), thereby dismissing the issue in a single statement.

The debate, although potentially insoluble, remains an important one. Both the perspectives have their value and need to be taken with a more sensitive degree of understanding about what is at stake. For it cannot be denied that the position of the outsider is fraught with the possibility of fictional space recreating the very same hierarchy that Dalit literature is fighting against. On the other hand, it appears unjust to condemn texts dealing with issues urgent and necessary or understanding the Dalit movement because the author's outsider position automatically invalidates it. Possibly, a further division of Dalit literature itself into texts written by Dalits and texts written by non-Dalits could, to a certain extent, resolve the matter. Such a division would allow a text to be categorised at once based on the position of the author and on the themes and issues dealt with. The Tamil play *Nandan Kathai* by Indira Parthasarathy could, as the critical note by the translator C. T. Indra mentions, also be read as a Dalit text as it deals with the ways in which being a *paraya* affects the life of its seventh-century protagonist Nandan and describes the processes by which Nandan is made a saint, thereby dissolving his caste-identity by adding a suffix to his name marking sacredness in Tamil i.e. converting *Nandan* to *Nandanar*. At the same time, a play like Vijay Tendulkar's *Kanyadaan* cannot be strictly called a Dalit play although it has a Dalit as one of its main characters, simply because it does not exclusively depict the travails of being a Dalit in the world. Tendulkar's play, as the citation to the Saraswati Samman mentions, does touch upon the politics involved in the Dalit movement itself, but does not bring the caste identity of the protagonist to bear upon the action of the play.

In other words, a Dalit text could perhaps be defined as a text, be it produced by a Dalit or a non-Dalit, if it deals with the way in which one's caste identity affects the events in the life of the characters. In this, one may find Jaidev's use of the concept of *mamatva* in his essay 'Not by Law alone: *Doulati* as a National Allegory' helpful. Drawn from Sanskrit poetics (and perhaps for that reason alone open to suspicion), *mamatva* describes a sense of understanding, empathy and sympathy, not condescension. In using this idea in his analysis of Mahasweta Devi's works, Jaidev praises her ability to imaginatively bring out the travails and problems of oppressed classes and classifies her works as Dalit or protest literature. *Mamatva* then can usefully be invoked as an ideal that allows an author/ text to address issues which may even be out of her / his experiential confines. It is this feeling of *mamatva* in texts like *Karukku* and *Angaliyat* as well as in women's literature such as *Breaking Ties* and *The Moth-eaten Howdah of the Tusker* which enables these texts to operate as discursive spaces where the battle for caste and gender rights can be fought.

The success of the translations of both *Karukku* and *Angaliyat* is a happy testimony to the growing awareness of Dalit literature and through literature, of the issues involved. In other words, both *Karukku* and *Angaliyat* use formal as well as thematic methods to centre stage Dalit rights and Dalit experience.

## Gender and Legal Reforms: *Breaking Ties* and *The Moth-eaten Howdah of the Tusker*

Like caste, gender operates as yet another instrument of social suppression. To say that women have traditionally played a secondary role in most societies is perhaps to state the obvious. The nationalist movement sought to change this in many ways. While some saw the home-bound, husband-worshipping Hindu wife as an ideal Hindu woman, leaders like Gandhi sought to bring women into the public sphere during the freedom struggle. Although Gandhi's ideas are today much criticised, this was a move necessitated by the contrasting picture of the 'free' British woman that the Indian community came to be acquainted with. Early attempts to secure a better position for women, however, openly discarded the imitation of the *angrezi mem* (witness the large numbers of lampooning of this character in fiction and essays in regional languages). Yet it cannot be denied that this very *angrezi mem* showed contrastively all that the Indian woman lacked, namely, fundamental rights of decision-making, education and even life expectancy. Among the social evils given much publicity were the practice of *Sati*, often glorified in Rajput discourses of heroism. The other such practice less talked about is female infanticide, still practised at an alarmingly high rate.

With Independence, the new government and its successors necessarily had to pay attention to the subordinate position of women and fortunately the Constitution and the legal system offered the means of bettering it. It is in this context that Sara Aboobacker's Kannada novel *Chandragiri Teeradille*, translated into English as *Breaking Ties* is read here.

One of the functions of the legal system is to help curb adverse social and communal practices. We saw in the discussion of the two Dalit texts that passing laws and legislations does make possible conditions for changing attitudes and belief systems. Dalits have successfully been using the legal system to their advantage while at the same time bringing out in creative and discursive writings the strengths and weaknesses of the present system. The same, however, is not true of women. Both the Dalit texts dealt with in this chapter did, to some extent, grapple with the problems of Dalit women leading to a much debated question of whether or not caste and gender issues can be treated together and on par.

While caste and gender do work as two of the most ubiquitous oppressive paradigms in the Indian scene, they have different social and cultural implications. Neither of them is a homogeneous mass and both have various dimensions to their concerns. Caste can especially disrupt the possibility of unity among women. A caste-Hindu woman may be oppressed in different ways from a Dalit woman, but the chances of her feeling a sense of solidarity with her Dalit counterpart are very less. In fact, quite alarmingly, reports of cases of Dalit women being forced to eat human excreta as punishment for warding off advances of upper caste males also mention that upper caste women too perpetrate these atrocities. Oppression practised in one major but unorganised sector where most women are employed—that of domestic service—is another instance of women being alienated from other women on the basis of caste. Another such divisive force is religion because women of one religion may feel greater solidarity with the men of that religion rather than with oppressed women of other religions. Nivedita Menon draws upon the opinions of Gail Omvedt and Gabrielle Dietrich to demonstrate that caste and religious communities are more powerful determining factors in women's lives than gender. She also adds that violence against minorities and Dalits merely serves to strengthen the hand of patriarchy within the family, thereby nullifying politically active and useful (and subversive) feminine bonding.

The law can of course function as a site wherein such disruptions can be mended, but unfortunately, it seems merely to reinforce them. Nowhere is this seen more clearly than in family and personal laws as depicted in the novels chosen for discussion here. These laws concern issues of marriage, inheritance, divorce, custody of children etc. After Independence, the Indian Constitution adopted the policy of making India a sovereign socialist secular democratic republic, which ideally implies that a single law must govern all her citizens in all aspects. This idea of a uniform civil code, however, has become the centre of much acrimonious debate and criticism. Even in Nehru's time, the idea was bandied about only to be shelved. Subsequent governments have chosen to view the issue of a uniform civil code as a minority rights issue rather than as pertaining at least partly to gender. Despite the feeling among many feminists in India that the Indian State is patriarchal, there is also the accompanying hope that the pressure of democratic movements can make the State or the law reconsider its stance. This too, however, is fraught with contradictions. Most of the amendments in the Indian legal system regarding women have been made for the Hindu woman. It is said that the Hindu woman is the most powerful among all categories of women in India.[7] Among the important legal amendments made in this respect have been the Hindu Marriage Act of 1955 and the Hindu Succession Act of 1956; the latter giving more rights to women in inheritance. Such acts have attempted to give to the Hindu woman some equality that her religion—at least as it was practised at the time of Independence and before—denied her. In effect then, what these laws amounted to was a reform of the religion itself. It was this important implication that led to a total neglect of reforms in the personal and family laws in other religions. The idea was that passing such laws would tantamount to interference in these religions. That this would go against the idea of a secular India was one of the arguments put forward to justify the neglect of these vexing questions. Archana Parashar points to the paradox in this situation. The law cannot evade its responsibility of redeeming the Dalits from their plight just because untouchability is part of and permitted by Hindu religion. Yet it does refrain from using its resources to change the plight of women in the minority communities on this very pretext. Parashar's argument sees the law itself as having encouraged division between and among women.

We must also keep in mind the form that 'feminism' took in the nationalist movement. Partha Chatterjee in his essay, 'The Nationalist Resolution of the Woman's Question', analyses the ways in which the movement, while seeming to work for women, only served to preserve certain existing scheme of values. He sees this in the context of the 'inside–outside' divide. The reach of Western ideas on the 'outside' reflected in clothing, language etc., was not a cause for concern so long as the 'inside', governed by religious notions, belief and value systems, remained Indian and *desi*. In this context, the woman was persuaded to relate herself to the 'inside'; she has been literally inside the house and metaphorically the harbinger of values and hence, her 'modernisation' was strictly to be within traditional norms. That it is the woman who has to pass on traditional values to future generations has become a staple and accepted idea still propagated by tele-serials and films. This discourse is today connected to that of 'responsibility' whereby the woman is made to feel 'good' and responsible for this task and her worth is judged according to how she manages to do it. Invariably then, this discourse, like others, has been internalised to an extent that any woman deviating from it runs the risk of ostracism by other women as well. Added to this is the very practical fallout that moving out of traditional ideas of femininity often implies moving out of the family as well. The family is still the central social unit in India and is the place of emotional and psychological support even if it is simultaneously the place where different kinds of violence are inflicted upon women. For most desperate women, moving out of the family offers little alternative. At the same time, such a moving out also involves an intense stress making the women's travails far more personal and emotionally traumatic than the Dalit experience. This is an important point of difference between the two which underscores the fact that most changes, as far as woman is concerned, need to come from within the family in the Indian context. If this is the case, then, family and personal laws can become an important front for such changes to take place, at least over a period of time.

*Breaking Ties* is set against the background of a rural Muslim family in which the elder daughter Nadira is made a victim of the system of unreformed and falsely practised Muslim family laws. The English translation of the novel has been published alongside a short autobiography titled 'A Muslim Girl Goes to School,' a piece that begs comparison with Bama's *Karukku* in the importance it gives to education. This is not without significance.

Education works here, as in the case of Dalits, as a means of creating awareness, among others, of one's legal rights. In its absence, the less privileged section of society—here, the women—can be easily manipulated by the privileged section, that is, the men. This is especially true in the case of family and personal laws, since it is the men in any society who control and interpret family and religious laws. This places them in a position of power and makes it easier for them to convince women that to question these laws is sacrilegious. Yet, circumstances—everyday circumstances—may arise where many of the religious laws taken for granted may appear absurd to the most ordinary of women. It is a pity that they cannot challenge religious and personal laws because there seems to be no option outside the family.

*Breaking Ties* tells the story of precisely such a predicament. At the heart of the novella is the raging debate in the Muslim community over a woman's right to divorce her husband, the validity of divorce by the husband saying '*talaaq*' three times and that of remarriage of divorcee women.

The issue of *talaaq* has time and again been taken up for discussion by the Muslim community itself. Traditionally, the Ulema or clerics claimed responsibility for safeguarding the Shariat which is the source for most of the family and personal law as followed by the Islamic community. It was understood that the Shariat could be interpreted *only* by the Ulema. It is this which is at the heart of much of the action that takes place in *Breaking Ties*. For though the Koran does allow dissolution of a marriage by the woman under certain circumstances, there has not been enough consensus on what constitutes these certain circumstances.

However, according to the Hanafi law, converting out of Islam was an option for women out of undesirable marriages. Since this was a move adopted by many women, the Ulema decided in 1935 by the Shariat Bill to allow 'Muslim judges to dissolve a marriage on the initiative of a woman' (Parashar, *Women and Family law Reform*, 151). However, the bill rejected conversion as a means out of marriage and thereby the right to grant divorce was retained with the men. Very typically, the Shah Bano case (1985)[8] was given the guise of a minority rights issue whereas the basic question of women's fundamental rights was shelved in the name of national integration.

The government contends that demands for changes in the family and personal laws of minority communities must come from within those communities, but texts like *Breaking Ties* and *The Moth-eaten*

*Howdah of the Tusker* put forward the very pertinent question of *who* from within the community would make such demands. Both the novels, as will be seen, have good-willed, good-natured and quite liberal men as heroes (Rashid and Indranath), but both the heroes shy away from questioning any of the laws that give them power because of their gender. As we will see, while Indranath is ready to give up part of his land to his tenant farmers, he is loath to give up the powers that his masculinity confers upon him. The same is true of *Breaking Ties* as well.

Formally, *Breaking Ties* is cast in the form of a love story – not a traditional one as in *Angaliyat*, but nevertheless, the story of a couple deeply in love and forced to separate due to human agencies and forced to continue this separation due to the laws that govern interpersonal relationships. Here again, as in both *Angaliyat* and *Jhadajhadati*, human frailties and peculiarities have to be taken into consideration. Nadira's father Mahammad Khan's greedy and wicked nature stands in total contrast to the loving and caring nature of her husband Rashid. What makes Mahammad Khan's plans work is the manner in which Islamic laws regarding divorce are practised. Heavy stress is laid in the text and in its accompanying piece on the fact that the way in which these Islamic laws are practised is not in keeping with what the Holy Koran advocates. Moreover, there is also an implicit criticism of the government's refusal to reform these laws. The absence of a sustained attempt from within the community itself to reform or ask for religious reforms also comes under attack.

Two basic issues regarding Islamic religious and personal laws are dealt with here – the question of *talaaq* or divorce and that of women's remarriage. The first of these becomes, in fact, the cause for the action in the novella as Mahammad Khan makes use of the practice whereby the husband is allowed to say '*talaaq*' three times *even in the absence of his wife* and such a divorce is considered valid. Khan's greed for money makes him lie to both Rashid and Nadira, convincing both of them that the other wanted the divorce. At the same time, since the novel is cast in the form of a love story, the disaster takes on romantic overtones, with the language and the events described taking on definite the tenor of what in classical Sanskrit theory would be called *viraha sringar rasa* or the *rasa* of love in separation. As in *Angaliyat*, the love story form—a favourite with the media—serves to make the issues all the more poignant. Nadira is forced stay in her father's house is replete with memories of the days she spent with Rashid in quite a cinematic flashback manner (21–22). The description of Rashid's state of mind is (24) just as evocative of *viraha sringara rasa*.

What is interesting from the point of view of this study is that such descriptions of the separation between husband and wife are embedded in various social and religious issues. Even before the dubious motif of *talaaq* is introduced, that of female education is brought in. Rashid's letter to Nadira asking her to meet him on the banks of the Chandragiri river is left unanswered because Nadira cannot write. She owes even her ability to read to her husband. Nadira's friend's response is typical, 'Are you serious? Why do women need to know reading or writing?' (32). In an atmosphere where the education of women is taken not even as a luxury, but as a totally unnecessary exercise, it is not surprising that Nadira, although having learnt to read haltingly, cannot write. It is only when she receives Rashid's letter that she realises the importance of what she does not have: 'Today, she cursed herself for her foolishness. If only she had learnt to read and write properly, she could have poured her heart out to him through letters and kept in touch with him' (33). To place the value of women's education in the traditional context of family and marital love may appear to be romanticising it, but it nevertheless provides a space to critique tradition from within. Nowhere in the text does Nadira break away from tradition – perhaps that is her tragedy. From one perspective this method of asking for women's education is akin to the method adopted by the nationalist movement of assuring society that education need not make a woman go astray. In many ways, the text and the accompanying piece fail to move out of patriarchy. The author seems to fail to seize the opportunity to make a frontal attack on her patriarchally motivated religion. While Nadira's lack of education is brought out in her inability to maintain a romantic relationship with her husband, Sara's education is seen primarily as her father's attempt to make a statement to his community. Hence, Sara's desire to represent her school in a basketball match is frustrated because her father feels that it would reiterate the idea that education will make a woman over-reach herself.

> You're the first Muslim girl in our community to set foot in a school. When just the act of your attending schools has raised so many eyebrows, what will people say if you went out of town to play? You must take care not to err in any way. If you do, then no other Muslim girl in this town will ever even glimpse a school". (97)

The ultimate aim of education remains in this case merely to recreate patriarchal notions of femininity while the woman is not allowed to take responsible decisions for herself.

Part of Nadira's problem in *Breaking Ties* is that she has been taught to internalise patriarchal values as universal and unquestionable. Therefore, when events do bring her to the point of questioning them, she is unable to act upon these questions and challenges.

In a household where the men hold the reins and the women have no official role to play as individuals, it is not surprising that Nadira is unable to stand up to her father. It is interesting that even after getting education and despite having a liberal father, Sara too is not allowed to take her own decisions. Such similarities between the novella and the autobiography force us to consider religious rules within the social context. Hence, although Sara's father quotes from the Koran to justify her education: 'Nowhere does the Qua'ran [sic] say that girls should not receive education. In fact, Prophet Mohammad has preached that women who are responsible for bringing up future citizens are in greater need of education than men' (95), the fact of their living in a rural Indian society makes them behave in a reactionary manner.

Added to this socially sanctioned subordination of women is the equally socially sanctioned violence that Mahammad Khan unleashes upon his family to keep himself in control. Instances of his violence begin right from the description of his wedding night with Fatimma.

The final authorial comment becomes all the more poignant in the light of the fact that Fatimma's father himself takes her to Mahammad Khan the following day despite her refusals saying, 'but would it do to give so much value to a woman's tears? Scolding and spanking her, Fatimma's father had carried her to Khan's room himself and consoled *him*! "Please don't feel bad. These girls behave like this until they get used to us"' (5, italics in original). As in *Jhadajhadati*, silent irony works as an excellent tool for exposing reactionary social and religious laws.

Mahammad Khan's violent nature is reinforced in various other ways and situations as well – his refusal to allow his wife to visit her nephew and his reaction to her late return from her sister's house: 'You filthy whore, where have you been, so late? Gone looking for your paramours?' (6) is but one of them. The description of him as a good-for-nothing who 'went on without a care, knowing full well that Fatimma would somehow manage and provide for the family' (2) only goes to buttress this image. Reinforced here is the idea of a woman working both within the house to 'run' it and provide for its income. This is an idea we already noticed in *Karukku* and it comes out strongly – the double burden that women bear in making these two spheres operate smoothly and the precious little assistance they receive in this matter is only to be lamented. Even her two daughters—especially Jamila—learn to roll beedies when they are still young and so provide for the family. The predicament of the woman is such that they run the family completely, but have absolutely no power whatsoever. The social sanctions given to such unequal distribution of power and labour make it even more difficult for the women to think about these situations as being unequal. It is to the voice of the narrator that we need to turn for such comments. The irony implied in statements such as 'After all, wasn't woman created for the service of man' (4) after elders reason out that 'It's always good to marry a young girl, because when the man grows old and is bed-ridden, the woman will have the strength to nurse him!'(4) is quite obvious. The open critique of Mahammad Khan only makes this clearer: 'Mahammad Khan was one of those who believed in the masculine principle to the total negation of the feminine' (39) and is brought out clearly in most of Khan's actions.

In the light of such brutalities, Khan's one saving grace is his monogamy, especially since the religion and therefore the law allows polygamy. Fatimma sees this as something to be thankful for, exemplifying the traditional notion that a woman can bear anything except to share her husband. It is almost as if in the light of this one 'goodness,' all of Khan's brutalities fade into insignificance in her eyes. It is doubtful whether the text itself asks this to be read in Khan's favour, but it does sadly betray the complete dependence of the wife on the man.

Set against such a brutal man like Khan, Nadira's husband Rashid emerges almost as godly, an aspect brought out again on their wedding night (9–10). The romantic images of two tender hearts opening out their wings (9) and the various ways and means by which Rashid shows his love for Nadira are a relief from customary male brutality and insensitivity. But Vanamala Vishwanatha argues in her introduction that he is both a victim as well as a victimiser, though the second role is played more subtly and unconsciously. What brings about the central action is, as already mentioned, Khan's ploys to get a divorce for Nadira from Rashid using the practised principles of Islamic laws in order that Nadira can be married to a rich old man.

This again brings us back to the idea of human agency. Widow and divorcee remarriage is one of the progressive aspects of Islam, but in the face of the greed of people like Khan, it gets twisted out of shape ironically turning the beneficiaries—the women—into victims.

Despite the fact that Nadira and Rashid already have a child, Khan manages his trick quite well. Yet again, we may take recourse to the narrative voice to understand his attitude:

> In his eyes, a woman was a creature without a heart, without feelings. She had to implicitly obey her father, husband and then her sons. As far as he was concerned, the child was Rashid's and so it was his responsibility. It was generous of them that they'd taken care of the baby all these months. In his scheme of things, Nadira didn't have much to do with the baby. Equally, if her father were to say, 'you don't need this husband: I'll find you another,' Nadira had to consent. The same applied for the relationship between husband and wife. If the word '*talaaq*' was uttered, everything was over between them. From that moment onwards, they were total strangers. If she possessed any of his belongings, they had to be sent back immediately. After the *talaaq*, he was no longer her man, but a stranger. Three and a half months later, she was free to marry another – this time span was allowed only to make sure that she was not pregnant by that husband. (38–39)

What Khan believed in were the practised principles of Islamic family and religious laws, laws which Aboobacker's autobiography implies, are more man-made (not woman-made) than Koranic:

> My mother herself taught me the scriptural texts of Islam. The Muslim myths and legends are available all over Kerala . . . . I learnt that Muslim women those days were not imprisoned within the house. I've read that Muslim women used to wield the sword in war and fight alongside men in the battlefield. (93).

By so historicising the subordinate position of women within practised Islamic law, Aboobacker implicitly makes a plea for changes from within the community to better the status of women by providing them greater justice and decision-making powers in matters regarding marriage, divorce, remarriage and custody of children. The issue of inheritance is not touched upon here.

What these practised laws amount to is psychological violence against women – violence that is potentially self-destructive. The way in which Khan secures a divorce for Nadira from Rashid is outright cheating. This is made possible largely because of the practice whereby the man is given the right to utter '*talaaq*' three times and divorce his wife even in her absence. This is precisely what Rashid does: 'I pronounce talaaq once, twice, three times to release my wife who is Mahammad Khan's daughter Nadira from wedlock' (48). Yet again, the narrative voice gives vent to its bitterness: 'The maulvi, Mahammad Khan and two others who were present acted as witnesses. All of them left having partaken in an act *that Allah was most averse to*' (48, italics mine). This method of divorcing is one where the power is vested entirely in the hands of the man. It makes even a meek person like Nadira question laws that she would otherwise never have dreamt of interrogating:

> But what kind of a law was this that the man who called himself 'husband' should pronounce *talaaq* three times from wherever he was, and the marriage was null and void! Startled by such thoughts, she was repentant the next moment: 'Who am I to question the sacred laws? Don't the maulvis keep saying in their sermons that the law of God should never be questioned. O Allah, forgive me . . .'(49–50)

Naturally, given her background and her understanding of religious laws, this would be blasphemy. Yet, the text itself makes it clear that the method generally adopted to divorce one's wife—of uttering '*talaaq*' three times—is not drawn from the Koran, but is a deliberate patriarchal misinterpretation in order to endow power with the men:

> People have no sense. No one bothers to read the Qua'ran properly. When we say that the husband has to utter *talaaq* three times, it does not mean he can say it all in one breath. He has to say it separately, over three months. That is the Qua'ran's way of giving us another chance to think. We really have to think long and hard before we say it the third time. Only when the husband is convinced that he cannot live with his wife should he use this option. Until the end of these three months, they should live under the same roof. If they can come together even after the second *talaaq*, the divorce is nullified and they can start afresh. But if one has to marry the same person again after the third *talaaq*, the wife should be married to another

> and then she should seek divorce from him because they are truly incompatible. Nowhere does the qua'ran decree that the wife has to go through a one-day marriage to remarry her first husband. These are ploys employed by selfish men for their convenience. (76)

What is most striking is that it is a maulvi who utters these remarks although he is one of the 'keepers' of religious law. Technically, for legal amendments to be made to religious and family laws, the demand should come from people such as him. But he follows his long comment with a telling statement: '"Keep your questions to yourself. I'm not prepared to fight the establishment." . . . he chided the boy who was throwing stones into the lake, "Hey, don't do that, the water will get muddy"'(76) thereby symbolically suggesting that he does not want to struggle against existing modes. The clerics remain the sole authority in interpreting Islamic laws and this makes it all the more clear why, as Parashar says, women continue to suffer religio-political inequality. When neither people like this Maulvi nor well-meaning men like Rashid even attempt to bring about changes—even within the spheres where they do have control—the issue of women asking for reforms in family and personal laws from within minority communities remains a distant dream.

Two other issues complicate the matter – that of custody of children and remarriage. The first is clarified by Khan himself in the passage quoted earlier – the child is the father's responsibility and the mother has little right over it. This is the religious sanction that allows Rashid and his mother to kidnap the breastfeeding child. In fact, Umma—usually a kind and loving mother-in-law—justifies her action using this discourse: 'who asked her permission? The child belongs to the father, all right. The baby is ours, after all' (43). However, Rashid and his mother do this in the hope that Nadira would defy her father and come at least for the child. This turns out to be a vain hope, as Nadira, brought up with a terrible fear of her father, is unable to defy him in any way. Moreover and most importantly, to return to Rashid means she has to cross the Chandragiri river – something she, as a woman, cannot do alone, as the society in which she lives would be outraged.

The metaphorical importance of the river increases as Nadira's grief and agonies do, for it becomes at once her tears, a means of meeting with Rashid, a barrier between them. and finally, her grave.

Rashid himself is not so much a victimiser as a victim of the same family and religious laws as is Nadira, although to a much smaller degree. It is perhaps to highlight the unjust nature of these laws to both men and women that the text takes up substantial space in describing Rashid's agony as well. Yet, his agonies remain purely emotional and have little of the psychological violence that Nadira's imply. This reaches a head when Khan asks Nadira to marry a rich old man only to get his money. The suggestion—an affront to her sexuality and another attempt by her father to control her sexuality—finally makes her defy her father: 'You married me off once, and that'll do. If you try again, I'll kill myself by jumping into the Chandragiri!' (54). Used to having his way all his life, Khan is unable to face this unforeseen belligerence and even begins negotiations for Nadira's remarriage with Rashid. Once again, religious and family laws come in the way; for it is required that the wife be married to another man for a night and that he voluntarily give her *talaaq* after which she can remarry her old husband. This attempt on the part of the law to regulate and control her sexual life and desires is revolting to her.

What Nadira is faced with here is violence—psychological violence from all sides—from her greedy father whose violent nature is made all the worse for the sanction it gets from religion, from religious laws as interpreted by male clerics to the detriment of the women, and from social customs that make it impossible for her even to move about alone. It is her understanding of all these and the deep feeling of being victimised that forces Nadira to initially agree to the one-night wedding and finally throw herself into the Chandragiri rather than face the affront to her sexuality.

Nadira's suicide is possibly the only decision she takes on her own and can be read as a sharp castigation of the religious and social laws that she is subject to. For her sister's suggestion that she and Rashid ignore the society and marry anyway is a thought not even to be considered. One legal option available here is the Special Marriage Act of 1956 according to which civil marriages can be performed overruling religious laws. This was one of the alternatives offered by the government, an optional law that people can choose. It is conspicuous by its absence. It might be mentioned that the Muslim clerics saw it as an affront to Islamic laws and demanded that a special clause be attached barring Muslims from using it – a request that was turned down. The fact that this option is not even considered only confirms the idea that legal reforms, although necessary, also need to be publicised and the beneficiaries made aware of their position as beneficiaries. Yet, it is doubtful whether awareness too would have allowed Rashid and Nadira to follow it in the face of hostility from their own religious establishment.

The novel acts therefore, as a bitter chastisement of the Islamic personal, religious and family laws as they are practised, bringing out the injustice and inequality that women are forced to endure as well as the internalisation of these laws and one's subordinate position by the women themselves. As in *Jhadajhadati*, here too we see how the space of fiction has been used as a discursive one, giving voice to the problems faced due to unjust laws and by implication, the failure of the government to alter these laws.

The impact of the novel can perhaps best be judged by the critical comments it provoked. Vanamala Vishwanatha mentions in her introduction that the novel, first published in Lankesh's little magazine (that should be clue enough to its anti-establishment attitude), was indulgently received under the impression that it was written by a man with a female pseudonym. When it came to be known that Sara was indeed a woman, it was charged that she was not a true Muslim. The implication is obvious. The novel questions the authority not so much of the Koran, but of the clerics who interpret the Koran and who, in the absence of state intervention, have been given sole authority to interpret and implement the Shariat. Such questioning by a woman, it is feared, would lead to more questions and shake the male establishment.

The ways in which the women of the community get together and help each other therefore almost forms a counter discourse to patriarchal hegemony. It is Nadira's female neighbour who acts as the carrier of messages between her and Rashid and even reproaches Rashid and his mother for snatching the child away from the feeding mother. This is recaptured in the autobiography as well:

> Though one was a Hindu and the other a Muslim, they were not sworn enemies like the members of RSS and Jamayat Islam who were at each other's throats. They were two people with human hearts who responded to the suffering and pain of another woman and helped her in every possible way. (94)

Yet another of such incidents is the exchange of religious ideas between Sara's mother and her Hindu neighbours: 'My mother would share many ideas from our scriptures with them. Equally, she would listen to the stories from the *Ramayana* and the *Mahabharata*. My mother, a staunch Muslim would compare the two and whenever she found something in common, she would laughingly say, 'So our religion and yours are the same then" ' (95). The image we get is that of a community of women wherein politicised enmities between religions do not matter much.

The autobiographical piece brings out an entire way of life of the Muslim community in the village of Kosuragodu on the banks of the Chandragiri. The introduction mentions that Sara is one of the few Muslim voices in Kannada literature and in the autobiographical piece, we get a glimpse of the social life of the Muslim community and the ways in which a young girl may feel stifled in it. The admonitions Sara's father had to face on account of her education and the fact that she went without a burkha, the ways in which she was treated by girls of other communities (some treated her as an untouchable while others gave her due respect), the openings that her education gave her etc., all form part of this piece.

What the novel and its accompanying piece foreground is the life of a minority female rural community – a community wherein internally the girls are oppressed due to misinterpretation of religious laws, and are also victimised in the name of secularism and freedom of religion by the state which has taken few steps to assure equality or indeed, give these women any choice.

*Angaliyat* and *Breaking Ties* deal, completely or otherwise, with the sexuality of women in minority communities. The sexual repression faced by women belonging to upper caste and 'ruling' families is no less a theme for novels. As already mentioned, caste often acts as a barrier in the formation of a feminine community and the internalisation of modes of behaviour can act in a similar way. Indira Goswami's Assamese novel *The Moth-eaten Howdah of the Tusker*[9] (originally published as *Datal Hatir Une Khowa Howdah* in Assamese) chosen for the Bharatiya Jnanpith Award in 2001, deals precisely with these issues. Set in the Kamrup district of Assam and more specifically within the Vaishanavite *sattras*[10] or monasteries, the novel deals with a range of subjects – the fall of an older feudal order which has gone rotten from within (along the lines of novels like Giriraj Kishore's *Dhai Ghar*), the influx of Communism and Marxist ideology into a feudal system and, what this analysis will focus primarily upon, the miserable state of widows in the *sattras* and the vicious circle they created by internalising various modes of behaviour.

One constant in the review of *Howdah* and indeed of Goswami's novels as a whole is the lack of overt ideology in them. More than one critic has spoken appreciatively of her 'human-ness' and non-ideological approach. Sisir Kumar Das, for instance, finds her work praiseworthy because there is no manipulation or endeavour to establish ideology in them (*Hindustan Times* SS). Similarly, D. K. Baruah mentions that although a feminist strain can be discerned in her treatment of certain themes, Indira Goswami primarily works with a 'larger canvas'. He further says that Indira Goswami is not really a feminist as she keeps the struggles of the women in her novels at an individual level and does not make them part of a 'common cause' (SS). Prafulla Kotoky reiterates these points when he says that the sympathy for the sufferers in Indira Goswami's novels is not doctrinaire nor an offshoot of political ideology, but is rather based on a belief in human compassion and values (SS). As has been constantly urged in our discussions, one important role that criticism can play is to construct precisely such an ideological and theoretical framework against which to analyse texts and arrive at a means of reading certain social and cultural constructs. Although the discussion on *Jhadajhadati* and *Breaking Ties* has, to a certain extent questioned the validity of the law and political machinery in correcting certain social distortions, there can be little doubt that battles of the oppressed sections of society need to be waged on many grounds: political, legal and even literary. So we beg to differ with D. K. Baruah that the struggles of the main characters are not made part of a common cause. While the text itself may contain no lines where any of the characters or even the narrative voice links up these struggles with the plight of women in general, there can be little doubt that the sufferings of the three widows of the Gossain household as well as that of Eliman are squarely because of their gender situation and insofar as this is true, their problems are part of the common struggle of women living within a set of socio-religious norms.

The setting of the novel—both temporally and spatially—is significant. Situating a text in this way not only marks out its cultural coordinates; but in the context of protest literature, it also brings out the various contours along which resistance has to take place. The struggle in *Breaking Ties* was primarily within a socio-religious framework and the same is the case here. We had also mentioned in our discussion on *Breaking Ties* that after Independence, the government chose to make changes to various aspects of Hindu family and religious laws. *Howdah* is set initially in the period immediately following freedom (it begins in 1948), but before any reforms had been handled or considered by the indigenous government. Within the *sattras*, only ancient laws related to caste and gender hierarchy that have been propagated and safeguarded by the male *sattradhikars* operate. The position of women therefore remains peripheral and they suffer some of the most inhuman kinds of oppression. This is not to deny that some laws enforced by the British government like the marriageable age of girls continued to operate in independent India. These laws nonetheless remained remote from social realities so that in *Howdah* girls are still married off before puberty to avoid excommunication of their fathers. Despite attempts to make laws known to the common people, there is little regard for them and in all ignorance and innocence, people take recourse to male-interpreted religious laws.

In the figures of the three widowed women in the *sattra*, the novel depicts the various ways in which modes of oppression have been internalised. The violence done to the human body and the disregard for basic human rights for decent living under the guise of tradition and 'culture' are sharply denounced in the novel. Moreover, being set at a time when India as a nation was moving into what it considered a 'modern' phase, traditionally ordained hierarchies of caste and class are questioned by the intervention of the newly formed government: witness the Land Ceiling Act and 'equality of all' proclaimed under the law. However, the hierarchies of gender remain as before and the already weak position of women is only reinforced by the new laws.

The depiction of the state of the widows in the *sattras* is one of the most poignant in the novel. The position of these women cannot very clearly fall into binaries of dominant or suppressed, for as members of the *sattras* and Gossain families, they occupy the highest caste status in the society. The novel even makes it clear that they are not on equal terms with 'ordinary Brahmins' and Indranath finds that his family priest has strong views on Gossains marrying girls from ordinary Brahmin families: 'Have you ever heard of a Gossain sending betrothal gifts to an ordinary brahmin girl? In this *sattra*, no Gossain has ever married an ordinary brahmin girl' (641–42).

However, this position of power operates differently for the women. We go back to the traditional Hindu notion of the sanctity attached to the 'married woman' (*suhagan*) and the consequent impurity that came to be attached to widowhood. This discourse has taken quite deep roots and finds expression in various ways. Apart from the inhuman ways in which widows have been treated—from physical abuse to verbal and psychological violence—it is also at the root of the primacy given to marriage in a woman's life in India and the sanctity attached to her 'husband's house' as against her mother's house. The latter may be a sanctuary in times of ill health and delivery, but can never become a permanent place of residence for an Indian woman. The social stigma attached to a married woman staying in her natal home is one more manifestation of the same discourse. These expressions almost always take the form of honour and social respectability so that the perpetrators of such oppressive practices appear to be women themselves. This has, in turn, led to other points of view that see women as the victims as well as the victimisers. It needs only a few minutes of reflection to understand that such perpetrations are often unconscious and motivated by the elusive 'family honour' and 'tradition' which society has enjoined a woman to uphold.

In such a context, any power or authority that women possess is solely because of their married status. Their belonging to a dominant class and caste operates more as a hindrance than as a source of help, for it merely puts more restrictions upon widows. Yet, in this discourse of respectability and social honour, the very restrictions are in fact seen as a means of attaining '*punya*'. In the figures of the three widows of the *sattra* in *Howdah*, we see three different ways of coping with the situation. The *sattradhikar* Gossain Mahaprabhu's sister Durga, his brother's wife Saru Gossainee and his young daughter Giribala offer three different pictures of brahmin widowhood. All three have been forced to follow most of the restrictions imposed upon their kind: their diet is strictly restricted to boiled rice and vegetables, their days are expected to be spent in religious rites, they ought to worship their dead husband's sandals and most importantly, they need to immerse their husband's ashes in the Holy Ganga to attain salvation. The underlying motive in most of these practices is the control of the sexuality of the women; widows and unmarried young girls who have attained puberty need to have their sexual urges controlled by tradition and custom. It is this that makes the *sattradhikar* marry off his young daughter Giribala to a debauched man who himself broke all rules of caste and class (510).

While such debauchery is allowed for men and even tolerated with indulgence, the women are made to bear the burden of culture, tradition and their maintenance. Hence, while Giribala's dead husband could do non-violent *prayaschit* (penance) for eating and sleeping with a low-caste woman, Giribala herself has to undergo severe beating, punishment and rebuke for eating 'flesh' as a widow. More than one issue is at stake here. On the one hand, we can easily discern how women are castled as the custodians of tradition. *Howdah* is set *after* Independence and it is striking that not a whiff of the social issues related to freedom can be caught. The *sattra* is conspicuously untouched by any of these concerns. In such a scenario, one wonders whether the demarcation of the inside–outside that Partha Chatterjee talks about is confined to the freedom movement alone. It appears rather that this underlying pattern was already present in the thought processes and that was perhaps why it operated so strongly even in movements which sought to benefit women. Regarding the difference in the positions of men and women, Giribala's statement to Mark towards the end of the novel is very telling:

> After I came of age, all those Gossainees on the river bank used to tell me: you are an angel, you are a sweet angel! But do you know? That husband of mine, who often visited that notorious woman, the opium thief, he used to say, 'What's so great about your beautiful body? That lady of Kiniari! Even though she is a low caste opium seller, her body glows with exciting sexuality . . . you are nothing in comparison . . . They say she always goes about sniffing at men, like a botch in heat, but where's that lustful current of blood flowing in the veins of Gossainee girls like you.' (646)

This statement underscores the centrality of sexuality in life in general. One of the commendations that Indira Goswami has received from critics is for her unashamed revelation of feminine sexual desires. The commendation is not without merit in this context too, for *Howdah* depicts the deleterious effects of sexual repression of widows. This repression comes out most strongly in the case of Giribala for it is she who is the youngest and therefore feels the strength of her sexuality the most. Moreover, among all the three widows, it is she alone who had not enjoyed conjugal love with her husband and hence, is all the more aware of the system which makes her a victim without giving her any choice in the matter.

Saru Gossainee offers yet another picture of Gossainee's widowhood – a woman who has courage enough to manage her own household and advise her disciples, thereby acting as a spiritual head as well. Yet, the respect she commands is not so much for her administrative and managerial skills as for her ability to perform all these without moving out of her house:

> Good gracious! We are ladies of the Gossain family! Go out there and expose ourselves? Saru Gossainee gets things done through her disciples. She has never set foot on the land herself. That is why she is respected so much by everybody . . . She knows how to keep the dignity and honour of the family intact! (392)

Just as Giribala feels a strong physical attraction for Mark, the British historian who is writing the history of the *sattra*, Saru Gossainee too feels the attraction for Mahidhar, a Brahmin who helps her in administering her lands. The sexual overtones are deliberate and bring out exactly the truth of Bhavaankaka's statement in *Angaliyat* regarding the practicality of the custom of widow remarriage. We can easily discern how the notion of sexual purity of upper caste women and the consequent branding of women of other communities as impure smacks of hypocrisy.

Yet, neither Giribala nor Saru Gossainee is able to come close to fulfilling her desires. Giribala's story ends in tragedy as she kills herself in the fire lit for purifying her after she is caught in the company of Mark. Mahidhar Babu, taking advantage precisely of the fact that Saru Gossainee will not go out and risk her family honour, tries to cheat her of her lands and money. Both Giribala and Saru Gossainee eventually become victims of a social order which puts enormous restrictions on their female sexuality and attempts to regulate the lives of women in general.

While both Giribala and Saru Gossainee transgress the system in their own ways—Giribala openly and Saru Gossainee covertly—Durga has internalised most of the restrictions and the attendant discourses of honour and salvation. This repression in turn makes her repressive towards Giribala. Giribala's father in fact, asks her to follow Durga as her role model and it is Durga who is most shocked at Giribala's eating 'flesh' and at her going out with Mark. She has internalised the system so thoroughly that she does not realise that she herself is its victim. Her one wish that she would be taken to her husband's house and die there remains a dream ironically enough because of the belief that it is the woman whose 'stars' are responsible for the luck of the family. This feeling is augmented by later developments:

> After her departure, her father-in-law's elephant had captured a wild tusker of high value. He had made a huge profit of it. Then a disciple had come from Mayang and built a temple at Chikarhati with donations of abundant gold and jewellery. He had given away seven

> bhigas of land too! Rumours floated . . . that now the inauspicious woman had gone, good luck and prosperity had flooded the sattra to enrich its soil. (395)

We can see here in all its gory reality the traditional dictum that all events occur due to the activities of the woman in the house. Far from giving the women a sense of superiority or centrality, as propagandists of this discourse asserted, it causes endless suffering and trauma, leading to a sense of loneliness: 'An intense abhorrence for life had cast a shadow of melancholy . . . She is childless . . . Her nature always had a tinge of pessimism which had now become darker, more frightening' (394–95).

The psychological violence inflicted upon the widows in the *sattras*, as was already mentioned, was a sure way of regulating the sexual lives of the women. Such repressed sexuality erupts in the novel in the form of intense physical attraction outside and beyond the bounds of society and religion – Giribala's for Mark and Saru Gossainee's for Mahidhar. Not allowed a natural and socially acceptable expression, this repression is ultimately symbolised by the titular elephant – the *must* or mad elephant that begins to kill in its way even the people it once loved. As Giribala's attraction for Mark increases and as she herself becomes more and more aware of it, the madness of the elephant seems to accentuate. It is tempting to read this as yet another manifestation of the mad woman in the attic syndrome,[11] but it also needs to be pointed out that *Howdah* is not *only* about the women / widows in the *sattras*. It places this issue in the context of other issues and concerns important at that time and in this context, the mad elephant takes on various other symbolic overtones as well.

The suffering and oppression of the Brahmin widows is set in the context of several social and economic changes which take place in Assam. Chief among them is the slow decay of the *sattra* as an institution and the influx of Marxist ideas that threaten to upturn class hierarchy. The Communists having made a mark among the disciples of the *sattradhikars* and labourers, the traditional awe with which the *sattradhikars* were once seen gives way to demands that the land would belong to the tillers themselves and that the *adhikars* should themselves till the land. Although these changes are viewed with a sense of disbelief, the protagonist Indranath, it appears, is not averse to them. Indications are that due to government intervention—through the Land Ceiling Act—the amount of property owned by the *sattradhikars* would be severely curtailed, thereby causing a change in power relations. Alongside these issues of economics, laws and power relations are also painted pictures of opium addiction that almost ate up most of Assam during the British rule. The efforts taken by the native government to rehabilitate the addicts also forms an important part of the novel.

It may superficially appear that these themes concerning the decay of the feudal order and women's oppression are two disconnected strands. Yet, when taken together, they offer a powerful critique of government policies, of the *sattras* as well as of historiography itself. The old feudal order is shown to be decaying due to a variety of reasons – the influx of Marxist ideas, internal problems and government intervention. The cumulative effect of these is to threaten the existing hegemony of the *sattradhikars* over their disciples or the workers. Yet, the fact remains that despite all these, the inequality between the genders and between the castes remains. If anything, Saru Gossainee, as proxy *adhikar*, feels threatened by the Communists in her lands. The impact of these new 'equalising' forces on the gender issue is less than negligible. What is even more disappointing is the fact that the protagonist Indranath, while supporting the claims made by the Marxists, appears to disregard completely the problems of gender. Although shown as a very liberal person who encourages Giribala's association with Mark and also thinks well of a possible association between them, he is absolutely inept when it comes to action. As a historian, Mark has the power to bring to light some of these oppressive structures and the atrocities against the widows and thereby induce the desire for change even within the community. Yet, by asking him to set aside Giribala's experience as 'merely one more' instance, Indranath is effectively blocking the possibility of bringing about social change through creating awareness.

Indranath's indecision in matters relating to gender leaves more than one woman affected. Eliman, waiting for Indranath to 'rescue' her from her opium-smuggling Brahmin household is kept waiting in vain, for Indranath is quite unable to break out of the position of power that his caste and gender 'naturally' give him. The Assamese tradition that necessitates that a girl be married before the onset of puberty forces even the most loving fathers to send their daughters to living hell for fear of excommunication, besides creating rifts between the women themselves. The image of older women waiting in open spaces to see if girls have 'stained their dress' is a recurring image that spells horror for the girls and ultimately leads to their destruction. Indranath appears quite unable to break most of the rules of gender inequality. Perhaps even the most liberal of minds finds it difficult to give up the position of power. Such a portrayal of Indranath, as of Rashid in *Breaking Ties*, is not without reason, for it questions the government's assumption that communities will themselves ask for changes and that passing laws will automatically be followed by their implementation. The novel can be read as subtly hinting that the ill-treatment of women, thanks to the unbridled power afforded to the male *sattradhikars,* is one reason for the decay of the old feudal order. This is only reinforced by the symbol of the mad elephant Jagannath who stands simultaneously for the repressed sexuality of the women and for the decayed feudal order. That his madness is ultimately traced to a rusted nail on the side of the ornamental *howdah* only nails down the truth that the source of destruction lies right within the *sattras* themselves.

As Vaishnavite monasteries, the *sattras* also operated as the source of dispersal of religion and religious ideas. In dealing with the last few years of the life of the *sattra*, *Howdah* also exposes the way in which Vaishnavism was practised in Assam. It must be remembered that for centuries, Vaishnavism was an important religious force in Assam and the Bhakti period was primarily the period of its resurgence and establishment. The emotional power that characterised that kind of Vaishnavism has, however, decayed into mere scriptural quoting in the novel. We find Sanskrit *?lokas* liberally splattered through the novel, and used primarily as a means of establishing scriptural authority for maintaining caste and gender inequality. The edition of the translation used here is a trifle inconsistent as only some of the *?lokas* are translated. But the impact is clear: any incident which appears to threaten the superiority of men or the *sattradhikars* or the Brahmins is met with a rigorous quoting from the scriptures. For instance, the Brahmin priests caught smuggling opium quote the Vedas to proclaim the holiness of the Brahmin body: 'In this world, there are many holy places. These holy places exist in the oceans also . . .and the same holy places can be found on the lotus feet of the brahmins too!' (491) and add, 'It is also written that in the hand of a brahmin exist heaven and Lord Hari . . . and in his limbs are found the most auspicious pilgrimage places and *yagyas* . . . in his arteries exist *trigunatmik prakriti* and in his neck there is *gayatri* *mantra*' (491). The same scriptures are quoted to impose rigorous penance on a widow if she broke any rules.

The presence of these scriptural quotations in the text shows the ways by which religion has been used to serve the interests of a particular section of society—the Brahmin male—in defiance of the laws (known or unknown). What is also brought out is the way religious ideas of marriage get embroiled with social customs and work to the detriment of women, again making women the victimisers as well as the victims. The importance given to the *suhaagan* status mentioned earlier is just one of them.

The centrality of religious sanction and the use of scriptures for vindication of certain practices is important as the *sattras* acted also as monasteries and the *sattradhikar* as the religious head who could interpret the scriptures for the people in his *sattra*. That the Gossain and the family priest were unscrupulously changing and altering the scriptural tenets for their own ends only reinforces the idea that once the hierarchy placing Brahmin men at the top has been set, it remains so unless challenged by a very strong counter-force. The same duty of spiritual headship is performed by Saru Gossainnee and the text explicitly projects the deviations she makes in scriptures as meant for human ends as against the selfish ends of the *sattradhikar* and the family priest: 'It was all a play for making some quick money. Of course, she herself was not averse to a slight change which served some beneficial human purpose' (574).

The text goes on to describe one such instance when she made alterations and it is an issue concerning women – polygamy. Her response to the pleas of a man come to ask her advice about taking another wife is given without consulting religious texts:

> 'A woman who deliberately destroys the household happiness of another man's wife, deserves contempt and I will give her a curse that will destroy her family lineage . . .'
>
> After hearing these words from the Gossainee, the *mahout* dared not take the other woman into his house and all ended well, *though in the scriptures, having more than one wife was allowed*" (574–75; italics mine)

What is implied is that religion need not be about an ontological reality, but merely offers a way of running one's life and community according to certain values. That Gossain and the priest alter religious rules for *their* convenience and not for humane ends like Saru Gossainee does highlight the fact that religion is used mainly as an institution by the powerful—here the men—for their benefit. The unasked question is why the same religious rules cannot be bent in favour of women.

The figure of Mark Sahib offers a point of contrast to most of the decadent men and women of the *sattra*. Apart from offering an escape route to Giribala from her sexual repression, Mark also undertakes to write the history of the *sattra* from old manuscripts, some of which are reproduced verbatim. It is notable that as a historian Mark has come so close in contact with the plight of Giribala and that Giribala should herself have helped him in unearthing ancient manuscripts. Perhaps as far as Giribala is concerned, the incident reiterates that it is inevitable that one reckons with sexuality as a necessity; that its repression will only have disastrous effects. For Giribala finds that given her repression, neither the quest for historical manuscripts (knowledge) nor the religious teachings of Hinduism nor Christianity (philosophy and theology) offer any solace to her. As a person forced to renounce her sexuality, she, like Nadira in *Breaking Ties*, finds suicide to be the only solution. Yet, her role in finding the ancient manuscripts is important, for it stresses in some way the role played by women in maintaining, preserving and unearthing tradition of a different kind, a tradition that needs to be written and made known to the world. It is equally telling that society virtually ignores this role, for the tradition which Brahmin women are usually expected to maintain demands staying indoors and observing rituals and does not permit the kind of activity that Giribala indulges in. Witness the comments when she is bitten by a snake:

> 'Why should it not bite her? That girl, to help that Christian, roams about through all the villages in search of manuscripts. She has left out none! In the *dhekal* of Kallapara's *jajamani* brahmin, she climbed up to the attic in search of manuscripts. There, that nasty snake attacked her. Those people had pleaded with her, not to go up into the attic. But that girl! Would she listen?' (456)

In his role as historian, as already mentioned, Mark has the power to bring to light various aspects of life in the *sattras*. In this context, it is important that he is painted as a compassionate and understanding man, a man who does not look at local customs with the contempt of an Orientalist. The history of the *sattra* from the pen of such a historian is capable of opening the possibility for changes. But this again is not to be, as after Giribala's death, he is forced to leave the town. In a way then, we can argue the novel itself fills the gap which he leaves. The novel writes part of the history of the *sattra* – a history in which the manuscripts of ancient times that Mark finds become a part, a history in which Mark's story itself forms a part, a history that talks of the beginning of the decline of the feudal order and most importantly, a history in which the sufferings of women loom large. As in the other novels discussed here, these sufferings are narrated as human stories and dramas, not as statistical data or theoretical assumptions. That pieces from the government's documents, legal reforms etc. form part of this 'history' highlights the role that such interventions can play. Ironically, in this novel by incorporating them, only their inefficiency is thrown into relief.

The effect of making such legal documents, local legends, etc. a part of this text is to evoke an entire era and a milieu. They also bring out the issues that the newly formed government considered important – removal of opium addiction, and conservation of natural resources. The novel also hints in the various interludes describing opium addiction and the Congress members' speech to the addicts that the period was one when the government felt it to be its duty to collect data and statistics and present it to the world, giving the idea that the image of the nation will be built on such data. Some of these amendments, in fact, make it possible for Indranath to get Eliman's prospective aged groom—a Brahmin—arrested for smuggling opium, thereby creating a rupture in caste hierarchies. The government's orders and rules regarding the killing of the mad elephant also show the intervention of the State in what would earlier have been merely an internal matter for the *sattra*. Yet, as already mentioned, these interventions in no way affect the role, position or place of women for whom traditional rules of religion and purity, interpreted by male members, still apply. The novel then can be said to view the government itself as an institution that shies away from actively altering existing social hierarchies – especially those that are practised in the name of religion. In effect, the legal system, while seeming to provide new and equal opportunities for hitherto repressed sections of society, actually fails to intervene in the social structure.

If this was true in *Breaking Ties* of minority communities where it was seen that the government actively refused to intervene to reform family and religious laws, it is equally so in the case of majority communities where, despite seeming reforms, the social structure remains rigid and reactionary. *Howdah* too raises disturbing questions regarding the role to be played by the State and religion in correcting social evils and much like the other novels discussed, seems to hint that both have so far not served the purposes satisfactorily. It depicts the problems and harrowing experiences of women of the upper castes, when their superior caste status in fact becomes a burden.

## Notes

1. This is true especially of countries in the African continent and authors such as the Somali writer Nuruddin Farah have critiqued this dependency in their novels.
2. Unless otherwise stated, all material for *Jhadajhadati* have been taken from the archives of the Saraswati Samman, especially Marathi *bhasha samiti* reports, abbreviated as SS hereafter.
3. The Lalit-Dalit controversy, Rita Kothari explains in her Introduction to *Angaliyat*, refers to the debate concerning whether Dalit experiences are aesthetic enough for literary expressions.
4. M. G. Ramachandran (1917–87), Tamil matinee idol, who later became Chief Minister of Tamil Nadu.
5. *Sthalapurana* refers to the history of a town/ city/ place of worship; it is usually an amalgam of myth, history and legend.
6. *Mother India* (1957) was a famous and path-breaking Hindi film directed by Mehboob Khan with Nargis in the lead role. It depicted the rebuilding of a village by a woman and has come to represent the Indian woman as resilient and as the major force behind the formation of a family/ community.
7. Many ideas with regard to family and personal laws are taken from a workshop on gender awareness conducted by The Centre for Peace and Conflict Resolution Studies, University of Madras.
8. In 1979, Shah Bano, a 60-year-old woman went to court asking for maintenance from her divorced husband. The Supreme Court in 1985 ruled in her favour, entitling her to maintenance with an upper limit of Rs 500 a month under Section 125 of the Criminal Procedure Code. Islamic orthodoxy saw this as a threat to and attack on Islam. That being an election year (1986), the Congress government buckled under pressure and fear and enacted the Muslim Women (Protection of Rights on Divorce) Act which gave the Muslim woman right to maintenance only upto three months or the period of *iddat*, after which the responsibility was shifted to her relatives or the Wakf Board.

9. 'Howdah' is the ornamental seat placed on an elephant on which the aristocracy and royalty rode.

10. *Sattras* are Vaishnavite monasteries where the head—the *Sattradhikar*—acts as landlord as well as the spiritual head.

11. Proposed by Sandra Gilbert and Susan Gubar in their path-breaking *The Madwoman in the Attic: The Woman Writer and the Nineteenth Century Imagination* (New Haven, Yale, 1979), the 'mad woman in the attic' symbolises a socially disruptive and violent self in the woman's unconscious. This is mostly fed by the disjunction between her natural desires and the social expectations of behaviour imposed upon her. Gilbert and Gubar's text read many archetypal fairy-tale characters like the witch and marginalised literary characters like Bertha Mason in *Jane Eyre* as manifestations of this mad woman syndrome.

## References

Aboobacker, Sara. *Breaking Ties*. 1984. Trans. Vanamala Viswanatha from Kannada into English (Chennai: Macmillan India Limited, 2001).

Anand. S., ed. *Touchable Tales: Publishing and Reading Dalit Literature* (Pondicherry: Navayana, 2003).

Bama. *Karukku*. 1992. Trans. Lakshmi Holmström from Tamil into English (Chennai: Macmillan India Limited, 2000).

Chatterjee, Partha. 'The Nationalist Resolution of the Woman's Question'. Eds. Kumkum Sangari and Sudesh Vaid. *Recasting Women: Essays in Colonial History* (New Delhi: Kali for Women, 1989), 233–53.

Davidar, David. *The House of Blue Mangoes* (New Delhi: Penguin, 2002).

Gandhi, M. K. *Hind Swaraj or Indian Home Rule*. 1928. Trans. M. K. Gandhi From Gujarati into English. *The Selected Works of Mahatma Gandhi*. Ed. Shriman Narayanan. Vol. 3 (Ahmedabad: Navjivan Publishing House), 1968.

Goswami, Indira. *The Moth-eaten Howdah of the Tusker*. 1984. Trans. Indira Goswami from Assamese into English. *The Search for the Sea: The Fictional World of Indira Goswami (Mamoni Raisom Goswami)*. Ed. Satarwala Kaikous Burjor (New Delhi: B. R. Publications, 2002), 187–338.

Hasan, Zoya. 'Muslim Women and the Debate on Legal Reforms'. *From Independence Towards Freedom: Indian Women Since 1947*. Eds. Bharati Ray and Aparna Basu (New Delhi: Oxford UP, 1999), 67–98.

Imayam. *Koveruk Kazhudaigal* (Beasts of Burden). Translated from the Tamil by Lakshmi Holmstrom (Chennai: East West Publishers, 2001).

Jaidev. 'Not by Law Alone: *Douloti* as a National Allegory'. *The Politics of Literary Theory and Representation*. Ed. Pankaj. K. Singh (New Delhi: Manohar, 2003), 25–52.

Khaund, Malaya. Collection of Criticism on Indira Goswami. Report of Assamese *Bhasha Samiti* on Indira Goswami. Saraswati Samman Archives (New Delhi: K. K. Birla Foundation).

Kothari, Rita. 'Short Story in Gujarati Dalit Literature'. *Economic and Political Weekly*, 27 May 2003. <http://www.ambedkar.org/shortstory>

Limbale, Sharankumar. *Akkarmashi* (The Outcaste). Trans. from the Marathi by Santosh Bhoomkar (New Delhi: Oxford UP, 2003).

*Longman Dictionary of Contemporary English*. International Edition (Essex: Pearson Education Ltd., 2004).

Macwan, Joseph. *Angaliyat*. n.d. Trans. Rita Kothari from Gujarati into English (New Delhi: OUP, 2004).

Markandeya, Kamala. *Nectar in a Sieve* (New York: John Day, 1954).

Mendelsohn, Oliver and Marika Vicziany. *The Untouchables: Subordination, Poverty and the State in Modern India* (Cambridge: Cambridge UP, 2000).

Menon, Nivedita. *Themes in Politics Series* (New Delhi: Oxford UP, 1999), 72–95. Referred to hereafter as *Themes*.

Nimbkar, Jai. 'Disturbing and Depressing: A Look at a Marathi Novel'. *Indian Review of Books*. Report of Marathi *Bhasha Samiti* on Vishwas Patil. Saraswati Samman Archives (New Delhi: K. K. Birla Foundation).

Parashar, Archana. *Women and Family Law Reform in India: Uniform Civil Code and Gender* (New Delhi: Sage Publications India Pvt. Ltd, 1992).

Parthasarathy, Indra. *The Legend of Nandan*. Trans. C. T. Indra from Tamil into English (New Delhi: Oxford UP, 2003).

Patil, Vishwas. *Jhadajhadati*. 1990. Trans. Gajanan Chauhan from Marathi into Hindi (New Delhi: Vani Prakashan, 1995).

———. 'A Man, Fair Enough to Understand their Grief'. Interview with Rajee Suri. No source. Report of Marathi *Bhasha Samiti* on

Vishwas Patil. Saraswati Samman Archives (New Delhi: K. K. Birla Foundation).

Pillai, Thakazhi Sivasankara. *Kayar* (Coir). Trans. N. Sreekantan Nair from Malayalam into English (New Delhi: Sahitya Akademi, 1997).

Sarup, Anand and Sulabha Brahme. *Planning for the Millions* (New Delhi: Wiley Eastern Ltd, 1990).

Sreedhar, M. V. 'Reaching the Unreached: Enabling Dalit Girls to Get Schooling'. *Manushi* 111 (1999): 10–20.

*The Manorama Year Book 2001* (Kottayam: Malayala Manorama, 2002).

*The New Penguin English Dictionary* (New Delhi: Penguin Books, 2000).

# TOWARDS A CONCLUSION

> A million mutinies, supported by twenty different kinds of excess, sectarian excess, religious excess, regional excess; the beginnings of self-awareness, it would seem, the beginnings of an intellectual life, already negated by old anarchy and disorder. But there was in India now what didn't exist 200 years before; a central will, a central intellect, a national idea. The Indian Union was greater than the sum of its parts . . .
>
> V S Naipaul, *India: a Million Mutinies Now (517–18)*

The discipline of change management tries to identify different phases of change in any organisation. Drawn from the broader discourse of Business Management, change management also tries to identify ways and means by which an organisation can cope with varied and differing attitudes to change. An early model of change management called the Kurt Lewin Model identifies three stages of change: namely *unfreezing*, followed first by the *change* itself and later by *refreezing*. A later model called the ADKAR model views change as consisting of not three, but five discernible stages: *a*wareness (of why change is needed), *d*esire (to participate in the process of change), *k*nowledge (about how to bring about a change), *a*bility (to implement the skills required for the change) and *r*einforcement (to sustain the change).

Taken together, these two models can help us understand the paradigm shifts that characterise the literary cultural ethos in India since the 1980s.

*Unfreezing* is the overcoming of inertia regarding an older model or the dismantling of an existing idea. Very similar to the concept of defamiliarisation proposed by the Formalist school of criticism, this stage is closely related to *awareness*. It is only when one becomes aware of the shortcomings of an earlier discourse can the complacency regarding that discourse be shaken off.

This phase is discernible in almost all areas in literary studies in India in the period we are considering, allowing for the number of discursive / critical positions to greatly multiply. This unfreezing has been made possible by a number of non-literary factors. The growing importance given to smaller matrices of identity in Indian culture and politics today, the suspicion with which majoritarian or even potentially majoritarian discourses are viewed along with the increasing numbers of media that disseminate information (notably the huge number of television channels, each giving different versions of news) have made it possible for the average Indian to become conscious of different, perhaps even contradictory, subject positions from which any cultural, social or political phenomenon can be viewed. The discussion in the first chapter about the postcolonial model can be a good example here. While the model 'unfroze' earlier Eurocentric notions of literary canon and form, this model itself was 'unfrozen' by the growing awareness that it could not easily accommodate *bhasha* literatures. This was reinforced by the growing importance given to regional languages and ethnic identities in all spheres and by the fear that a canon consisting of purely English literature would misrepresent India.

However, such an unfreezing would remain a mere idea unless it were to be complemented by a *desire* felt by constituent parts to participate in the change that is felt to be needed, by the *knowledge* to conceptualise the changes and the *ability* to implement them.

The growing number of subject positions from which discourses have been read, critiqued and 'unfrozen' are perhaps testimony enough for the desire by various groups to participate in a different model for reading and critiquing, not merely creative but also discursive literature. While Dalit intellectuals use models such as poststructuralism or deconstruction to reappraise foundational culture and traditional notions of literature and criticism, there has been a corresponding move by writers to discuss different issues in different, definitely anti-traditional ways. This has been further complemented by the rise of ideologically conditioned publishing houses (such as Navayana) that give visibility to such writings and by the increasing openness of colleges and universities—in India and elsewhere—to include Dalit literature in their syllabi. That many such texts have been considered for literary awards has given a further impetus to it.

Recent publications such as *Dalit Aesthetics* by Sharankumar Limbale and the various publications by Navayana try to establish different models for reading, appreciation and evaluation of this differential literary trend, thereby demonstrating the ability to conceptualise as well as bringing about an actual change.

Yet, this move is itself almost immediately critiqued. The discussion first in the second and later in the fifth chapter brought out arguments that saw this visibility given to Dalit writing itself as being ideologically orchestrated, thereby nullifying any subversive potential in it.

Such constant 'unfreezing' is one feature that characterises the literary–cultural scene in India in recent years. No sooner has one point of view or subject position been foregrounded than it is critiqued and other, earlier subsumed or silenced voices that come out into the open. Thus, for instance, if criticisms against the postcolonial model foregrounded regional or ethnic identities, these regional identities were further seen as comprising many marginalised streams which needed to be made visible. Thus, while *Red Earth and Pouring Rain* questioned colonial interpretations of Indian history, the Gopallapuram Chronicles and The Memory of Elephants offer a challenge to viewing only the pauranic model as the alternative model of historiography.

Such constant unfreezing does not allow any one model to '*refreeze*' or sustain itself for too long a period. This has virtually given rise, to draw from Naipaul, to a 'million mutinies' in the Indian literary cultural scene; a million voices, each asking for their rightful place and visibility. But while Naipaul saw these mutinous millions as an excess that needs to be purged, we might also celebrate the redefinition of India that they offer. India as a concept and idea still remains intact, for some political and cultural positions certainly require that the grand narrative of nationalism be reiterated. But this India is very different from say, the nationalist understanding of India that believed that national identity can be achieved only by denying smaller (regional, gender, caste) identity matrices. India—and consequently, Indian culture and literature—is no longer simplistically a 'unity' in 'diversity'—the diversities are what define India.

It would perhaps be futile to speculate on where we are going, although the fear or anticipation of what is to come is certainly one emotion that we have to cope with when dealing with any kind of change. One can only hope that we move towards a point where as many voices as possible make themselves heard, without necessarily prioritising any one voice, where ideas are critiqued for themselves and not for the subject position that articulates them, where even suspect methods can be fruitfully adapted to suit one's own ends and where disciplines and discourses flow into each other, allowing us to see any one of them as part of a cultural continuum.

## References

Naipaul, V. S. *India: A Million Mutinies Now*. (1990; rpt. New Delhi: Minerva, 1993).

Desai, Boman. *The Memory of Elephants.* (1988; Kent: Sceptre, 1990).

Limbale, Sharankumar. *Towards an Aesthetic of Dalit Literature: Histories, Controversies and Considerations*. Trans. Alok Mukherjee (Delhi: Orient Longman, 2004).

# A SELECT BIBLIOGRAPHY

## *Novels*

Aboobacker, Sara. *Breaking Ties*. 1984. Trans. Vanamala Vishwanatha from Kannada into English. Chennai: Macmillan India Limited, 2001.

Aiyer, B. R. Rajam. *The Fatal Rumour*. Trans. Stuart Blackburn from Tamil into English. New Delhi: Oxford UP, 1998.

Anantanarayanan, M. *The Silver Pilgrimage*. New Delhi: Arnold Heinemann, 1975.

Bama. *Karukku*. 1992. Trans. Lakshmi Holmström from Tamil into English. Chennai: Macmillan India Limited, 2000.

Baraney, Inez. *Neem Dreams*. New Delhi: Rupa and Co., 2003.

Chandra, Vikram. *Red Earth and Pouring Rain*. New Delhi: Penguin, 1995.

———. *Love and Longing in Bombay*. New Delhi: Penguin, 1997.

Davidar, David. *The House of Blue Mangoes*. New Delhi: Penguin, 2002.

Desai, Boman. *The Memory of Elephants*. 1988. Kent: Sceptre, 1990.

Divakaruni, Chitra Banerjee. *The Mistress of Spices*. London: Black Swan, 1997.

Gangopadhyay, Sunil. *First Light*. Trans. Aruna Chakravarti from Bengali into English. New Delhi: Penguin Books, 2001.

Ghosh, Amitav. *The Calcutta Chromosome: A Novel of Fevers, Delirium and Discovery*. New York: Avon Books, 1997.

———. *The Shadow Lines*. New Delhi: Oxford UP, 1988.

———. *In an Antique Land*. New Delhi: Ravi Dayal Publishers, 1992.

Gokhale, Namita. *Mountain Echoes: Reminiscences of Kumaoni Women*. New Delhi: Lotus Collection Roli Books, 1998.

Goswami, Indira. *The Moth-eaten Howdah of the Tusker*. 1984. Trans. Indira Goswami from Assamese into English. *The Search for the Sea: The Fictional World of Indira Goswami (Mamoni Raisom Goswami*) Ed. Satarwala Kaikous Burjor. New Delhi: B. R. Publications, 2002, 187–338.

Gupta, Sunetra. *The Glassblower's Breath*. New Delhi: Penguin Books, 1993.

———. *A Sin of Colour*. New Delhi: Penguin, 1999.

Hariharan, Githa. *When Dreams Travel*. London: Picador, 1999.

———. *In Times of Siege*. New Delhi: Penguin, 2003.

Hussain, Attia. *Sunlight on a Broken Column*. New Delhi: Penguin, 1979.

Hyder, Qurratulain. *River of Fire*. 1959. Trans. Qurratulain Hyder from Urdu into English. New Delhi: Kali for Women,1998.

Jung, Anees. *Unveiling India: A Woman's Journey*. New Delhi: Penguin, 2000.

Imayam. *Koveruk Kazhudaigal*. Trans. from the Tamil by Lakshmi Holmstrom. Chennai: East West Publishers, 2001.

Karanjia, B. K. *More of an Indian*. New Delhi: Orient Paperbacks, 1970.

Kesavan, Mukul. *Looking Through Glass*. New Delhi: Ravi Dayal Publisher, 1995.

Kishore, Giriraj. *The Knight's Move*. Trans. Prajapati Sah from Hindi into English. New Delhi, Sahitya Akademi, 1996.

Limbale, Sharankumar. *Akkarmashi: The Outcaste*. Trans. from the Marathi by Santosh Bhoomkar. New Delhi: Oxford UP, 2003.

Macwan, Joseph. *Angaliyat*. n.d. Trans. Rita Kothari from Gujarati into English. New Delhi: OUP, 2004.

Markandaya, Kamala. *Nectar in a Sieve*. New York: John Day, 1954.

Nair, M.T. Vasudevan. *Kaalam*. Trans. Gita Krishnankutty from Malayalam into English. Mumbai: Disha Books, 1998.

Nagarkar, Kiran. *Cuckold*. New Delhi: HarperCollins Publishers, 1997.

———. *Ravan and Eddie*. New Delhi: Penguin Books, 1995.

Nambisan, Kavery. *The Scent of Pepper*. New Delhi: Penguin Books, 1996.

Nemade, Bhalchandra. *Cocoon*. 1963. Trans. Sudhakar Marathe from Marathi into English. Chennai: Macmillan, 1997.

Patil, Vishwas. *Jhadajhadati*. 1990. Trans. Gajanan Chauhan from Marathi into Hindi. New Delhi: Vani Prakashan, 1995.

Pillai, Thakazhi Sivasankara. *Kayar* (Coir). Trans. N. Sreekantan Nair from Malayalam into English. New Delhi: Sahitya Akademi, 1997.

Rajanarayanan. Ki. *Gopalla Gramam*. Tamil. Sivagangai: Selma, 1976.

———. *Gopallapurathu Makkal*. 1990. 2nd ed. Tamil. Sivagangai: Selma, 1993.

Rushdie, Salman. *Midnight's Children*. 1981. London: Picador, 1982.

———. *Shame*. New Delhi: Rupa and Co., 1983.

Sethu. *Pandavapuram*. Trans. Prema Jayakumar from Malayalam into English. Macmillan Modern Novels in Translation. Madras: Macmillan, 1995.

Vishwanatha, Vanamala et al. *Routes: Representation of the West in Short Fiction from South India*. Chennai: Macmillan India Ltd. and the British Council, 2000.

### *Drama*

Parthasarathy, Indra. *The Legend of Nandan*. Trans. C. T. Indra from Tamil into English. New Delhi: Oxford UP, 2003.

## CRITICAL WORKS

### *Books and Essays*

Ahmed, Aijaz. 'Jameson's Rhetoric of Otherness and the "National Allegory"'. *Post-colonialism: Critical Concepts*. Ed. Diana Brydon. Vol. 2. Critical Concepts in Literature and Culture Studies Series. London: Routledge, 2000, 565–88.

Aloysius, G. *Nationalism Without a Nation in India*. New Delhi: Oxford UP, 1997.

Anand. S., ed. *Touchable Tales: Publishing and Reading Dalit Literature*. Pondicherry: Navayana, 2003.

Anderson, Benedict. *Imagined Communities: Reflections on the Origin and Spread of Nationalism*. 1983. Rev. Ed. London: Verso, 1991.

Arnold, David. 'A Time for Science: Past and Present in the Reconstruction of Hindu Science, 1860–1920.' Ed. Daud Ali. *Invoking the past: the uses of history in south-asia*. New Delhi: Oxford UP, 1999 156–78.

Ashcroft, Bill, Gareth Griffith and Helen Tiffin. *The Empire Writes Back: Theory and Practice in Post-colonial Literature*. 2nd ed. London: Routledge, 1989.

Basnett, Susan and Harish Trivedi, eds. *Post-colonial Translation*. London: Routledge, 1999.

Bhabha, Homi, ed. *Nation and Narration*. 1990. London: Routledge, rpt. 1991.

Bharucha, Nilufer and Vilas Sarang, eds. *Indian-English Fiction: 1980–1990: An Assessment*. New Delhi: B. R. Publishing Corporation, 1994.

Blackburn, Stuart and Vasudha Dalmia. Introduction. *India's Literary History: Essays on the Nineteenth Century*. Eds. Stuart Blackburn and Vasudha Dalmia. New Delhi: Permanent Black, 2004.

Burjor, Satarwala Kaikous, ed. *Indira Goswami (Mamoni Raisom Goswami): The Search For the Sea*. New Delhi: B. R. Publications, 2002.

Chaudhuri, Amit. Introduction. *The Picador Book of Modern Indian Literature*. Ed. Amit Chaudhuri. London: Picador, 2001.

Chatterjee, Partha. 'The Nationalist Resolution of the Woman's Question'. Eds. Kumkum Sangari and Sudesh Vaid. *Recasting Women: Essays in Colonial History*. New Delhi: Kali for Women, 1989, 233–53.

Clarke, T. W., ed. *The Novel in India*. London: George Allen and Unwin, 1970.

Dasgupta, Sudha Chakraborty, ed. *Regionality and Comparative Literature: Papers in Comparative Literature: Seminars and Workshops 1993–1998*. Jadavpur: Jadavpur UP, 1998.

Dev, Amiya, ed. *Narrative: A Seminar*. New Delhi: Sahitya Akademi, 1994.

———. 'Conscience, Activism and Intellect: Jaidev's Location'. *The Politics of Literary Theory and Representation*. Ed. Pankaj K. Singh. New Delhi: Manohar, 2003, 67–73.

Devy, G. N. *After Amnesia: Tradition and Change in Indian Literary Criticism*. Bombay: Orient Longman, 1992.

———. *Of Many Heroes: An Indian Essay in Literary Historiography*. Mumbai: Orient Longman, 1998.

———. 'History and Historiography in Pre-colonial India'. *Indian Literary Criticism in English*. Critics, Texts, Issues Series. Ed. P. K. Rajan. New Delhi: Rawat Publications, 2004, 230–51.

Diertrich, Gabrielle. 'Women, Ecology and Culture'. *Gender and Politics in India*. Ed. Nivedita Menon. Themes in Politics Series. New Delhi: Oxford UP, 1999, 72–95.

Gandhi, M. K. *Hind Swaraj or Indian Home Rule*. 1928. Trans. M. K. Gandhi from Gujarati into English. *The Selected Works of Mahatma Gandhi*. Ed. Shriman Narayanan. Vol. 3. Ahmedabad: Navjivan Publishing House, 1968.

Guha, Ranajit. Introduction. *A Subaltern Studies Reader: 1986–1995*. Ed. Ranajit Guha. New Delhi: Oxford UP, 1997.

Gupta, Akhil. Introduction. *Post-colonial Developments: Agriculture in the Making of Modern India*. New Delhi: Oxford UP, 1998.

*Encyclopedia of Indian Literature*. 4 vols. New Delhi: Sahitya Akademi, 1987.

Harris, V. C. Introduction. *Pandavapuram*. Sethu. Trans. Prema Jayakumar. Macmillan Modern Novels in Translation. Madras: Macmillan, 1995.

Hasan, Zoya. 'Muslim Women and the Debate on Legal Reforms'. *From Independence Towards Freedom: Indian Women Since 1947*. Eds. Bharati Ray and Aparna Basu. New Delhi: Oxford UP, 1999, 67–98.

Hoffman, Michael. J and Patrick D. Murphy, eds. *Essentials of the Theory of Fiction*. 2nd ed. London: Leicester UP, 1996.

Holton, Robert. J. *Globalisation and the Nation–State*. London: Macmillan, 1998.

Huntington, Samuel P. *The Clash of Civilisations and the Remaking of World Order*. 1996. New Delhi: Penguin, 1997.

Iyengar, Srinivasa K. R. *Indian Writing in English*. 1962. Rev. ed. Bangalore: Sterling Publishers Pvt. Ltd, 1987.

Jaidev. *The Culture of Pastiche: Existential Aestheticism in the Contemporary Hindi Novel*. Shimla: Indian Institute of Advanced Study, 1993.

———. 'Not by Law Alone: *Douloti* as a National Allegory'. *The Politics of Literary Theory and Representation*. Ed. Pankaj. K. Singh. New Delhi: Manohar, 2003, 25–52.

Jain, Jasbir. *Creating Theory: Writers on Writing*. Delhi: Pencraft International, 2000.

———. 'Towards the 21st Century: The Writing of the 1990s.' *Indian Writing in English: The Last Decade*. Ed. Rajul Bhargava. Jaipur: Rawat Publications, 2002.

Jain, Jasbir and Vina Singh, eds. *Contesting Post-colonialisms*. New Delhi: Rawat Publications, 2000.

Jameson, Fredric. 'Third-World Literature in the Era of Multinational Capitalism'. *Post-colonialism: Critical Concepts.* Ed. Diana Brydon. Vol. 2. Critical Concepts in Literature and Culture Studies. London. Routledge, 2000, 541–62.

Jogdand P. G, ed. *Dalit Women: Issues and Perspectives*. New Delhi: Gyan Publishing House and University of Pune, 1995.

Kapadia, Novy. *Parsi Fiction*. Vol. 1. New Delhi: Prestige Books, 2001.

Kapoor, Kapil. *Literary Theory: Indian Conceptual Framework*. New Delhi: Affiliated East West Press Pvt. Ltd., 1998.

Khair, Tabish. *Babu Fictions: Alienation in Contemporary Indian English Novels*. New Delhi: Oxford UP, 2001.

Kirpal, Viney. *The Third World Novel of Expatriation: A Study of Émigré Fiction by Indian, West African and Caribbean Writers*. New Delhi: Sterling Publishers, 1989.

———. ed. *The New Indian Novel in English: A Study of the 1980s*. New Delhi: Allied Publishers, 1990.

Kishwar, Madhu. *Off the Beaten Track: Rethinking Gender Justice for Women*. New Delhi: Oxford UP, 1999.

Kumar, V. L. V. N. Narendra. *Parsee Novel*. New Delhi: Prestige Books, 2002.

Lakshmi, C. S. *The Face Behind the Mask: Women in Tamil Literature*. Women in Society Series. New Delhi: Vikas Publishing House Pvt. Ltd, 1984.

———. *Payanappada Padaigal: Katchi Vadiva Varalatrup Payilarangil Penn Kalaignargalin Padivugal*. (Tamil). (*Untrodden Paths: Sound and Picture Archives on Women Artistes*). Compiled by. A. Srinivasan and M. Shivasubramanian. Mumbai: SPARROW (Sound and Picture Archives for Research on Women), 2001.

Limbale, Sharankumar. *Towards an Aesthetic of Dalit Literature: Histories, Controversies and Considerations*. Trans. Alok Mukherjee. Delhi: Orient Longman, 2004.

*Longman Dictionary of Contemporary English*. International Edition. Essex: Pearson Education Ltd., 2004.

Machwe, Prabhakar. 'The Regional Novel and Neo-Realism'. *Four*

*Decades of Indian Literature: A Critical Evaluation*. New Delhi: Chetana Publications, 1976.

Madiyazhagan, M. *Naveena Ilakkiya Sindanaigal*. Tamil. (Thoughts on Modern Literature). Pondicherry: Breith Veliyeettagam, 1995.

*The Manorama Year Book 2001*. Kottayam: Malayala Manorama, 2002.

*Masterpieces of Indian Literature*. 3 vols. Ed. K. M. George. New Delhi: National Book Trust, 1997.

McHale, Brian. 'From "Chinese Box Worlds"'. *Postmodern Fiction*. London: Methuen, 1987.

Mehrotra, A. K, ed. *A History of Indian Literature in English*. London: Hurst and Company, 2003.

Mendelsohn, Oliver and Marika Vicziany. *The Untouchables: Subordination, Poverty and the State in Modern India*. Cambridge: Cambridge UP, 2000.

Menon, Nivedita. Introduction. *Gender and Politics in India*. Ed. Nivedita Menon. Themes in Politics Series. New Delhi: Oxford UP, 1999.

Michael, S. M., ed. *Dalits in Modern India: Vision and Values*. New Delhi: Vistaar Publications, 1999.

Mohanty, Manoranjan. *Class, Caste, Gender.* Readings in Indian Government and Politics Series. New Delhi: Sage Publications, 2004.

Mukherjee, Meenakshi. *Realism and Reality: the Novel and Society in India*. New Delhi: Oxford UP, 1985.

———. 'The Anxiety of Indianness: Our Novels in English'. *Postcolonial Literature in English*. Ed. Nilufer Bharucha and Vrinda Nabar. New Delhi: Vision Books, 1998, 78–93.

Mukherjee, Sujit. *Translation as Discovery*. Sangam Books, 1981.

Nabar, Vrinda. *Caste as Woman*. New Delhi: Penguin, 1995.

Nagendra, ed. *Literary Criticism in India*. Meerut: Sarita Prakashan, 1976.

Naik, M. K. *A History of Indian English Literature*. 1982. New Delhi: Sahitya Akademi, 1995.

Naipaul, V.S. *India: A Million Mutinies Now*. 1990. Rpt. New Delhi: Minerva, 1993.

Nandy, Ashis. *The Intimate Enemy: Loss and Recovery of the Self under Colonialism*. New Delhi: Oxford UP, 1983.

Narasimhan, Raji. *Sensibility Under Stress: Aspects of Indo-English Fiction*. Delhi: Ashajanak Publishers, 1971.

Narayan, Kirin. *Storytellers, Saints and Scoundrels: Folk Narrative in Hindu Religious Teaching*. New Delhi: Motilal Banarsidass Pub. Pvt. Ltd, 1992.

Narayan, Shyamala A. *Raja Rao: Man and his Works*. Bangalore: Sterling Publishers Pvt. Ltd, 1988.

Naval, Nandakishore. *Hindi Alochana ka Itihas*. (Hindi). (The History of Hindi Criticism). New Delhi: Rajkamal Prakashan, 1981.

*The New Penguin Dictionary*. New Delhi: Penguin Books, 2000.

Padma, V. 'Neither on Either Side nor In-between: the Anglo-Indian and Post-colonial Indian Fiction in English'. *Presentations of Postcolonialisms in English*. Ed. Jaydeep Sarangi. New Delhi: Authorpress, 2007, 127–44.

Pandey, Sudhakar and R. Raj Rao, eds. *Image of India in the Indian Novel in English: 1960–1985*. Mumbai: Orient Longman Ltd, 1993.

Panikker, Ayyappa. *A Perspective of Malayalam Literature*. Madras: Anu Chitra Publishers, 1990.

———. 'The Oral Narrative Tradition in Malayalam'. Anu Chitra Publishers, 39–42.

———. 'The Narratology of Thakazhi's *Kayar*'. Anu Chitra Publishers, 101–9.

———. 'Literary Criticism in Malayalam'. Anu Chitra Publishers, 121–30.

———. 'Towards an Indian Theory of Literary Translation'. *Translation: From Periphery to Centrestage*. Ed. Tutun Mukherjee. New Delhi: Prestige Books, 1998, n.p.

Paranjape, Makarand, ed. *Nativism: Essays in Criticism*. New Delhi: Sahitya Akademi, 1997.

———. *Towards a Poetics of the Indian English Novel*. Shimla: Indian Institute of Advanced Study, 2000.

Parashar, Archana. *Women and Family Law Reform in India: Uniform Civil Code and Gender*. New Delhi: Sage Publications India Pvt. Ltd, 1992.

Pathak, R. S., ed. *Indian Fiction of the Nineties*. New Delhi: Creative Books, 1997.

Pillai, Thakazhi Sivasankara. 'Excerpts from Acceptance Speech'. *Jnanpith Puraskar: 1965–1990*. (Hindi). Ed. Bishen Tandon. New Delhi: Bharatiya Jnanpith Prakashan, 1991.

Pollack, Sheldon, ed. *Literary Cultures in History: Reconstructions from South Asia*. New Delhi: Oxford UP, 2003.

Prem and Ramesh. *Ki. Rajanarayanan: Ezhuthulagam*. (Tamil). (The World of Ki. Rajanarayan's Writing). Chennai: Kalaignan Padippagam, 2000.

Premchand, Munshi. *Kuch Vichar: Nibandh*. (Hindi). (Some Thoughts: Essays). New Delhi: Diamond Pocket Books, n.d.

Preston, P. W. *Development Theory: An Introduction*. 1996. Oxford: Blackwell (Indian Rpt.), 2001.

Rai, Girija. *Sahitya ka Naya Shastra*. (Hindi). (A New Aesthetics for Literature). Illahabad: Shalini Prakashan, 2000.

Raja, Kunhan. C. *Survey of Sanskrit Literature*. Bombay: Bharatiya Vidya Bhavan, 1962.

Rajan, P. K Ed. *Indian Literary Criticism in English: Critics, Texts, Issues*. Jaipaur: Rawat Publications, 2004.

Rajashekhara. *Kavyamimamsa*. Trans. Sadhana Parashar from Sanskrit into English. New Delhi: D. K. Printworld Pvt. Ltd., 2000.

Ramachandran, C. N. 'Critical Responses to Rushdie'. *Writers of the Indian Diaspora*. Ed. R. K. Dhawan. New Delhi: Prestige Books, 2001, 27–35.

Ramamurthy, K. S. *Rise of the Indian Novel in English*. Bangalore: Sterling Publishers, 1987.

Rege, Sharmila, ed. *Dalit Women: Issues and Perspectives*. Pune: Gyan Publishing House and University of Poona, 1995.

Rushdie, Salman. *Imaginary Homelands: Essays in Criticism: 1981–1991*. London: Granta Books, 1991.

———. 'Exclusive Interview.' *Salman Rushdie: The Essential Guide: Midnight's Children, Shame, The Satanic Verses*. London: Vintage, 2003.

Rushdie, Salman and Elizabeth West, eds. Introduction. *The Vintage Book of Indian Writing: 1947–1999*. London: Vintage, 1997.

Said, Edward. *Representations of the Intellectual: The 1993 Reith Lectures*. London: Vintage, 1994.

Said, Edward. *Reflections on Exile and Other Literary and Cultural Essays*. New York: Penguin Books, 2001.

Sardar, Ziauddin. Introduction. Ashis Nandy. *Return from Exile*. New Delhi: Oxford UP, 1998.

Sarup, Anand and Sulabha Brahme. *Planning for the Millions*. New Delhi: Wiley Eastern Ltd, 1990.

Satyapremi, Purushottam ed. *Dalit Sahitya: Sṛjan ke Sandarbh*. (Hindi). (Dalit Literature: The Contexts of its Creation). New Delhi: Kāmna Prakāshan, 1999.

Sharma, Neeta. *Banabhatta: A Literary Study*. Delhi: Munshiram Manoharlal, 1968.

Sharrad, Paul. *Raja Rao: Culture and Tradition*. New Delhi: Sterling Publishers, 1987.

Shastri, Pushpendra. *Introduction to the Puranas: The Lighthouse of Indian Culture*. New Delhi: Rashtriya Sanskrit Sansthan, 1995.

Shiva, Vandana. *Staying Alive: Women, Ecology and Survival in India*. New Delhi: Kali for Women, 1988.

Shiva, Vandana and Maria Mies. *Ecofeminism*. New Delhi: Kali for Women, 1993.

Shivakumar, R. (Unpublished Dissertation). 'Literary Avant-gardism in American Little Magazines with Special Reference to *Poetry* and *The Little Review*'. M. Phil. University of Madras, 1989.

Sivasankari. *Knit India Through Literature*. 4 vols. Chennai: East West Books Pvt. Ltd, 1998.

Srivastava, Bina. *Hindi Upanyas ka Vikas aur Madhyavargeeya Chetana*. (Hindi). (Bourgeois Mentality and The Growth of Hindi Literature). New Delhi: Macmillan India Ltd, 1981.

Srivastav, Paramanand, ed. *Samakaleen Hindi Alochana*. (Hindi). (Contemporary Hindi Criticism). New Delhi, Sahitya Akademi, 1998.

Subramaniam, K. N. *Vimarisana Kalai*. (Tamil). (The Art of Criticism). Chennai: Narmada Padippagam, 1984.

Tandon, Bishen, ed. *Jnanpith Puraskar: 1965–1990*. (Hindi). (Jnanpith Award: 1965–1990). New Delhi: Bharatiya Jnanpith Prakashan, 1991.

Thapar, Romila. *Interpreting Early India*. New Delhi: Oxford UP, 1992.

Thapar, Romila. 'Some Appropriations of the Theory of the Aryan Race Relating to the beginnings of Indian History'. Ed. Daud Ali. *Invoking the Past: the Uses of History in South-Asia*. New Delhi: Oxford UP, 1999, 15–36.

Tharu, Susie and Lalitha, eds. *Women Writing in India.* 2 vols. New Delhi: Oxford UP, 1991.

Tiwari, Nityanand. *Aadhunik Hindi Sahitya Mein Itihas Bodh*. (Hindi). (Historical Sense in the Modern Hindi Novel). New Delhi: Vani Prakashan, 1982.

Trivedi, Harish and Meenakshi Mukherjee, eds. *Interrogating Post-colonialism: Theory, Text and Context*. Shimla: Indian Institute of Advanced Study, 1996.

Vishwanathan, Gauri. *Masks of Conquest: Literary Study and British Rule in India*. London: Faber and Faber, 1989.

Waugh, Patricia. *Metafiction: The Theory and Practice of Self-conscious Fiction*. New York: Methuen and Co., 1984.

Wilfred, Felix. 'Whose Nation? Whose History?'. *The Struggle for the Past: Historiography Today*. Eds. Felix Wilfred and Jose D. Maliekal. Chennai: Department of Christian Studies, University of Madras, 2002, 71–99.

Young, Robert. J. C. *Post-colonialism: An Historical Introduction*. Oxford: Blackwell Publishers, 2001.

## *Articles from Journals and Newspapers*

'All For English'. Editorial. *The Hindu*, 14 Feb. 2003, 10.

Asher, R. E. 'Kerala's Greatest Modern Writers'. *Malayalam Literary Survey*. 21, 2 (Apr.–Jun. 1999), 26–32.

Ashokamitran. 'Tharkala Ulaga Ilakkiyathaip Pattri Talavay Sundar-athidam Ashokamitran Pesugirar'. (Tamil). ('Ashokamitran Talks to Talavay Sundaram about the Position of Contemporary World Literature'). *Kumudam International: Deepavali Malar*, 4 Nov. 2002, 280–87.

Bharucha, Nilufer. E. 'Reflections in Broken Mirrors: Diverse Diasporas in Recent Parsi Fiction'. *Wasafiri*, 21 (Spring 1995), 32–35.

Chaudhuri, Amit. 'Gods, Monkeys and Englishmen'. Review of *Red Earth and Pouring Rain* by Vikram Chandra. *Times Literary Supplement*, 2 Jun 1995, 20.

Futehally, Shama. 'Classic Let-down'. Review of *River of Fire* by *Qurratulain Hyder. Indian Review of Books* 8, 4 (16 Jan.–15 Feb. 1999), 36–37.

Ghosh, Shohini. 'A Transcreation'. Review of *River of Fire* by *Qurratulain Hyder. The Book Review* 23, 1 & 2 (Jan.–Feb. 1999), 69–70.

Gokhale, Shanta (Interview with Rushdie). 'Writing in the Oral Tradition'. *The Indian Express Magazine*, 4 March 1984, 5.

Hussein, Aamer. 'Chaos and Upheaval'. Review of *River of Fire* by Qurratulain Hyder. *Times Literary Supplement*, 6 Nov. 1998, 25.

Kumar, Sukrita Paul. 'The Old Order Changeth, Does it?' Review of *The Knight's Move* by Giriraj Kishore. *The Book Review* 22, 4 (April 1998), 38.

Kurian, Sangeeth. 'Successful, Yet Losing Count?' *The Hindu Metro Plus*, 29 Jan 2003, 1.

Malak, Aman. 'The Shahrazadic Tradition: Rohinton Mistry's *Such a Long Journey* and the Art of Story-telling'. *Journal of Commonwealth Literature*, 29 (1993), 109–16.

Menon, V. K. Narayana. 'Thakazhi Sivasankara Pillai: Jnanpith Award Winner'. *The Book Review* 10, 2 (1986), 7–9.

Nair, S. Guptan. 'Thakazhi Sivasankara Pillai'. *Pratibha India,* 5, 1 (1985), n.p.

Padmanabhan, Mukund. 'Drenched in Déjà Vu'. Review of *Red Earth and Pouring Rain* by Vikram Chandra. *Indian Review of Books* 4, 8 (1995), 2–3.

Rao, N. Susheela. 'Review of River of Fire' by Qurratulain Hyder. *World Literature Today* (Summer 1999), 597.

Reddy, Sheela. 'Midnight's Orphans'. *Outlook*, 25 Feb. 2002, 54–63.

Satchidanandan, K. 'English vs. Bhashas?' *Sunday Express*, 2 March 2003, 17.

Sreedhar, M. V. 'Reaching the Unreached: Enabling Dalit Girls to Get Schooling'. *Manushi*, 111 (1999), 10–20.

Srivastava, Paramanand. 'The Story of a Dying Order'. Review of *The Knight's Move* by Giriraj Kishore. *Indian Literature* 37, 1 (Jan.–Feb. 1994), 112–16.

Tamizhnadan. 'Mudal Indiya Navalgal'. ('The First Indian Novels'). *Melum* (November 1990), 1–7.

Vanajam, Ravindran. 'This Mortal Coil'. *Indian Review of Books* 7, 11 (16 Aug.–5 Sep. 1998), 39–44.

Varma, Nirmal. 'Nammul Uraiyum Kadal.' ('The Raging Sea Within Us'). Interview with B. A. Krishnan. *Kalachuvadu*, 37 (Sept–Oct 2001), 32–40.

Walker, Richard. 'Plaiting History and Fiction'. Review of *Red Earth and Pouring Rain* by Vikram Chandra. *The Book Review* 19, 10 (1995), 26–27.

## *Online Sources*

'"ADKAR"–a Model for Change Management'. *Change Management Tutorial Series*, 30 Sept.. 2007. <http://www.change-management.com/tutorial-adkar-overview.htm>

Bama. Interview with S. Gopinath. n.d. 22 Feb 2004. <http://www.outlookindia.com>

———. Interview with Sucheta Behal. *The Hindu*, 22 Feb 2004; 6 Mar. 2003. <http://www.thehinduonline.com>

Basu, Anjana. 'The Asylum of Memory'. Review of *The Memory of Elephants*. *Gowanus*. Spring 2001. 11 Sept. 2002. <http://www.gowanusbooks.com>

Chandra, Vikram. 'The Cult of Authenticity'. *Boston Review*. Feb–March 2001; 15th June 2001. <http://www.bostonreview.com>

Ghosh, Amitav. 'Ghosh Letter to Administrators of Commonwealth Writers Prize', 18 March 2001; 23 Nov. 2001. <http://www.amitavghosh.com>

Goswami, Indira. 'Writing for Social Awareness: Interview with Indira Goswami'. *Deccan Herald,* 7 Apr. 2002; 22 Nov. 2002. <http://www.deccanherald.com>

Kothari, Rita. 'Short Story in Gujarati Dalit Literature'. *Economic and Political Weekly*, 27 May 2003. <http://www.ambedkar.org/shortstory>

'Lewin's Change Management Model: Understanding the Three Stages Of Change'. 30 Sept. 2007. <http://www.consultpivotal.com/lewin's.htm>

Memon, Md. Umar. 'Modern Urdu Literature: An Introduction'. 22 Feb 2002. <http://www.shelterbelt.com>

Paksoy, H. B. 'Dastan Genre in Central Asia'. 6 Feb 2002. <http://www.ku.edu.>

Palakeel, Thomas. 'Experimental Novels and the Problems of Imagined History'. *Urdu Journal*, 4 Oct. 2001. <http://www.shelterbelt.com>

Rollason, Christopher. 'Vikram Chandra's *Red Earth and Pouring Rain:* Entwining Narratives and Intertextuality'. *IndiaStar Review of Books*, 23 March 2001. <http://www.indiastar.com>

Roy, Nilanjana S. 'Judgement Day: An Analysis of the Booker Prize and its Literary Cohorts'. *Biblio: A Review of Books* 6 (7 & 8) Nov.–Dec. 2000. 1 page. 26 March 2003. <http://www.biblio-india.com/archives>

*Sahitya Akademi: India's National Akademi of Letters*. 27 Feb. 2002. <http://www/sahitya-akademi.org>

Sen, Sudeep. 'Not So Little Magazines: A Survey of Literary Magazines in the Subcontinent'. *Biblio: A Review of Books* 6, 7 & 8 (Nov.–Dec. 2000), 15 Dec. 2002. <http://www.biblio-india.org>.

## Other Sources

*Bharatiya Jnanpith Souvenir, 2001*.

Bhatia, H. S. 'Meta Criticism and the State of Panjabi Literary Criticism'. Paper. *The State of Literary Criticism: Trends, Texts and Issues*. Seminar. Sahitya Akademi Auditorium, Rabindra Bhavan, New Delhi, 21–23 Feb. 2002.

Chandra Chari. Editor. *The Book Review*. Personal Interview, 15 March 2002.

Deshpande, Shashi. 'Indian Literature'. Keynote Address. Seminar. 'Indian Literature'. Stella Maris College, Chennai, 18 Sept. 2002.

Dinesh Mishra. Director in-charge, Bharatiya Jnanpith. Personal Interview, 15 March 2002.

Indra, C. T. 'People's Narrative as Alternate History: A Study of Ki. Rajanarayanan's *Gopalla Gramam* (Tamil)'. Paper. *Translation and Mediation*. International Conference, University of Warwick, 6–8 July 2001.

Khaund, Malaya. Collection of Criticism on Indira Goswami. Report of Assamese *Bhasha Samiti* on Indira Goswami. Saraswati Samman Archives, K. K. Birla Foundation, New Delhi.

M. H. Venkateswaran, Officer on Special Duty, Sahitya Akademi. Personal Interview, 16 March 2002.

Minutes of Meeting. East Kshetra Samiti. 5 October 2001. Saraswati Samman Archives. New Delhi: K. K. Birla Foundation.

Mirajkar, Nishkant D. 'Exploring the Full Potential of the Genre'. *Indian Literature*. Report of Marathi Bhasha Samiti. Saraswati Samman Archives. New Delhi: K. K. Birla Foundation. Report of Marathi *Bhasha Samiti* on Vishwas Patil. Saraswati Samman Archives. New Delhi: K. K. Birla Foundation.

Mohanty, P. K. 'Towards a Search for a Pan-Indian Literary Theory'. Paper. *The State of Literary Criticism: Trends, Texts and Issues*. Seminar. Sahitya Akademi Auditorium, Rabindra Bhavan, New Delhi. 21–23 Feb. 2002.

Nimbkar, Jai. 'Disturbing and Depressing: A Look at a Marathi Novel'. *Indian Review of Books*. Report of Marathi *Bhasha Samiti* on Vishwas Patil. Saraswati Samman Archives. New Delhi: K. K. Birla Foundation.

Patil, Vishwas. 'How the Novel was Born'. Trans. Keerti Ramachandra from Marathi into English. Report of Marathi *Bhasha Samiti* on Vishwas Patil. Saraswati Samman Archives. New Delhi: K. K. Birla Foundation.

———. 'A Man, Fair Enough to Understand their Grief'. Interview with Rajee Suri. No source. Report of Marathi *Bhasha Samiti* on Vishwas Patil. Saraswati Samman Archives. New Delhi: K. K. Birla Foundation.

Reports of *Bhasha Samities*. Saraswati Samman Archives. New Delhi: K. K. Birla Foundation.

*Sahitya Akademi Souvenir, 2001.*

*Saraswati Samman Souvenir, 1999–2000.*

*Sarda, Sankar*. 'Jhadajhadati'. Report of Marathi *Bhasha Samiti* on Vishwas Patil. Saraswati Samman Archives. New Delhi: K. K. Birla Foundation.

Sarma, Gobinda Prasad. 'Fiction of Protest'. Report of Assamese *Bhasha Samiti* on Indira Goswami. Saraswati Samman Archives. New Delhi: K. K. Birla Foundation.

Tripathi, Ravindra. 'Hindi Mein Alochana: Ek Sandighdh Upastithi?' (Criticism in Hindi: A Doubtful Existence?). Paper. *The State of Literary Criticism: Trends, Texts and Issues*. Seminar. Sahitya Akademi Auditorium, Rabindra Bhavan, New Delhi, 21–23 Feb. 2002.

# INDEX

## D



## E



## F



## G



## H

## M



## N



## O



## P

## T



## U



## V

## W



## Y



## Z

METRO

O. No. - 3622 (27/01/26)

Bill No. - 3852 (20/02/26)

Rs. - 1295.00